Aline McKenzie

How To Find What You Want In The Library

How To Find What You Want In The Library

Charlotte Gorden

Formerly Teacher, Curriculum Advisor, and Resource Center Coordinator
Yellow Springs Public School System, Yellow Springs, Ohio

Barron's Educational Series, Inc.
Woodbury, New York • London • Toronto • Sydney

All inquiries should be addressed to:
Barron's Educational Series, Inc.
113 Crossways Park Drive
Woodbury, New York 11797

Library of Congress Catalog Card No. 77-12534

International Standard Book No. 0-8120-0696-8

Library of Congress Cataloging in Publication Data
Gorden, Charlotte.
  How to find what you want in the library.
  Includes index.
  1. Libraries—Handbooks, manuals, etc. I. Title.
Z710.G67   021'.28   77-12534
ISBN 0-8120-0696-8

PRINTED IN THE UNITED STATES OF AMERICA

567   510   9876543

For Ray, Greg, Karen, and Esther
—with thanks and love.

TABLE OF CONTENTS

LIST OF PROBLEMS AND ANNOTATIONS

* Descriptive note only.

x | * Descriptive note only.

Problem

Literature

Page

Science and Mathematics

* Descriptive note only.

| * Descriptive note only.

PREFACE TO THE TEACHER AND THE INDIVIDUAL LEARNER

This book has been designed for anyone who wants to plug into the memory bank of civilization commonly called the library or instructional materials center. It is organized to be used either in group instruction, individualized supervised instruction, or self-instruction. It will be helpful to teachers, librarians, student teachers, paraprofessional aides, and students in middle and high school, as well as to adults who want to be more effective in their use of the local public library, or to help their children use either the public library or the school library. After a general description of the organization of the book that is relevant to all readers, there is a special note for teachers and another for the self-instructing person.

In the author's twenty years of experience (as a teacher, librarian, and curriculum advisor) she discovered that her colleagues and students found most of the books on how to use the library often lacked essential *coverage*, rarely made any attempt to involve the student in an *active approach* to learning, and often were impractical in their *organization*. We feel that this book is a step forward in each of these three dimensions.

First, the coverage is more complete in that we give complete bibliographic descriptions and annotations of a large number of general references and reference works specialized in mathematics and science, history and government, literature, and biography. Here we have made a special effort to include recent reference works on minorities including blacks, Catholics, Indians, and Jews. We have also included a final section on doing the library research for a reference paper. This section concentrates on how systematically to find and accumulate information from the library that is relevant to the theme of the paper.

Second, to facilitate the student's active approach to the library, we have provided Self-Checking Exercises at the end of each of the three chapters in Part I and have included Search Questions and Clues for parts of Part I and for each of 77 general and specialized reference works in Part II.

The Self-Checking Exercises are paper-pencil checks to see whether the student has understood what has been read. The Search Questions require that the student *apply* what has just been read and be able to use it to find information.

To help with this we have provided a set of Clues after each set of Search Questions. These Clues explain to the student who is having trouble just how to go about finding the answer, but the Clues do not tell what the answer is nor the page on which it can be found. If the student still cannot find what he or she is looking for, of course the teacher or librarian will have to help, but in our actual experience using this material, these times have been rare.

Here we would like to offer some suggestions we found vital for use of the Search Questions and Clues. These Search Questions were selected to highlight the type of content unique to each reference. In looking up specific answers, the student naturally will become aware of this content. But the emphasis needs to be on how to use the reference and on the kinds of questions that a particular reference will answer, not on the answer to any specific question. Regardless of whether the Search Questions are used as class assignments or to help a single learner work on an individual need, the learner should report only the volume and page number where the answer can be found and *not* be required to copy or report on the answers to the Search Questions. This is vital to student morale and to the sanity of the teacher trying to keep up with student work.

Once free of the burden of copying, memorizing, or summarizing the answers to the Search Questions, the learner begins to catch the spirit of the detective using the Clues to track down the culprit, or of the explorer for whom the Clues constitute the map and landmarks of the territory to be crossed. Students learn that although some of the Search Questions are not those uppermost in their minds at the moment, they have found the keys for unlocking portions of civilization's memory bank and can now use them to find answers to the questions which are most relevant to them personally.

The third valuable dimension of this book is its organization into three sections according to use. Part I deals with the card catalog and with two major periodical indexes, the *Readers' Guide* and the *New York Times Index*. It also describes the location in the library of fiction and nonfiction. This whole first section is the basic core and should be assimilated first by all of the students.

Part II deals with reference works only and is built upon the assumption that the reader understands the previous section. Unlike the first section, Part II need not be read from beginning to end; it is a collection of annotated reference books with Search Questions and Clues to help the student become familiar with each of these. To assist the reader in finding what is needed, the discussion of references is arranged in two parts: general references and specialized references. The general references are divided by form into encyclopedias, almanacs, and dictionaries. The specialized references are divided by field into biography, literature, history and government, and science and mathematics. At the beginning of each section there is an outline of the references which follow. Each section and

subsection has a short introduction on the general nature of these references.

Part III is for the person who is faced with the task of writing a reference paper. It focuses on the systematic gathering and accumulation of materials needed for writing the paper.

The answers to the Self-Checking Exercises are in the appendix. We cannot supply the page locations of the answers to the Search Questions because every library has different editions of the reference works.

A SPECIAL NOTE TO THE TEACHER

The extent to which this book should be read by the student instead of providing information to be passed on orally by the teacher, librarian, or paraprofessional aide, depends upon the level of the student and whether the unit on library use is to be a class project or a series of independent study assignments selected to fit the needs of an individual student.

You must take two preparatory steps that could not be supplied in this book because they depend upon the contents of your particular library. First, in order to decide which Search Questions to assign, you must determine which of the reference books your particular library has. Second, for each of the Search Question assignments you plan to use, make an answer sheet showing the page numbers on which the answers to the Search Questions can be found in your particular editions of the references. By using the Clues to each assignment, a paraprofessional aide can make up the answer sheet. This can also be done by interested student assistants working ahead of the class.

If many students are to be assigned Search Questions at the same time, it is important to rotate the questions to avoid a rush for the same book.

One additional aim of this book is to help the classroom teacher have more influence on the content of the school library. Even though very few school libraries have all of the reference works cited, there is always an opportunity in the future to expand the holdings of the library. The teacher who is aware of the reference works available and how they relate to his or her field of teaching can urge that acquisitions be made to enrich the instruction for students.

A SPECIAL NOTE TO THE SELF-INSTRUCTED

If you are not already very familiar with the organization and use of the *Card Catalog* and the *Readers' Guide* you should first read Part I. If you are not sure how well you understand them, try some of the Search Questions supplied at the end of Part I.

Then select an area of specialized references such as biography, literature, history, government, science, or mathematics and use the Search Questions and Clues provided in that section to begin your systematic exploration of the library.

After you have covered the Search Questions related to several of the specialized references, you can then launch on a search for the answers to your own questions in that area. At this point you will find Part III — *Gathering Information* — very helpful.

Remember, your focus should be on how to use these references and how to learn the general kinds of questions they answer, not on answers to these specific questions. The main benefit to you lies in what you learn by actively exploring the library and becoming familiar with the search process.

ACKNOWLEDGMENTS

I appreciate the help given me by Bruce Thomas, Joe Cali, and Carolyn Dearnaley of the Antioch College Library and by Fran Rickenback of the Yellow Springs Public Library. I would like especially to acknowledge the help of Paul Simmons and his staff at Wright State University media services. Thank you all.

AN OVERALL VIEW

Since the word *library* comes from the Latin word *liber* meaning book, we sometimes make the mistake of thinking of a library as just a collection of physical objects called books. Actually, a library is as important to modern life and society as a brain is to a person. Without a brain a person cannot remember the past and, therefore, would never learn from experience. It is obvious that without a brain the human race would not have survived. It is equally true that without libraries modern civilization would never have developed. The library is the memory bank of civilization. It contains the distilled experience of mankind and provides the information needed for both understanding the past and planning for the future.

Primitive societies, in contrast to civilizations, have a very small memory bank, even after thousands of years of survival. Since they have no writing, there are no books or libraries to store the human experience. The people of each generation pass onto the next only what they can remember of their own experiences and of what their parents have told them. This is not enough information to develop the sciences or a wide variety of arts or to build a civilization.

This book will help you discover the kinds of information our civilization has stored in the library and will show you how to retrieve the bits that you need or are interested in. To do this effectively requires skill.

What would you do with a tennis court if you did not know how to play tennis or with a typewriter if you did not know how to type? Of what use is a library if you do not know how to use it? Of course you might try to use the tennis court or the typewriter or the library by your own trial-and-error system and you might even work out some interesting or helpful approaches. But in the meantime you will have lost a lot of valuable time; perhaps you will also have run out of patience or interest in using these things.

Effective use of a library, like the effective use of a tennis court or a typewriter, is not an inherited skill, but one that has to be learned. Our purpose is to help you learn in a general way how to use all libraries and to help you use some of the specific reference tools usually found in libraries. Obviously you don't want to fill your mind with a myriad of details such as Ulysses Grant was born on April 27 or Texas has 23 morning newspapers. It is important, however, to learn the general principles of locating information.

The library skills you learn in this book will help you in any library or resource center. The phrase *resource center* or *materials center* is now often used, particularly in schools, instead of *library* to show that the collection includes materials other than books. Such centers often contain tapes, slides, filmstrips, records, film loops, or movies as well as the equipment to use them. These "non-book" materials are usually catalogued, arranged, and circulated according to the same general principles as the book materials in that particular center.

This book has three parts. Part I discusses things everyone must know to use a library easily and effectively: using the card catalog, locating materials in the library, and using indexes.

To be sure that you understand what you have read, there are three Self-Checking Exercises. These are not tests to be graded by; the answers are in the Appendix. They are tests to help you spot the areas you do not understand thoroughly so you can go back and read about them again to learn.

Part II describes both general and specialized reference books that help you answer specific questions. The general reference books are divided into encyclopedias, almanacs, and dictionaries; the specialized references are divided into the areas of biography, literature, history and government, and science and mathematics. At the beginning of each of these areas there is an outline of the references in that section, a kind of shopper's guide to show where to find a description of the contents of a particular reference book.

To be sure that you really can use these references, there are Search Questions about most of them. If you can find the answers to these Search Questions, you really know how to use the reference. If you have trouble, read the Clues that follow the questions, and you will learn how to use that reference. With these Search Questions, the important thing is not the answers to the questions but whether you can use the reference to find answers.

You may not remember the names of all the special references, but you should remember what *kinds* of references exist so you can refer to them as you need them.

Part III is to help the student who is preparing to write a reference paper, sometimes called a term paper, research paper, or report. Instead of dealing with how to find a specific kind of information in the library, this shows you how to make a systematic search of the library for information from a variety of sources which relate to a particular topic or set of questions. This is quite different from just finding interesting tidbits of information to answer a specific question.

If it seems to you that plugging into civilization's memory bank is a bit complicated, remember that you do not have to learn it all at once. Take one step at a time. It takes much less effort to learn to use the library well than it did to learn to read, and the small additional investment needed will pay you large dividends.

THE CARD CATALOG

When you go to a new town for the first time, you soon have certain landmarks that help you get around. The grocery, the school, the gas station, the main street, a new friend's house — all these help you to begin to orient yourself and form an outline in your mind which you fill in gradually as you have time to observe more details.

When you go to a new library, you also have certain landmarks that help you get around. The card catalog, the arrangement of books, the location of pamphlets and audio-visual (AV) materials, the procedures for using materials, the people who are there to help you — these are the signposts the new user of a library must find in order to find his or her way around. Usually the first and most important thing to find is the card catalog.

The catalog cards are kept in a cabinet of small drawers in some central place in the library. The cards may fill a few drawers or several rooms. The cards are filed alphabetically in these drawers and the drawers are alphabetically arranged in the file.

The card catalog is the master key to all the materials in the library. It tells you whether the library has a particular book or other form of information on a special subject. There is at least one card for each book, record, or filmstrip the library owns.

Sometimes you may be looking for a book called *Half Magic,* or sometimes you may be looking for any book by Isaac Asimov, or sometimes you may be looking for something about building boats. So to make the catalog easy to use, books are generally listed in the catalog in all three places: title, author, and subject.

CARDS FOR AUTHORS

If you know who wrote the material you are looking for, look under his or her name in the card catalog. The author card is filed under the writer's last name. If there are several authors with the same last name, cards for their books are filed by last name, then alphabetically by the first names. If an author has written several books, the cards will be filed under his or her name and then alphabetically by title. Here is a possible list of author cards in the order they would be found in the catalog.

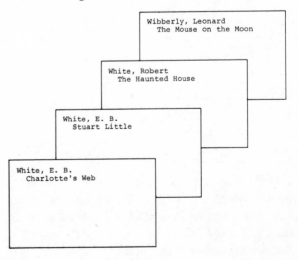

1

CARDS FOR TITLES

Sometimes you know the title of the material you want but not its author. Look for the title card filed alphabetically in the catalog. Knowing a few filing rules will help you use this file:

(1) *A, An,* or *The* at the beginning of a title are not considered when these cards are filed. For example: *A Time for Dreams* would be filed under *T*.

(2) Titles that begin with numbers or abbreviations are filed as though the words were spelled out. For example: *100 Cats* would be filed under *One*. Also, you would look for *St.* or *U.S.* as if they were written *Saint* or *United States*.

(3) Last names beginning with *Mc* are filed as though they were spelled *Mac*. So you would look for McCarthy and McNamara as if they were spelled MacCarthy and Mac-Namara.

(4) Nothing comes before something; the space between words is counted as nothing. So you would look for *All is Well* before *Allen Jones*.

Here is a possible list of title cards in the order they would be found in the catalog:

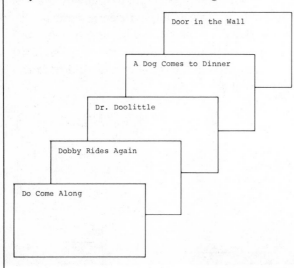

Sometimes an additional card is made for a book in a series so it can be found under its series title. For example, the book *Israel*, which is part of the *Life World Library Series*, would have a card in the catalog under both *I* and *L*.

CARDS FOR SUBJECTS

If you are interested in finding all the material the library has on a particular subject, the subject cards will help you. If you are interested in peanuts, but don't know any of the authors who have written about peanuts, look under that subject heading in the card catalog. Sometimes there will be divisions within a general subject like PEANUTS — FARMING and PEANUTS — USES.

The books and materials with the same subject headings are arranged within that subject by author. To make these subject headings stand out, they are usually typed in red or in capital letters. Here is a possible list of subject cards in the order they would be found in the catalog:

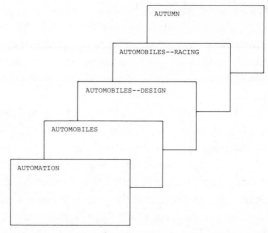

One important deviation in the alphabetical order of subject cards in the card catalog occurs in historical subjects. Historical subtopics are arranged *chronologically under the main subject*. For example, the subject U.S. — HISTORY might have subtopics filed in this order:

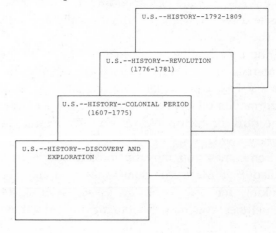

Libraries differ sometimes in the names they use for subjects in the card catalog. One library may use FARMING in its subject file while another may use AGRICULTURE for that same subject.

Sometimes you need to use some imagination to find a subject in the catalog. You might not find any subject cards under FOOTBALL. You would have to ask yourself what other subject might be used to include this one.. What other different name could this subject be listed under? In this case SPORTS could be the answer. A book about sports might contain information about football.

CROSS REFERENCE CARDS

The card catalog often contains some special cross reference cards to help you find a subject used in that library. Would you find a book about *tides* under OCEAN or SEA? If you looked for information under SEA you might find a card that says:

```
    SEA
        See
  OCEAN
```

That cross reference card tells you that library uses OCEAN as the subject heading for all books about seas or oceans.

Another kind of cross reference card will refer you to a related subject the library also has. If you look for a book on SPIES you might find several cards filed under this subject, and the last card under the subject of spies might read:

```
    SPIES
        See also
  SECRET SERVICE
```

The card catalog is suggesting to you that the library has related information you might also be interested in.

EXTRA HELP FROM THE CARD CATALOG

At first you may be only interested in knowing whether or not the library has a certain book and if so how you can locate it. Some time, however, you may want help selecting material. Here the card catalog gives you some extras to help you decide whether material might be useful. Cards often tell you:

(1) whether the book is illustrated or has charts and maps.

(2) publication information for the book including the date — this could be especially important for topics demanding recent information.

(3) the number of pages in the book — this should give you some idea how extensive the information would be.

(4) whether the book contains a bibliography — this could lead you to other information on the subject.

(5) a note about the contents of the book — sometimes a list of chapters.

CARDS FOR NON-BOOK MATERIAL

Libraries that catalog records, filmstrips, and other audio-visual materials often distinguish cards for these "non-book" materials in different ways.

All card catalogs make a distinction in the call numbers to show the kind of non-book material involved. For example, you might find the following call numbers for non-book materials:

Record	Filmstrip	Tape (cas)
973.1	582.16	973
Lif	Met	Mur

Sometimes these designations are abbreviated: Rec, FS, or T.

In addition some card catalogs call attention to non-book materials by using colored cards or color-banded cards as well as the distinguishing call numbers. In large libraries a different color card may be used for each kind of non-book material.

When you first encounter a new card catalog, you need to find out how many parts, or how many alphabets, the card catalog is filed in. For example, some libraries file author and title cards together in one alphabet and subject cards in a separate alphabet.

A few minutes of getting acquainted with the card catalog will often save you much time and confusion. Look at the catalog in your library:

(1) Are authors, titles, and subjects filed together or separately?

(2) Are records and filmstrips filed with books or are these in separate files? Are these non-book materials specially marked?

(3) Are there any special files, such as a file of bound periodicals, or a file of subjects to be found in the vertical file? Are these separate or filed in with the book catalog cards?

Once you have located the cards in the catalog for the materials you need, the call numbers in the upper left-hand corner of each card will tell you where in the library to find the material. They are the home address for the book. In large libraries people write the number of a book they want on a slip of paper which they give to the librarian to "call for" or request the book. So "call number" has come to mean the classification number of a book. The next section tells how these numbers help you locate what you want.

Look over the following summary; then try to answer the questions in the Self-Checking Exercise to be sure you have understood what you have read about the card catalog. Check your answers with those given in the appendix and reread any part you are not sure you understand.

SUMMARY — CARD CATALOG

If you know the author, look for the *author card*

```
Fic
P 23 1  Parks, Gordon
            The learning tree. Fawcett
        World Library. 1963.
```

If you know the title, look for the *title card*

```
Fic
T 57 h  The hobbit
        Tolkien, J.R.R.
            The hobbit or there and back
        again, illus. by the author.
        Houghton. 1938.
```

Books about a certain subject can be found by the *subject card*

```
641.5    COOKERY
R 66 j  Rombauer, Irma S. and Marion
        Becker. The joy of cooking.
        Bobbs-Merrill.
```

Books in a series are also found under the *series card*

```
915.6   Life World Library Series
Sa 5 i  St. John, Robert
            Israel (Life World Library).
        Time-Life, New York 1968.
```

If the material is not a book, it is described by *non-book card*

```
Record
940.53  Historic voices and music from
            World War II. American
            Heritage. UB-487/8. c1966.
        1 record, 2 sides, 12", 33 1/3 rpm
```

If there is additional related material in the library, there will be a *see also card*

```
        SPORTS
                    See also
        FOOTBALL
```

If the library does not use a subject, to refer you to the subject they do use, there will be a *see card*

```
        PREHISTORIC MAN
                See
        MAN, PREHISTORIC
```

Problem 1 — Card Catalog

SELF-CHECKING EXERCISES

1. What is the library user's guide to all the books in the library?

2. What three cards do most nonfiction books have in the catalog?

Following are sample cards found in a catalog. Answer the questions about each.

Card A

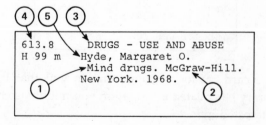

3. Which number points to each of the follow-ing in Card A? If none does, answer with X.
   a. The author?
   b. The title?
   c. The subject?
   d. The call number?
   e. What letter would this card be filed under?

Card B

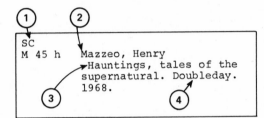

4. Which number points to each of the follow-ing in Card B? If none does, answer with X.
   a. The author?
   b. The title?
   c. The subject?
   d. The call number?
   e. What letter would this card be filed under?

Card C

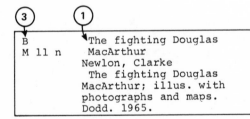

5. Which number points to each of the follow-ing in Card C? If none does, answer with X.
   a. The author?
   b. The title?
   c. The subject?
   d. The call number?
   e. What letter would this card be filed under?

Card D

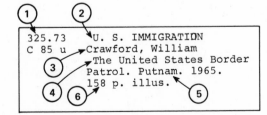

6. Which number points to each of the follow-ing in Card D? If none does, answer with X.
   a. The author?
   b. The title?
   c. The subject?
   d. The call number?
   e. What letter would this card be filed under?

7. Under what letter would books written by these authors be found?
   a. Louisa May Alcott
   b. Robert McCloskey
   c. Phyllis A. Whitney
   d. Mary O'Hara
   e. Isaac Asimov
   f. Meindert DeJong
   g. C. S. Forester

8. In what order would the following titles be found in the card catalog? Put 1 after the letter of the title that would be found first, 2 after the letter of the title that would be second, etc.
   a. St. Nicholas Anthologies
   b. The Scalp-Hunters
   c. First Book of Baseball
   d. 900 Buckets of Paint
   e. A Bit of Blue
   f. Abby

9. Number the following subjects according to the way they would be found in the card catalog. Put 1 after the letter of the subject that would be found first, 2 after the subject that would be second, etc.
   a. SCHWEITZER, ALBERT
   b. PLANETS see also ASTRONOMY
   c. FOLKLORE — U.S.
   d. BALLET
   e. FOLKLORE
   f. HIGHWAYS see TRANSPORTATION — HIGHWAYS
   g. FOLKLORE — AFRICA
   h. U.S. HISTORY — REVOLUTION (1764-1782)
   i. U.S. HISTORY — CIVIL WAR (1860-1865)

10. Would you expect the library that has the subject cards listed in question 9 to have material listed under each of the following? (Answer yes, no, or can't tell for each).
    a. PLANETS?
    b. HIGHWAYS?
    c. FOLKLORE — INDIAN?

LOCATING MATERIAL

EXPLORING THE LIBRARY

We said that the call number on the card was the home address of the book, filmstrip, or record. However, when you are looking for a person in a strange city, before you can find the address, you need a map. It is the same when looking for something in a new library. Some large libraries will give you a map, but more often you will need to walk around to locate things for yourself.

When you first begin using a new library, you need to know the location of the card catalog so that you can discover what's in the library. You need to know where the check-out desk is so that you can check out a book once it is found. You should discover if there is a special information desk where the librarian or another person can help you if you run into problems. Then of course you have to know where the different kinds of books and other materials are located.

A library usually has areas for separate collections of fiction, biography, nonfiction, reference, periodicals, and pamphlets. These may all be contained in one room, or there may be an entire room devoted to each collection, depending on the library and whom it serves. There may also be special areas or rooms for children's books, for music, or for special collections like mystery or science fiction.

All of the books, of course, are on shelves, but there are other types of materials such as pamphlets, maps, clippings, and pictures that are kept in file drawers usually called the Vertical File or the Information File which is often located with the reference books. Each piece of material is given a subject heading and then filed in a folder for that heading. Some Vertical Files are arranged alphabetically by subject, while others are filed alphabetically within types of materials like maps, reports, or pamphlets. Your library may subscribe to one of the useful series of pamphlets such as Public Affairs Pamphlets, Headline Series, Focus, or Facts on File. Browse through the Vertical File in your library to see what kinds of things it includes and how they are arranged.

You should explore the whole library to make a mental map of the location of the different collections. Even though the card catalog tells you that the library has a certain book and the call number tells you that it is in the reference section, you still need to know where the reference books are kept. Your mental map should give you the answers to the following kinds of questions:

- How do you get to the fiction collection?
- Where do you find biographies?
- Where is the nonfiction material?
- Where are the reference books?
- Where are the vertical files?
- Where are the bound volumes of magazines and periodicals?
- Where are the current magazines?
- Are there any special areas or collections of materials?

Find out where each of these areas is so you can follow the directions the call numbers in the card catalog give you.

LEARNING THE RULES

Once you know where things are in the library, you need to know how you are supposed to obtain and use the various kinds of materials. All libraries make their own rules. If you learn these rules when you first start using the library, you can save yourself some frustration and embarrassment. You should read the rules of the library or talk with the librarian to find the answers to the following questions:

- Once you have the call number can you go directly to the shelf yourself, or do you write the call number on a slip requesting the librarian to get the materials for you?
- Are all types of material — books, vertical file material, magazines, records, filmstrips — obtained in the same way?
- What material may you take out of the library and what must you use there?
- How do you take material out?
- How long can you use the material outside the library?
- How long can you use the material inside the library?
- How much material may you check out at one time?
- What are you supposed to do with the materials you have used?

Now that you have explored the library and know the rules for using the materials, you need a more detailed understanding of the call number which is the book's home address.

THE ANATOMY OF THE CALL NUMBER

We have said that the call number is located in the upper left-hand corner of the card in the card catalog. It is also written on the book it describes so that the book can be put in the proper order on the shelf. We also pointed out that the purpose of the call number was to tell you where to find the book in the library. But we haven't yet explained to you how to read the home addresses.

The call number is made up of two parts. The first part which may be some or all of the top line tells you what *collection* the book is in. The first part may be an abbreviation standing for fiction, biography, or reference, for example, or it may be a number from the Dewey Decimal System used to classify books by the subject category. We will explain the Dewey Decimal System in detail later, but for the moment let's look at some examples of the first part of the call number.

Fic B 14 n	The first line tells us that this book is in the *fiction* collection.
B D 25 g	The B in the top line tells us the book is in the *biography* collection.
R 512 J 19 r	The R tells us that it is in the *reference* collection. The 512 tells us (according to Dewey Decimal System) that it is in the mathematical portion of the reference section.
739.5 P 63 m	The 739.5 on the top line tells us that the book is in the *fine arts* collection.

In every case above, the second line gives the location of the book on the shelf within the particular collection specified in the first part of the call number. The exact meaning of the bottom line will be explained in detail as we explain how to find books on the shelf in each type of collection.

FINDING FICTION BOOKS

Novels are usually classified as fiction and kept together in a special collection in the library. They are arranged on the shelves in alphabetical order by the author's last name. Sometimes a special number is used to help arrange books in alphabetical order. For example, depending on the library's system, Kate Seredy's book, *The White Stag,* may have any of the following call numbers:

Fic	Fic	Fic
S	Ser	S 64 w

Here the *S* is to help alphabetize books on the shelves according to the author's last name. Some librarians use more letters of the author's last name such as the *Ser* here in the second example. In the third example the *S* is the initial of the author's last name, the number comes from a table designed by John Cutter (on the theory that it is easier to arrange things by number than by alphabet), and the *w* is the first letter of the book title. Sometimes a particular library does not assign any number to its fiction, but still shelves the books in a special section alphabetically by author.

Whatever system is used for fiction, it is designed to help locate books on the shelves alphabetically by the author's last name, and then alphabetically by title. No matter which system is used, these books would appear on the shelves in the same order.

Enid Bagnold	Curtis Bishop	Curtis Bishop	Enid Blyton
NATIONAL VELVET	FAST BREAK	SIDELINE PASS	THE CIRCUS ADVENTURE
Fic B 14 n	Fic B 54 f	Fic B 54 s	Fic B 62 c

FINDING BIOGRAPHIES

A biography is not fiction but is a story about a real person. If the story is written by the person himself, it is called an *auto*biography. You know that in the fiction collection books are arranged alphabetically by the author's name, but in the biography collection[1] the books are arranged according to the name of the *person written about*. If the book is about one person, the first part of the call number is either a B for biography or the Dewey Decimal number 92 which stands for biography.

The call numbers for biographies differ depending on the system adopted by a specific library. We might find any of the following call numbers for Miriam Gurke's book about Clarence Darrow:

[1]All libraries do not have a separate biography collection, but many do. If your library has one, it will follow these principles.

92	B	B	B
D	D	Dar	D 25 g

In all of the examples *D* stands for the person the biography is about. In the last example, the number is to help us alphabetize and the *g* stands for the author's last name.

If the book contains a collection of biographies, it would be impossible to alphabetize it by the names of all of the people written about, so it must be alphabetized by the author or by the editor. It would be marked 920 and shelved with the other 920's in sequence by author. These would still be in the biography collection, but they would be on the shelves after all the individual biographies.

Here is an example of the order in which you would find biographies on a shelf

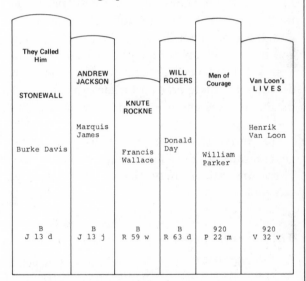

They Called Him STONEWALL	ANDREW JACKSON	KNUTE ROCKNE	WILL ROGERS	Men of Courage	Van Loon's LIVES
Burke Davis	Marquis James	Francis Wallace	Donald Day	William Parker	Henrik Van Loon
B J 13 d	B J 13 j	B R 59 w	B R 63 d	920 P 22 m	920 V 32 v

Regardless of the marking system used, biographies about one person will be found arranged alphabetically according to the person they are about. All biographies the library has on Thomas Jefferson will be together on the shelves, arranged within the group alphabetically by author.

NONFICTION AND MR. DEWEY

Nonfiction books other than biography are arranged on the shelf first numerically by the class number, then alphabetically by the author's last name. The purpose of the classification system is to keep books on one subject together. Before this system was devised, you might have had to find books arranged in the order in which they were acquired by the library, or by groups according to the person who had given them to the library. Or perhaps the books would not have been classified at all, and only the librarian's memory would help you to find them.

Two common systems used in libraries in this country are the Dewey Decimal Classification and the Library of Congress Classification. Although the numbers do not resemble each other, the underlying logic is the same: each is a way of keeping books on the same subject together. We will discuss the Dewey system first, since it is the most common in our public and school libraries.

If you would pick any number from 1 to 999 and then go to the shelves of books, you would find that all the books with that number are on the same subject. It is helpful to be acquainted with the general ten classes in the Dewey system and the overall logic of the plan of classification. You will remember a specific number when you do a lot of reading on a particular subject. In the meantime, it is enough to understand how the system works.

The hundreds place stands for the large, general category the subject of the book fits into. There are ten of these Dewey Decimal large categories:

The Numbers Between	Are Used For Books About
000–099	general things (encyclopedias, book lists, newspapers)
100–199	philosophy (psychology, ethics, logic)
200–299	religion (theology, mythology)
300–399	social sciences (political science, economics, law, education, holidays, etiquette, folklore)
400–499	language (dictionaries, books about foreign languages, language study)
500–599	science (mathematics, astronomy, physics, chemistry, geology, biology)
600–699	applied science or useful arts (medicine, engineering, agriculture, home economics, business, industrial arts)
700–799	fine arts (painting, sculpture, drawing, photography, music, sports)
800–899	literature (poetry, plays, essays, criticism)
900–999	history (ancient, modern, U.S., world)

Two special sections of the 900s have been reserved:

910–919	geography and travel
920–929	biography

Each of the ten general classes is subdivided as much as necessary. For example, the ten divisions of the 500–599 pure science classification begin:

510–519	mathematics
520–529	astronomy
530–539	physics
	etc.

Still further subdivisions can be made. For example, under the numbers 510–519 reserved for mathematics, you would find another ten subdivisions

511	arithmetic
512	algebra
513	geometry
	etc.

Still further, the 511 arithmetic category is broken down

511.1	numeration systems
511.2	fundamental operations
511.3	prime numbers
	etc.

Thus the call number 511.2 tells you: This book is in the general field of pure science, in the area of mathematics, more specifically, it is about arithmetic, and deals with fundamental operations.

While no one would want to clutter his mind with the entire Dewey system, it is helpful to understand the overall logic of the classifications.

At times it is also helpful to memorize the numbers related to a subject you are currently working on.

LIBRARY OF CONGRESS CLASSIFICATION

The Library of Congress system of classification uses the same principle as the Dewey system: it keeps books on the same subject on the shelves together.

The Library of Congress system allows more specific categories of subjects by using combinations of letters and numbers. This makes it especially useful for large libraries and technical libraries. Many college libraries also use this system.

During the Battle of Washington in 1814, the young Library of Congress was burned. The next year the government bought Thomas Jefferson's library to re-establish a library for congressmen to use. Almost at the end of the 1800s the Library of Congress was recatalogued and reclassified. The Library of Congress Classification was developed during that process.

In this system the first letter stands for the large, general category the subject of the book fits into. There are 20 of these large Library of Congress categories:

These Letters	Are Used For Books About
A	general things (encyclopedias, indexes, newspapers)
B	philosophy, religion (logic, psychology, ethics)
C	history — auxiliary sciences (archives, chronology, genealogy, heraldry)
D	history and topography (except for America)
E and F	America
G	geography, anthropology, sports
H	social sciences (statistics, economics, commerce, finance, sociology)
J	political science (constitutional history, local government)
K	law
L	education
M	music
N	fine arts (architecture, sculpture, graphic arts, painting)
P	language and literature (Greek and Latin, modern European, Oriental, African, American, Indian, artificial)
Q	science (mathematics, astronomy, physics, chemistry, geology, biology, physiology)
R	medicine
S	agriculture, plant and animal industry (forestry, fisheries, hunting, animal husbandry, horticulture)
T	technology
U	military science
V	naval science
W	bibliography, library science

Each of these large general classes is then divided, using a second letter. For example, the twelve divisions of the Q category of science begin

Q	science (general)
QA	mathematics
QB	astronomy
QC	physics
	etc.

Still further subdivisions are then made by using numbers. For example, under the QA category reserved for mathematics, you will find the following:

1– 99	general mathematics
101–141.8	arithmetic
150–271	algebra
273–280	probabilities, mathematical statistics
	etc.

The arithmetic category, for example, is broken down still further

101–107	textbooks
111	rapid calculators and short cuts
115	elementary operations (addition, subtraction, multiplication, division)

11

117   fractions, including proportion and ratio

etc.

Thus the call number QA 115 tells you: This book is in the general field of science, it is in the area of mathematics, more specifically it is about arithmetic and deals with fundamental operations.

The Library of Congress Classification number is followed by the first letter of the author's last name and a number which refers to the author. This is the same kind of system for identifying authors numerically that we discussed earlier. It helps get books of the same kind on the shelves alphabetically by author.

Again, you will not want to stuff your mind with the entire classification system. It is helpful, however, to understand the overall logic.

SUMMARY — LOCATING MATERIAL

Look over this summary and then go on to answer the questions in Problem 2 to be sure you have understood what you have read about locating materials in the library. The answers to the Self-Checking Exercises are in the Appendix. The Clues which follow the Search Questions should give you any help you need in finding the answers.

We have tried to show how the card catalog helps you find books. First, it can tell you whether the library has the book or other type of material you want. Second, the call number located in the upper left-hand corner of the catalog card gives you the location of the book in the library.

In the Library of Congress system, the letters of the call number tell you the broad subject area of the book. Books are grouped on the shelves alphabetically by these letters.

The following line of numbers further defines the subject. After the books are grouped alphabetically by the broad subject areas, they are arranged numerically by the smaller subject areas. Then within these groups, they are arranged first alphabetically by the author's last initial and then numerically by the author's number.

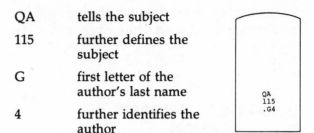

QA	tells the subject
115	further defines the subject
G	first letter of the author's last name
4	further identifies the author

This book would be found here

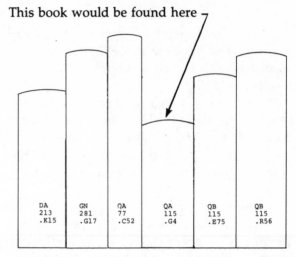

In the Dewey system the call number is divided into two parts. The first part tells you in which *collection* the book will be found. The second part tells you the *order* in which the book will be found among others in that collection.

Fic
K 6 i
    This book is with *fiction*. You will find it shelved alphabetically under K, the first letter of the author's last name, and then numerically under 6. (The *i* stands for the title).

B
W 19 o
    This book is with *biographies of individuals*. It is shelved alphabetically under W, the first letter of the last name of the *person the book is about*, and then numerically under 19. (In this case the *o* stands for the author's last name.)

920
R 89 m
    This book is with *biographies of several people* (collective biography). All the 920's would be in the biography collection following the individual biographies. In the 920s this book would be shelved under R, the first letter of the author's last name, and then numerically under 89. (The *m* stands for the title.)

SC
G 22 m
    This book is with *story collections* and is shelved alphabetically under G, the first letter of the editor or author's last name, and then numerically under 22. (The *m* stands for the title.)

R 810.3 · H 3 o *or* · R · 810.3 · H 3 o — This book is with the *reference collection* and is shelved numerically under 810.3. If there are several books with this number, it will be filed alphabetically under H, the first letter of the last name of the author. (The o stands for the title.)

973.7 · K 63 p — This book is with nonfiction, arranged on the shelves numerically by call number and then alphabetically by letter. (The p stands for the title.)

Call numbers are read from left to right. Lower numbers come before higher numbers. This book would be found here —

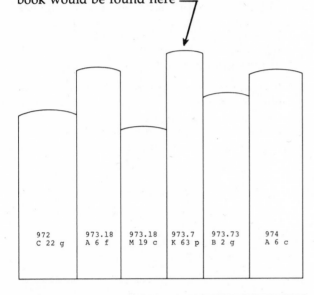

972 C 22 g | 973.18 A 6 f | 973.18 M 19 c | 973.7 K 63 p | 973.73 B 2 g | 974 A 6 c

Problem 2 — Locating Material

SELF-CHECKING EXERCISES

1. In items (a) through (i) below show in which collection the book with each call number would be found. Use the following key:
   (1) Fiction
   (2) Biography
   (3) Story collection
   (4) Reference
   (5) Nonfiction

   (a) B M 22 e (d) R 799 C 42 g (g) Fic H 67 j
   (b) SC R 34 g (e) 920 G 19 g (h) R 301 L 82 c
   (c) Fic K 23 g (f) 639 B 15 a (i) 935.7 M 37 s

2. Under what letter on the shelves of fiction would you find each of the following:
   a. Alistair MacLean, *Ice Station Zebra*.
   b. Alexandre Dumas, *The Three Musketeers*.
   c. Joan Aiken, *Nightbirds on Nantucket*.
   d. Robert Ruark, *The Old Man and the Boy*.
   e. Andre Norton, *The Time Traders World*.
   f. Gordon Parks, *The Learning Tree*.
   g. C. S. Lewis, *Out of the Silent Planet*.

3. Under what letter on the biography shelves would you find each of the following:
   a. Helen Keller, *The Story of My Life*.
   b. James Boswell, *Life of Dr. Samuel Johnson*.
   c. Geoffrey Bocca, *The Adventurous Life of Winston Churchill*.
   d. Albert Carr, *Men of Power: A Book of Dictators*.
   e. Olivia Coolidge, *Tom Paine, Revolutionary*.
   f. J. Alvin Kugelmass, *Ralph J. Bunche: Fighter for Peace*.
   g. Willie Mays and Charles Einstein, *Willie Mays, My Life In and Out of Baseball*.
   h. Sonia Daugherty, *Ten Brave Women*.
   i. Yogi Berra and Ed Fitzgerald, *Yogi: The Autobiography of a Professional Baseball Player*.

4. Write the following call numbers for nonfiction books in the correct order in which you would find them on the shelves. *Hint:* don't overlook a decimal point. 613 is larger than 612.25. On the library shelf 613.49 comes after 613.4 and before 613.5.

   620 M 18 | 620 B 51 | 621.56 W 93 | 616.9 Z 69 | 616.24 B 81
   616.94 B 91 | 620 B 81 | 616.3 K 82 | 616.8 J 15 | 616.99 S 36

SEARCH QUESTIONS[1]

Check yourself on your understanding of the arrangement of materials in the library. To answer these Search Questions you must go to the library but *do not use the card catalog*. Read the Clues below if you need help.

1. Is there a novel in your library by each of the following authors?
   a. Conrad Richter
   b. Donald Sobol
   c. Elizabeth Coatsworth
   d. Anne Emery
   e. Louisa Alcott
   f. C. S. Forester
   g. Fred Gipson
   h. Robert Heinlein
   i. Isaac Asimov

---

[1]Teachers: If this is a class assignment, you might want the students to write down the call numbers for a book by each of these authors they find on your library shelves. If your library does not use fiction or short story call numbers, they could write down the title of one book by each of these authors they find on the shelves.

j. James Thurber
k. Madeline L'Engle
l. Lois Lenski
m. Zilpha Snyder
n. Mary O'Hara

2. Is there a collection of short stories by each of the following writers in the library?

a. Edgar Allan Poe
b. Howard Haycraft
c. Ernest Hemingway
d. Mark Twain

3. Does your library have a book-length biography about the following people?

a. James Baldwin
b. Gandhi
c. Thomas Jefferson
d. Roy Campanella
e. Mozart
f. Shakespeare

CLUES

Of course we cannot say whether your library has a particular book which you are asked to find in the Search Questions, but we can give you some clues to help you find out.

1. Remember novels are fiction. All novels are in the fiction section of the library. The books in this section are arranged alphabetically by the author's last name. You don't need to look in the card catalog to find them. Walk along the shelves until you find the right alphabetical spot for the author's last name.

2. Most libraries put short stories on shelves together. These are arranged alphabetically by the author's last name. Find the right section of shelves for short stories and then look in the right alphabetical place.

3. Biographies are put on shelves together in the library and arranged in alphabetical order by the last name of the *person they are about*. Find the right section of the library and walk along the shelves looking for the place alphabetically for Baldwin, Gandhi, Jefferson, etc.

INDEXES

An *index* is a special kind of reference book. All reference books are meant to be referred to for bits of information rather than to be read from cover to cover. Reference books can be divided into two general types. One kind of reference (such as encyclopedias) contains the information you need. The other kind of reference — indexes — tells you where in collections of materials or books or where in collections of periodicals (magazines and newspapers) you should look to find the material you need.

You have already learned how to use the card catalog to discover whether the library has a particular volume and where it is located on the shelf. But what can you do if you want to know, for example, what magazine articles have been published on the American electoral college system? Should you start through ten years of *Newsweek* by looking at the table of contents in all of the 520 issues to see which articles are there? This would be too much work, particularly if your search only proved that the magazine had never published an article on that topic! Then how can you use magazines without having to subscribe to them and read every issue as they are printed? The answer is — use an index!

The index is the master key to the contents of periodicals and other collections within a volume just as the card catalog is the master key to books of all kinds. There is a vast store of interesting information, opinion, argument, analysis, and fiction contained in periodicals and collections, and indexes help you find these.

An index might classify thousands of items, it might get them from hundreds of different periodicals or collections, and the items might be classified under hundreds of topics. These are the things that make an index such a valuable time saver!

There are two basic kinds of indexes. There are general ones like the *Readers' Guide to Periodical Literature* and the *New York Times Index* and specialized ones like the *Applied Science and Technology Index*, the *Biological and Agricultural Index*, and the *Poetry Index*. We will show you how to use the two general ones, and this will give you the experience needed to use any index you want.

READERS' GUIDE TO PERIODICAL LITERATURE

Magazines — often called *periodicals* because they are published at regular periods — give us an important source of current material. Often they contain information that has not yet been written in books, and they can be used when the information in books needs to be updated. Magazines often present more viewpoints than ever written in books. Too often, however, people do not use magazines effectively, because they have no idea how to find the material they want.

If you were to visit Chicago and wanted to see your cousin, you would not rush frantically from house to house asking whether anyone knew an

Aileen Allan. Yet all too often a person who is looking for material on the latest space project starts thumbing hopefully through magazine after magazine. Luckily this is not necessary. There are indexes to periodicals which help us to find material. One you will use most often right now is a general index to magazines called the *Readers' Guide to Periodical Literature.*[1]

The *Readers' Guide* is a cumulative index. For example, an issue may appear in January and one in February. Then in March a cumulative issue will appear which will include in one alphabet all the entries in the January and February *Guides* as well as the new ones for March. An issue may appear in April and in May, and then another cumulative issue might appear in June which includes three months. Each year the quarterly issues are cumulated into one bound volume for the entire year.

This means that you need to have a period of time in mind before you begin to check the index and then select the issues of the index covering the dates you are interested in. For example, if you want information about relations between Russia and the U.S. during the first year of President Nixon's term in office, be sure to check the *Readers' Guide for 1969.* If you are interested in relations between Russia and the U.S. during the past six months, be sure to check the *Readers' Guide* for the appropriate dates. The dates indexed always appear on the outside of each of the *Readers' Guides.*

Each volume of the *Readers' Guide* is like a miniature card catalog. Magazine articles are listed according to author and according to subject. The author entries and the subject entries are listed together in one alphabet. The title of the article is not usually indexed. To save space many abbreviations are used in each entry. A key to these abbreviations appears in the front of each *Readers' Guide.*

Following is a typical entry listed by author:

ARMOUR, Richard
    East is East but West is best. Sat R 53:4 O
    3 '70

Translating this entry with the help of the key to abbreviations, we find that Richard Armour wrote an article entitled "East Is East but West Is Best" which appeared in the *Saturday Review* (volume 53, page 4) dated October 3, 1970. Notice that the *Readers' Guide* capitalizes only the first word and the proper nouns in the titles.

Following is a typical entry listed by subject:

BANKS AND BANKING
    Automated banking, fastest draw in the
        West, R. Hazelleaf. il Pop Sci 197:45 S '70

Again with the help of the key to abbreviations, we see that R. Hazelleaf has written an article called "Automated Banking, Fastest Draw in the West," which is illustrated and appears in *Popular Science*, volume 197, page 45, dated September 1970.

Like the card catalog, the *Readers' Guide* also gives you special help to find your subject. Large subjects are divided into narrower subjects by subheads and entries listed under the appropriate subhead. For example, under the subject UNITED STATES, you might find the following subtopics:

UNITED STATES — Air Force
                Atomic Energy
                Commission
                Bureau of Indian Affairs
                Cabinet

Any of these subtopics may again be subdivided. For example:

UNITED STATES — Air Force — education
                            forces in
                            Laos
                            history
                            officers

Also like the card catalog, the *Readers' Guide* gives you cross references to help you find your subject. There are "see also" entries which direct you to additional subjects. For example, you might find the following entry:

            INTERNATIONAL RELATIONS
                See also
                Peace

The *Readers' Guide* also has "see" entries which tell you that a certain subject heading is not used, but directs you to another. For example, you might find the following:

ARTIFICIAL diamonds. *See* Diamonds, artificial

---

[1]The *Readers' Guide* appears twice a month and indexes about 130 magazines. There is also an *Abridged Readers' Guide* which appears monthly September to June and indexes about 45 magazines. Although one indexes more magazines and is published more often than the other, they are organized the same way and give you the same help.

This is how these different kinds of entries look in the *Readers' Guide.*

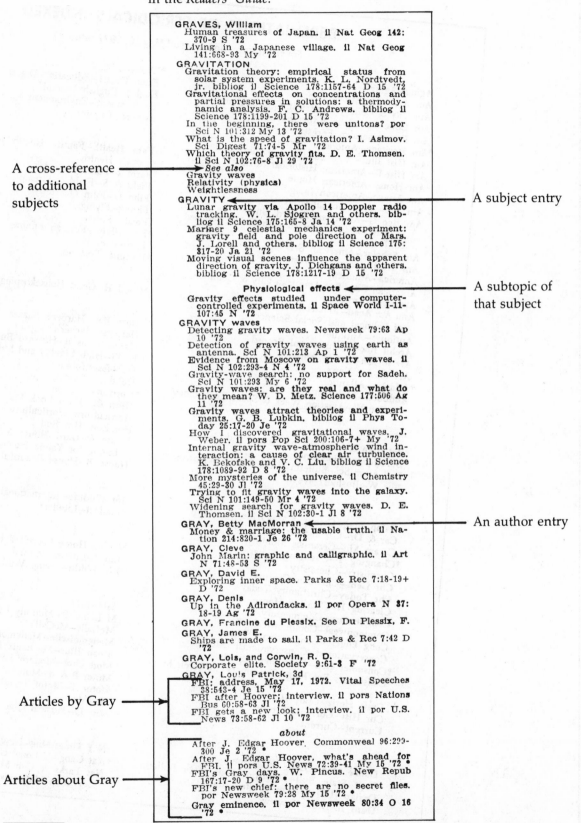

A cross-reference to additional subjects

A subject entry

A subtopic of that subject

An author entry

Articles by Gray

Articles about Gray

GRAVES, William
Human treasures of Japan. il Nat Geog 142:370-9 S '72
Living in a Japanese village. il Nat Geog 141:668-93 My '72
GRAVITATION
Gravitation theory: empirical status from solar system experiments. K. L. Nordtvedt, jr. bibliog il Science 178:1157-64 D 15 '72
Gravitational effects on concentrations and partial pressures in solutions: a thermodynamic analysis. F. C. Andrews. bibliog il Science 178:1199-201 D 15 '72
In the beginning, there were unitons? por Sci N 101:312 My 13 '72
What is the speed of gravitation? I. Asimov. Sci Digest 71:74-5 Mr '72
Which theory of gravity fits. D. E. Thomsen. il Sci N 102:76-8 Jl 29 '72
See also
Gravity waves
Relativity (physics)
Weightlessness
GRAVITY
Lunar gravity via Apollo 14 Doppler radio tracking. W. L. Sjogren and others. bibliog il Science 175:165-8 Ja 14 '72
Mariner 9 celestial mechanics experiment: gravity field and pole direction of Mars. J. Lorell and others. bibliog il Science 175:317-20 Ja 21 '72
Moving visual scenes influence the apparent direction of gravity. J. Dichgans and others. bibliog il Science 178:1217-19 D 15 '72

Physiological effects
Gravity effects studied under computer-controlled experiments. il Space World I-11-107:45 N '72
GRAVITY waves
Detecting gravity waves. Newsweek 79:63 Ap 10 '72
Detection of gravity waves using earth as antenna. Sci N 101:213 Ap 1 '72
Evidence from Moscow on gravity waves. il Sci N 102:293-4 N 4 '72
Gravity-wave search: no support for Sadeh. Sci N 101:293 My 6 '72
Gravity waves: are they real and what do they mean? W. D. Metz. Science 177:506 Ag 11 '72
Gravity waves attract theories and experiments. G. B. Lubkin. bibliog il Phys Today 25:17-20 Je '72
How I discovered gravitational waves. J. Weber. il pors Pop Sci 200:106-7+ My '72
Internal gravity wave-atmospheric wind interaction: a cause of clear air turbulence. K. Bekofske and V. C. Liu. bibliog il Science 178:1089-92 D 8 '72
More mysteries of the universe. il Chemistry 45:29-30 Jl '72
Trying to fit gravity waves into the galaxy. Sci N 101:149-50 Mr 4 '72
Widening search for gravity waves. D. E. Thomsen. il Sci N 102:30-1 Jl 8 '72
GRAY, Betty MacMorran
Money & marriage: the usable truth. il Nation 214:820-1 Je 26 '72
GRAY, Cleve
John Marin: graphic and calligraphic. il Art N 71:48-53 S '72
GRAY, David E.
Exploring inner space. Parks & Rec 7:18-19+ D '72
GRAY, Denis
Up in the Adirondacks. il por Opera N 37:18-19 Ag '72
GRAY, Francine du Plessix. See Du Plessix, F.
GRAY, James E.
Ships are made to sail. il Parks & Rec 7:42 D '72
GRAY, Lois, and Corwin, R. D.
Corporate elite. Society 9:61-3 F '72
GRAY, Louis Patrick, 3d
FBI: address, May 17, 1972. Vital Speeches 38:543-4 Je 15 '72
FBI after Hoover; interview. il pors Nations Bus 60:58-63 Jl '72
FBI gets a new look; interview. il por U.S. News 73:58-62 Jl 10 '72

about
After J. Edgar Hoover. Commonweal 96:299-300 Je 2 '72 *
After J. Edgar Hoover, what's ahead for FBI. il pors U.S. News 72:39-41 My 15 '72 *
FBI's Gray days. W. Pincus. New Repub 167:17-20 D 9 '72 *
FBI's new chief: there are no secret files. por Newsweek 79:28 My 15 '72 *
Gray eminence. il por Newsweek 80:34 O 16 '72 *

Excerpt from *Readers' Guide to Periodical Literature,* March 1972 to February 1973, p. 503. Copyright © 1972, 1973 by The H.W. Wilson Company. Reprinted by permission of the publisher.

ABBREVIATIONS OF PERIODICALS INDEXED

For full information, consult May 10, 1977 issue

Aging—Aging
Am Artist—American Artist
Am City & County—American City & County
Am Educ—American Education
Am For—American Forests
*Am Heritage—American Heritage
Am Hist Illus—American History Illustrated
Am Hist R—American Historical Review
Am Home—American Home
Am Imago—American Imago
Am Lib—American Libraries
Am Rec G—American Record Guide
    (Publication suspended with D '72; resumed
    N '76)
Am Scholar—American Scholar
Am West—American West
America—America
American City. See American City & County
Américas—Américas
Ann Am Acad—Annals of the American Academy
    of Political and Social Science
Antiques—Antiques
Archit Rec—Architectural Record
Art in Am—Art in America
Art N—Art News
*Atlantic—Atlantic
Audubon—Audubon
Aviation W—Aviation Week & Space Technology

*Bet Hom & Gard—Better Homes and Gardens
BioScience—BioScience
Bull Atom Sci—Bulletin of the Atomic Scientists
Bus W—Business Week

Camp Mag—Camping Magazine
Car & Dr—Car and Driver
Ceram Mo—Ceramics Monthly
*Changing T—Changing Times
Chemistry—Chemistry
Chr Cent—Christian Century
Chr Today—Christianity Today
Clearing H—Clearing House
Commentary—Commentary
Commonweal—Commonweal
Cong Digest—Congressional Digest
Conservationist—Conservationist (Albany)
*Consumer Rep—Consumer Reports
*Consumers Res Mag—Consumers' Research Mag-
    azine
Craft Horiz—Craft Horizons
Cur Hist—Current History
Current—Current

Dance Mag—Dance Magazine
Dept State Bull—Department of State Bulletin
Design (US)—Design (United States)
Duns R—Dun's Review

*Ebony—Ebony
Educ Digest—Education Digest
Engl J—English Journal
Environment—Environment
Esquire—Esquire

Fam Health—Family Health incorporatir
    day's Health
*Farm J—Farm Journal
Field & S—Field & Stream
Film Q—Film Quarterly
Flying—Flying
Focus—Focus
*For Affairs—Foreign Affairs
Forbes—Forbes
*Fortune—Fortune

*Good H—Good Housekeeping

Harp Baz—Harper's Bazaar
*Harpers—Harper's
Harvard Bus R—Harvard Business Rev
*Hi Fi—High Fidelity and Musical Ame
Hobbies—Hobbies
*Holiday—Holiday
*Horizon—Horizon
Horn Bk—Horn Book Magazine
Horticulture—Horticulture
Hot Rod—Hot Rod
House & Gard—House & Garden i
    Living for Young Homemakers
House B—House Beautiful

Int Wildlife—International Wildlife
Intellect—Intellect

*Ladies Home J—Ladies' Home Jour
Lib J—Library Journal
Liv Wildn—Living Wilderness

MH—MH
M Labor R—Monthly Labor Revie
McCalls—McCall's
Mademoiselle—Mademoiselle
Mech Illus—Mechanix Illustrated
Mod Phot—Modern Photography
Motor B & S—Motor Boating & S
Motor T—Motor Trend
Ms—Ms.
*Mus Q—Musical Quarterly

N Y Times Mag—New York Tim
*Nat Geog—National Geographic
Nat Parks & Con Mag—Nation
    servation Magazine

ABBREVIATIONS OF PERIODICALS INDEXED[1]

*Nat R—National Review (48p issue only, pub. in alternate weeks)
Nat Wildlife—National Wildlife
Nation—Nation
Nations Bus—Nation's Business
*Natur Hist—Natural History
Negro Hist Bull—Negro History Bulletin
New Cath World—New Catholic World
New Repub—New Republic
New Yorker—New Yorker
*Newsweek—Newsweek

Oceans—Oceans
Opera N—Opera News
Org Gard & Farm—Organic Gardening and Farming
Outdoor Life—Outdoor Life

Parents Mag—Parents' Magazine & Better Home-making
Parks & Rec—Parks & Recreation
Phys Today—Physics Today
Plays—Plays
Poetry—Poetry
Pop Electr—Popular Electronics including Electronics World
*Pop Mech—Popular Mechanics
Pop Phot—Popular Photography
Pop Sci—Popular Science
Progressive—Progressive
Psychol Today—Psychology Today
Pub W—Publishers Weekly

Radio-Electr—Radio-Electronics
*Read Digest—Reader's Digest
Redbook—Redbook
*Ret Liv—Retirement Living

SLJ—SLJ/School Library Journal
Sat Eve Post—Saturday Evening Post
*Sat R—Saturday Review

Sch Arts—School Arts
*Sci Am—Scientific American
Sci Digest—Science Digest
Sci N—Science News
Science—Science
Science and Public Affairs. See Bulletin of the Atomic Scientists
Sea Front—Sea Frontiers
*Seventeen—Seventeen
Sky & Tel—Sky and Telescope
Smithsonian—Smithsonian
Society—Society
Space World—Space World
Sports Car Graphic. See Motor Trend
*Sports Illus—Sports Illustrated
Sr Schol—Senior Scholastic including World Week (Scholastic Teacher's edition)
Suc Farm—Successful Farming (Midwest edition)
Sunset—Sunset (Central edition)

Time—Time
Todays Educ—Today's Education
Travel—Travel

UN Chron—UN Chronicle
UNESCO Courier—UNESCO Courier
*U.S. News—U.S. News & World Report

Vital Speeches—Vital Speeches of the Day
Vogue—Vogue

Weatherwise—Weatherwise
Wilson Lib Bull—Wilson Library Bulletin
World Week. See Senior Scholastic
*Writer—Writer
Writers Digest—Writer's Digest

Yachting—Yachting
Yale R—Yale Review

* Available for blind and other physically handicapped readers on talking books, in braille, or on magnetic tape. For information address Division for the Blind and Physically Handicapped, Library of Congress, Washington, D.C. 20542

[1]The *Readers' Guide* indexes these magazines.

Sample pages from *Readers' Guide to Periodical Literature,* March 1972 to February 1973, pp. iii and iv. Copyright © 1972, 1973 by the H.W. Wilson Company. Reprinted by permission of the publisher.

Often it is not easy to decide what word your subject may be listed under. If this happens to you, just look for the most important or the key word in your subject. If that does not happen to be the one the index uses, there will be a cross-reference.

Two special additional hints should help you find material more easily in the *Readers' Guide*. First, when you are searching for material related to a person who is frequently in the current news, you may find entries listed under his or her name in two separate alphabets. The first group lists things written *by* that person, and the second group lists things written *about* that person. Be sure you are looking in the right list for what you need.

The second hint is for times when you are interested in information about movies or plays. Important plays and movies are indexed in *Readers' Guide* under such headings as musical comedies, moving picture plays, or dramas. If, for example, you wanted a review of a recent movie, you would look in the *Guide* under the subject *Moving picture plays*; then under that in alphabetical order you would find the title. For example:

> MOVING picture plays
>> Single works
> Anne of the thousand days
>> America 122:170 F 14 '70
>> Look il 34:12-13 F 24 '70
>> Newsweek 75:75- S 29 '69
>> Time il 95:70 F 2 '70

The *Readers' Guide* has given us four sources of articles about this movie.

Most indexes have the same basic arrangement as the *Readers' Guide to Periodicals*. Taking a few minutes to become familiar with this index is like turning in your scrub board for an automatic washer. You can accomplish much more with a fraction of the effort and time.

SUMMARY — READERS' GUIDE

Author entry:	ARMOUR, Richard East is East but West is best. Sat R 53:4 O 3 '70
Subject entry:	BANKS AND BANKING Automated banking, fastest draw in the West. R Hazelleaf. il Pop Sci 197:45 S '70
Subtopics:	UNITED STATES — Air Force Atomic energy commission Bureau of Indian affairs Cabinet
Subtopics that are divided:	UNITED STATES — Air Force — education forces in Laos history officers
See also:	INTERNATIONAL RELATIONS *see also* Peace
See:	ARTIFICIAL diamonds. *See* Diamonds, artificial
Movie reviews:	MOVING picture plays Single works Anne of the thousand days America 122:170 F 14 '70 Look il 34:12-13 F 24 '70 Newsweek 75:75- S 29 '69 Time il 95:70 F 2 '70

NEW YORK TIMES INDEX

Another useful index to help you find current material you need is the *New York Times Index*. This is a subject index to the Late City Edition of the *New York Times* newspaper. Paperback indexes appear every two weeks and then are cumulated and bound in yearly volumes. The *NYT Index* began in 1851, and the earlier volumes covering the 19th century are reproductions of the originals. Some of the earliest are written by hand. If your library has these early indexes, take a minute to browse through to see what was making headlines before the Civil War. You'll find that Daniel Webster is a very busy man; Harriet Beecher Stowe's publisher announces *Uncle Tom's Cabin;* Ralph Waldo Emerson is making headlines; Indian Wars are being fought and treaties are being made. You can read these stories on microfilm as news.

The later editions of the *NYT Index* have a summary of the year in the foreward. The subject headings are arranged alphabetically. Some large subjects have subheadings and even second subheadings. Some entries give brief summaries of the articles, and all have date, page, and column references, e.g., Ja 5, 1:8, which means the article appeared January 5 on page 1, column 8. Sections of the Sunday paper are referred to by Roman numerals. There are many cross-references.

Excerpt from a reproduction of the early *New York Times Index*, September 1851 to September 1858. Copyright © 1967 by New York Times Company. Reprinted by permission.

Following are some sample entries from the *NYT Index* for 1971:

A subject heading

Cross-references

A subject subheading

Summary of article

This article is found in the January 31 paper on page 9, column 1.

Excerpt from the *New York Times Index*, vol. 59, 1972, p. 150. Copyright © 1972 by New York Times Company. Reprinted by permission.

Note the summaries of the stories. Sometimes they contain enough information so that you don't have to actually read the article, or at least they provide enough information to help you decide whether or not the article is what you need.

As with any periodical index, be sure you are using the volume that covers the period you are interested in. If you want information about Pearl Harbor, start with the *NYT Index* for 1941. If you want information about the McGovern-Nixon campaign, use the *NYT Index* for 1972.

There are other indexes available to help locate material from magazines in special fields:

> *Applied Science and Technology Index*
>
> *Art Index*
>
> *Biography Index* (for biographies appearing in periodicals)
>
> *Biological and Agricultural Index*
>
> *Book Review Digest*
>
> *Education Index*
>
> *Music Index*
>
> *Nineteenth-Century Readers' Guide to Periodical Literature*
>
> *Short Story Index*
>
> *Subject Index to Children's Magazines*

Most of these indexes are organized like the *Readers' Guide* — by author, title, and subject. The sample pages from some of these indexes show what kinds of things they contain. You probably will have no need to learn about all of these indexes right now, but you should remember that such specialized indexes exist.

Other kinds of indexes help locate paintings, plays, poetry, biographies, and short stories which have been collected in books. For example, in the *Index to Reproductions of American Paintings* reproductions of paintings found in 520 books are listed by artist, title, and subject. The *Index to Young Readers' Collective Biographies* lists alphabetically and by profession the important people who are in collections of biographies for elementary through junior high school readers.

The usefulness of indexes can spiral if you approach them with a bit of imagination. Obviously, if you were searching for material on Amelia Earhart you would check the *Biography Index*. But you might not think to check the same index if you were writing a paper on aerodynamics or searching for information about how women lawyers are portrayed in books for young people. The lists by professions in the *Biography Index* or the *Index to Young Readers' Collective Biographies* could be helpful for both of these.

When you are faced with the problem of gathering information, check early in your referencing to see what indexes are available to help you. Indexes often can reduce mountains to molehills.

Problem 3 — Readers' Guide

SELF-CHECKING EXERCISES

Following are entries from the *Abridged Readers' Guide*.[1] Parts of the entries are numbered. Using these numbers, answer the questions which follow. If there is no number that answers the question, use an *X*. If more than one number answers the question, use all which apply. (All the numbers are not used.)

FOOTBALL
(1) Devil's devil: Arizona State Sun Devils. il Newsweek 76:45 O 26 '70 (7)
(2) For Easterners, prospecting doesn't pay off: Colorado vs Penn State. D. Jenkins. (8) il Sports Illus 33:36-8 O 5 '70
(3) See also Football players (9) (10) (11)
(4) Anecdotes
(5) Everything you always wanted to know about football. R. Baker.
(13) *Read Digest* 97:59-60 O '70 (6)
FOOTBALL accidents. See Football — Accidents and injuries (12)

1. What is the subject of all the articles listed?

2. What is a subtopic under a subject heading?

3. What is a reference that sends you to additional information?

4. Who is the writer of the article?

5. What is the title of the article?

6. What is the magazine you would find the article in?

7. What is the page the article begins on?

8. What is the date of the magazine?

9. Who is the publisher of the magazine?

SEARCH QUESTIONS[2]

Use the *Abridged Readers' Guide*, Vol. 20 (June 1969 to May 1970) or the unabridged *Readers' Guide*, Vol. 29 (March 1969 to February 1970). Locate each of the following articles. Take time to read the entries to be sure you understand what it is telling you. If you need help, read the Clues.

---

[1]*Abridged Readers' Guide to Periodical Literature*, Vol. 21, December, 1970, p. 65.

[2]Teachers: If this is a class assignment, you might want the students to write only the numbers of the pages on which they find each entry.

1. Find an article on Ernest Hemingway that appeared in *Time*.

2. Find a review of the movie "Oh, What a Lovely War" that was in the *Saturday Review* or maybe it was *Harpers*.

3. Find a review of the play, *Hedda Gabler*.

4. Find something about music that is used in television.

5. Find some stories about Christmas.

6. Find something about People's Republic of China having gained a seat in the U.N.

7. Find an article on dog racing.

CLUES

1. a. Look first under Hemingway
   b. Next, find the listing for *Time*.

2. a. First look under the heading MOVING PICTURE PLAYS — Single works.
   b. Locate the title in the alphabetical list.

3. There are two ways to find this
   a. Find the title of the play under *H*.
   b. Follow the directions to see the author, H. Ibsen for the full entry.
      or
   a. Look first under DRAMA — Single works.
   b. Find the title in the alphabetical list.
   c. Follow directions to see the author.

4. If you chose MUSIC as your subject to check, follow the cross-reference that tells you to *see also* Television broadcasting — *or*
   If you chose TELEVISION as your subject to check, look under the subheading Music.

5. Look under CHRISTMAS stories.

6. a. Look under UNITED NATIONS
   b. Then look under the subheading China (People's Republic) — *or*
      Look under the subheading Membership — *or*

If you chose to look under CHINA (People's Republic) for your subject then follow the directions to "see also" UNITED NATIONS — China.

7. Look under DOG RACES.

Problem 4 — New York Times Index

SEARCH QUESTIONS[1]

Use the 1971 *New York Times Index*. Look for information about the following questions. If you need help, read the Clues.

1. What has been happening concerning women in Israel?

2. Carlos Montoya, the guitarist, gave a concert. What did the critics say about him?

3. What kind of growth did Canadian industry have this year?

CLUES

1. Look under WOMEN and then under the subheading "Israel."

2. You would find an article about Montoya under his name, but the review of his concert is not listed there. You need to check MUSIC, then the subheading Concerts, and then Montoya.

3. Look under CANADA — Economic conditions and trends. If you looked under INDUSTRY, a cross-reference sent you to U.S. — Economic conditions, but remember you're checking Canada.

[1]Teachers: If this is a class assignment, you might want students to write only the page numbers on which they find each entry.

PICASSO, Pablo—Reproductions—*Continued*
Portrait de Sébastien Juñer Vidal (1903)
Oeil no256:6 N '76 (col)
Le repas frugal (etch, 1904)
Art in Am 64:68 N '76
Connaissance Arts no296:20 O '76
PICHARD, Georges
Reproductions
Paulette, Ras-le-Bol Ville
R du Louvre 26 no3:224 '76
PICKER, Fred
Reproductions
[Icelandic terrain] (photo)
Art in Am 64:145 N '76
Art News 75:101 N '76
PICON, Gaëtan
Obituary
Connaissance Arts no296:13 O '76
PICOT DE LIMOËLAN DE CLORIVIÈRE, Joseph Pierre
Reproductions
Andrew Greene Simpson Semes (watercolor)
Antiques 110:1054 N '76
PICTURE frames and framing
Framing of Rembrandt's Night watch in the past and the new frame. C. J. de Bruyn Kops. bibl f il Bull Rijksmus 24:99-119 S '76
PICTURE hanging. See Pictures—Hanging
PICTURE writing, Egyptian. See Egyptian language—Writing. Hieroglyphic
PICTURES
Hanging
Framing of Rembrandt's Night watch in the past and the new frame. C. J. de Bruyn Kops. bibl f il Bull Rijksmus 24:99-119 S '76
Missing and found works
[Canvases by M. Craig-Martin incorporating "found" paintings] Rowan gallery, London; exhibit. Art Int 20:62 O-N '76
Caravaggio's Crowning with thorns in the Cassa di risparmi e depositi de Prato. il(p47) Art Int 20:66 O-N '76
Le curieux achat fait à Derain et à Vlaminck au Salon des Indépendants de 1905 ou deux tableaux retrouvés. M. Giry. bibl f il(pt col) Oeil no254:26-31 S '76
Marshal Blücher's booty; a rediscovered group of portraits. C. de Salis. il Connoisseur 193: 271-4 D '76
Rembrandt à vingt ans. E. Schlumberger. il(pt col) por(p 138) Connaissance Arts no296:68-75 O '76
PICTURESQUE
Eye for an I; the failure of the townscape tradition. R. Maxwell. il plan AD 46:534-6 S '76
PIEDMONT, Calif.
Schools
Functional simplicity in design for earthquake resistance [Piedmont junior high school] J. Nairn. il plans diags Archit Rec 160:141-4 S '76
PIER buildings. See Harbor buildings
PIERCE, Elijah
Phyllis Kind gallery, New York; exhibit. Artforum 15:60-1 Ja '77
il: Slavery time
Phyllis Kind gallery, New York; exhibit. Arts 51:34 D '76
il: Slavery time
PIERCE, Gerald
Benson gallery, Bridgehampton, N.Y; exhibit. Craft Horiz 36:56 O '76
il: Necklace of ancient stone beads and pendant from Mexico
PIERSON, William Harvey, Jr
Hammond-Harwood House: a colonial masterpiece. bibl f il(pt col) plans Antiques 111:186-93 Ja '77
PIETRO da Cortona (Pietro Berrettini)
Design and designers of Palazzo Barberini. P. Waddy. bibl f plans diags Soc Archit Hist J 35:151+ O '76
il (p 180-1): Drawing for the west façade of Palazzo Barberini (attrib); Villa Sacchetti (Villa del Pigneto)
Reproductions
Nativité de la Vierge
R du Louvre 26 no3:168 '76
Portrait of James Alban Gibbes (engr)
Burl Mag 118:696 O '76
Influence
Reproductions

PIGGOTT, Stuart
O. G. S. Crawford. Antiquity 50:185-6 S-D '76
PILGRIM, Anton, the younger
Reproductions
Organ podium, St Stephen, Vienna (1513)
Gesta 15 no 1-2:78 '76
PILGRIMS and pilgrimages
Constantine and Charlemagne. L. Seidel. bibl f il Gesta 15 no 1-2:237-9 '76
PILLEMENT, Jean Baptiste
Reproductions
Le pont de bois
Connaissance Arts no296:12 O '76
Ruins in a landscape (drwg, 1801)
Apollo ns 104:400 N '76
Influence
Reproductions
Aubusson chinoiserie tapestry (tapestry after J. B. Pillement)
Apollo ns 104:[front] 81 N '76 (col)
PILLSBURY, Edmund P.
Federico Barocci's Fossombrone Madonna: an unknown drawing. bibl f il Yale Univ Art Gal Bull 36 no 1:20-5 Fall '76
Lorenzo Sabatini and the Sala regia. bibl f il Oberlin Coll Bull 34 no 1:38-45 '76-77
Sala Grande drawings by Vasari and his workshop: some documents and new attributions [with documents from the Archivio di Stato, Florence] bibl f il Mast Draw 14 no2:127-46 Summ '76
PILOTY, Karl Theodor von
Reproductions
Christophe Colomb (1866)
R du Louvre 26 no4:262 '76
PIMENTEL, Alexandra de Serpa
Degree show 76; jewellery. il Design no335:38 N '76
PIMM, John
History and technique of japanning and the restoration of the Pimm highboy. J. H. Hill. bibl f il (with back cov) Am Art J 8:76-84 N '76
PINCUS-WITTEN, Robert
Entries. il Arts 51:17-20 O; 19 D '76
Howdy—Art nouveau in Houston [Institute for the arts, Rice university] il Art J 36 no 1:45-9 Fall '76
Jackie Ferrara: the feathery elevator. il Arts 51:104-8 N '76
PINEAU, Nicolas
Reproductions
Attributed works
Dessin d'un dessus de cheminée pour le château d'Ansbach (1731)
Gaz Beaux Arts ser6 v88:supp35 O '76
PINTO, Alfonso
Lilian Harvey gave a few light-hearted moments in the years before World war II [with list of films] pors Films in R 21:478-90 O '70; Addition. 27:639-40 D '76
PIOMBO, Fra Guglielmo del. See Porta, G. della
PIOMBO, Sebastiano del. See Sebastiano del Piombo
PIPE
See also
Tubes
PIPER, John
Reproductions
Spires of Oxford (watercolor)
Country Life 160:supp48a O 7 '76
PIRANESI, Giovanni Battista
Caisse nationale des monuments historiques: Hôtel de Sully, Paris; exposition. R du Louvre 26 no4:314 '76
il: Idea di un atrio reale
Piranesi: etchings and drawings [book review] A. Werner. Am Artist 40:27-8 O '76
PISANELLO (Antonio Pisano)
Reproductions
John VIII Paleologus (medal, 1438)
Apollo ns 104:407 N '76
PISANI, Vettor
Reproductions
Segno zodiacale del genio (1976)
Artforum 15:19 N '76
stella [installation view; Biennale, Venice 1976]

AVIAN nephrosis

Effect of infectious Bursal disease on the response of chickens to mycoplasma synoviae, Newcastle disease virus, and infectious bronchitis virus. J. J. Giambrone and others. bibl il Am J Vet Res 38:251-3 F '77

More research needed on bursal disease. T. H. Eleazer. Poultry Dig 36:92 F '77

Vaccination

Marek's breaks linked to Gumboro vaccination. G. Sharpe. Poultry Dig 36:92 F '77; Discussion. 36:157 Mr '77

Response of growing chickens to an inactivated IBD antigen in oil emulsion. G. A. Cullen and P. J. Wyeth. bibl il Vet Rec 99:418 N 20 '76; Discussion. 100:121 F 5 '77

AVIATION
See also
Airplanes

AVLOSULFON. See Dapsone

AVOCADOS

Chemical composition

Changes in the initiation of climacteric ethylene in harvested avocado fruits during their development. I. Adato and S. Gazit. bibl il J Sci Food & Agric 28:240-2 Mr '77

Discoloration

Latency properties of polyphenol oxidase in two avocado cultivars differing in their rate of browning. V. Kahn. bibl il J Sci Food & Agric 28:233-9 Mr '77

Some biochemical properties of polyphenoloxidase from two avocado varieties differing in their browning rates. V. Kahn. bibl il J Food Sci 42:38-43 Ja '77

Setting of fruit

Effect of temperature on floral behaviour, pollen tube growth and fruit set in the avocado. M. Sedgley. bibl il J Hort Sci 52:135-41 Ja '77

AWASI sheep

Possibilities of utilization of part lactation records for selection and progeny testing in Awassi sheep. E. Tuncel. bibl il Trop Agric (BWI) 54:15-19 Ja '77

AWNS (botany)

Role of multiple awns in determining barley yields. D. C. Rasmusson and R. K. Crookston. bibl il Crop Sci 17:135-40 Ja '77

AYRSHIRES

Length of gestation period of Ayrshire cows when mated with bulls of other breeds. R. Laird and E. A. Hunter. bibl il Animal Prod 24:63-7 F '77

AZADIRACHTA indica

Neem tree; commercial potential, characteristics and distribution. S. Radwanski. bibl il map World Crops & Livestock 29:62-3+ Mr '77

AZALEA blight. See Azalea flower spot

AZALEA flower spot

Therapy

Control of azalea flower blight with a new fungicide, Bay Meb 6447. H. N. Miller and K. A. Noegel. bibl il Plant Dis Rept 61:111-15 F '77

Effect of fungicides and application timing on control of azalea petal blight. J. L. Peterson and S. H. Davis, jr. bibl il Plant Dis Rept 61:209-12 Mr '77

AZALEA petal blight. See Azalea flower spot

AZALEAS

Chemical composition

2"-O-acetylquercitrin from azalea flowers. S. Asen and R. M. Horowitz. bibl il Phytochemistry 16:147-8 Ja '77

Flavonoids of the deciduous rhodendron of North America (ericaceae) B. L. King. bibl il Am J Bot 64:350-60 Mr '77

Diseases and pests
See also
Azalea flower spot

Laboratory experiments

Supercooling in overwintering azalea flower buds; additional freezing parameters. M. F. George and M. J. Burke. bibl il Plant Physiol 59:326-8 F '77

AZARA

Azaras. A. J. Anderson. il Garden 102:37-8 Ja '77

AZOOSPERMIA. See Spermatogenesis

AZOTOBACTER vinelandii

Alginate lyase from azotobacter vinelandii phage. I. W. Davidson and others. bibl il J Gen Microbiol 98:223-9 Ja '77

Generation of a transmembrane electric potential during respiration by azotobacter vinelandii membrane vesicles. P. Bhattacharyya and others. bibl il J Bact 129:756-62 F '77

Chemical composition

Purification and some biological properties of asparaginase from azotobacter vinelandii. S. A. Gaffar and Y. I. Shethna. bibl il App & Envir Microbiol 33:508-14 Mr '77

Selective inactivation of nitrogenase in azotobacter vinelandii batch cultures. D. Kleiner and J. A. Kleinschmidt. bibl il J Bact 128:117-22 O '76

AZOTURIA

Cattle

Some observations on paralytic myoglobinuria of cattle in Britain. P. H. Anderson and others. bibl Vet Rec 99:316-18 O 16 '76; Discussion. 99:364 O 30 '76

BK virus

Isolation and characterization of BK virus-transformed hamster cells. J. Seehafer and others. bibl il Virology 77:356-66 Mr '77

BMMV. See Bean mild mosaic virus

BABOONS

Monkey business; editorial. Vet Rec 99:283 O 9 '76

Observational learning of baboons and avoidance of mimics; exploratory tests. P. Jouventin and others. bibl il Evolution 31:214-18 Mr '77

BABOONS, Chacma

Defense of space and resources by chacma (papio ursinus) baboon troops in an African desert and swamp. W. J. Hamilton 3d and others. bibl il maps Ecology 57:1264-72 Aut '76

BACILLARY hemoglobinuria. See Hemoglobinuria, Bacillary

BACILLUS

Initiation of bacillus spore germination by hydrostatic pressure; effect of temperature. W. G. Murrell and P. A. Wills. bibl il J Bact 129:1272-80 Mr '77

Chemical composition

Enzymic assays for isomers of 2,6-diaminopimelic acid in walls of bacillus cereus and bacillus megaterium. A. Day and P. J. White. bibl il Biochem J 161:677-85 Mr 1 '77

Site-specific deoxyribonucleases in bacillus subtilis and other bacillus strains. T. Shibata and others. bibl il J Bact 128:473-6 O '76

BACILLUS anthracis
See also
Anthrax

BACILLUS brevis

Chemical composition

Electron microscopy of glycyl-tRNA synthetase from bacillus brevis. N. A. Kiselev and others. bibl il Acad Sci USSR Proc (Biochem Sec) 229:312-15 Jl '76

BACILLUS cereus

Chemical composition

Phospholipase C from bacillus cereus; evidence for essential lysine residues. B. Aurebekk and C. Little. bibl il Biochem J 161:159-65 Ja 1 '77

BACILLUS licheniformis

Light-induced inhibition of sporulation in bacillus licheniformis. C. Propst-Ricciuti and L. B. Lubin. bibl il J Bact 128:506-9 O '76

Morphological changes associated with novobiocin resistance in bacillus licheniformis. R. L. Robson and J. Baddiley. bibl il J Bact 129:1045-50 F '77

Chemical composition

Biochemical localization of the alkaline phosphatase of bacillus licheniformis as a function of culture age. J. A. Glynn and others. bibl il J Bact 129:1010-19 F '77

Electron microscope histochemical localization of alkaline phosphatase(s) in bacillus licheniformis. J. M. McNicholas and F. M. Hulett. bibl il J Bact 129:501-15 Ja '77

Penicillinase-releasing protease of bacillus licheniformis; purification and general properties. P. S. Aiya and others. bibl il J B

Sample page from *Biological and Agricultural Index*. New York, The H.W. Wilson Company. Copyright © 1975 by The H.W. Wilson Company. Reprinted by permission of the publisher.

READING—Achievements, Student—*Continued*

Comparison of reading achievement with teacher's effort. T. R. Blair. Read Improv 14:112-15 Summ '77

Effect of word imagery on reading performance as a function of reader ability. A. F. Jorm. bibl J Educ Psychol 69:46-54 F '77

Fifth-grade reading achievement as a function of selected school, classroom, and pupil variables. United States. Office of education. National center for education statistics. (NCES-76-310) U.S. Off Educ Pub 1976:99p

Is Johnny's/Mary's reading getting worse? R. Farr. Educ Lead 34:521-3+ Ap '77

Laterality and intelligence in relation to reading ability. C. E. Sawyer and B. J. Brown. Educ R 29:81-6 F '77

Reading attainment and family size: an anomaly. K. Richardson. bibl Brit J Educ Psychol 47:71-5 F '77

Reading performance of bilingual children according to type of school and home language. J. R. Cowan and Z. Sarmad. bibl il Lang Learn 26:353-76 D '76

Reading scores of American nine year olds: NAEP's tests. D. Lapp and R. J. Tierney. Read Teach 30:756-60 Ap '77

Relationship between performance on a Piagetian liquid conservation task and reading achievement in seven year old children. R. E. Orpet and others. Educ & Psychol M 36:1021-4 Wint '76

Resolving curricular conflicts in the 1970s: modifying the hypothesis. It's the teacher who makes the difference in reading achievement. H. Singer. Lang Arts 54:158-63 F '77

School achievement scores of hearing impaired children: national data on achievement status and growth patterns. R. J. Trybus and M. A. Karchmer. bibl il Am Ann Deaf 122:62-9 Ap '77

Sciencing activities as contributors to the development of reading skills in first grade students. A. Morgan and others. bibl il Sci Educ 61:135-44 Ap '77

Should you read aloud to your children? S. McCormick. bibl Lang Arts 54:139-43+ F '77

Student locus of control and teaching style in relation to college reading improvement. A. R. Allen and M. Harshbarger. Read Improv 14:104-8 Summ '77

Use of classroom time in high schools above or below the median reading score. W. C. Fredrick. Urban Educ 11:459-64 Ja '77

Visuothematic approach in the classroom. M. Jackson and G. Ackenstein. il Acad Therapy 12:327-37 Spr '77

Activities

CB reading center; a big 10-4. F. Wyatt. il Read Teach 30:887-92 My '77

Creating visual activities to enhance predictive behaviors. W. J. Valmont. il Lang Arts 54:172-5 F '77

Teaching for logical thinking is a prereading activity. J. R. Nevius, jr. Read Teach 30:641-3 Mr '77

Teaching students to read orally. G. R. Musgrave. Lang Arts 54:190 F '77

Administration

Arithmetic of reading. F. Silverblank. Read Improv 14:109-11 Summ '77

How to get more comprehensive reading programs at the secondary level. C. W. Peters. J Read 20:513-19 Mr '77

Aims and objectives

Affective component of the reading program. D. J. Strickler. Contemp Educ 48:161-4 Spr '77

Fresh look at secondary reading. N. P. Criscuolo and J. F. Rossman. bibl Clearing H 50:366-8 Ap '77

Jetting to utopia: the speed reading phenomenon. L. R. Mendelsohn. Lang Arts 54:116-20 F '77

Correlation with other subjects

Arts reader. R. S. Gainer. il Art Educ 30:33-8 Mr '77

Children's literature as a springboard to content areas. E. Billig. Read Teach 30:855-9 My '77

How content teachers telegraph messages against reading. B. J. Rieck. J Read 20:646-8 My '77

Math language ability: its relationship to reading in math. L. N. Knight and C. H. Hargis. Lang Arts 54:423-8 [Ap '77]

Curriculum

Extending the reading curriculum. H. Wartenberg. Read Teach 30:680-1+ Mr '77

Resolving curricular conflicts in the 1970s; modifying the hypothesis. It's the teacher who makes the difference in reading achievement. H. Singer. Lang Arts 54:158-63 F '77

Evaluation

Use of adapted classics in a reading program for deaf students. J. R. Anken and D. W. Holmes. bibl Am Ann Deaf 122:8-14 F '77

Diagnosis

Early intervention for the high risk child for reading instruction. R. D. Robinson. Read Improv 14:11-12 Spr '77

Getting the message, decoding the message; children of Chaldean immigrants. P. Rigg. Read Teach 30:745-9 Ap '77

Diagnostic tests

Performance by prospective teachers in distinguishing dialect features and miscues unrelated to dialect. W. J. Lamberg and J. L. McCaleb. J Read 20:581-4 Ap '77

Recall versus reinspection in IRI comprehension tests. J. P. Kender and H. Rubenstein. Read Teach 30:776-9 Ap '77

See also

Woodcock reading mastery tests

Difficulties

Auditory and visual evoked responses in children with familial reading disabilities. B. A. Weber and G. S. Omenn. bibl il J Learn Dis 10:153-8 Mr '77

Auditory-visual integration, auditory memory, and reading in retarded and adequate readers. N. A. Badian. bibl J Learn Dis 10:108-14 F '77

Cerebral dominance in disabled readers, good readers, and gifted children: search for a valid model. J. R. Kershner. bibl Child Devel 48:61-7 Mr '77

Children's reading processes revealed by pronunciation latencies and errors. A. F. Jorm. bibl J Educ Psychol 69:166-71 Ap '77

Dialogue: versatile tool in rescuing the reluctant reader. A. S. Escoe. Read Improv 14:13-16 Spr '77

Early intervention for the high risk child for reading instruction. R. D. Robinson. Read Improv 14:11-12 Spr '77

Effect of word imagery on reading performance as a function of reader ability. A. F. Jorm. bibl J Educ Psychol 69:46-54 F '77

Follow-up of slow readers after three years. R. Castallo and A. P. Conti. Read Improv 14:52-4 Spr '77

Helping teachers understand the needs of learning disabled children; simulated reading activity. J. C. Chalfant and G. E. Foster. il J Learn Dis 10:79-85 F '77

How to cause word-by-word reading. V. Froese. bibl Read Teach 30:611-15 Mr '77

Intervention in the motor domain: a training study with first- and second-grade slow readers. M. Potts and L. Leyman. bibl Psychol Sch 14:200-6 Ap '77

Language-based learning disabilities: reading is language, too! G. P. Wallach and S. C. Goldsmith. bibl J Learn Dis 10:178-83 Mr '77

Perceptual deficits are not a cue to reading problems in second grade. B. A. Hare. bibl Read Teach 30:624-8 Mr '77

Performance of learning (reading) disabled children on a test of spoken language. P. L. Newcomer and P. Magee. bibl Read Teach 30:896-900 My '77

Reversals in reading: diagnosis and remediation. S. B. Moyer and P. L. Newcomer. bibl Excep Child 43:424-9 Ap '77

Use of problem-solving strengths in dealing with disabled readers. N. E. Dworkin and Y. S. Dworkin. Read Improv 14:82-5 Summ '77

Verbal rehearsal and short-term memory in reading-disabled children. J. Torgesen and T. Goldman. bibl Child Devel 48:56-60 Mr '77

Research

How society creates reading disability. J. Downing. El Sch J 77:274-9 Mr '77

Reading of atypical learners. S. Weintraub and others. Read Res Q 12 no3:451-9 '76-77

Habits and skill

Is John[ny's]... reading ...[w]orse? R. Fa... 34:521...

Kumari. Abdullah, M. and Mathew, R.

Kumudini
  Teaching father
    Swaminathan, K. ed. The plough and
    the stars

"K'ung, I-chi." Lu, Hsün

Kung-tso, Li. See Li, Kung-tso

Kuo, T'uan
  The thoughtful mother
    Bauer, W. and Franke, H. eds. The
    golden casket

Kuprin, Alexander
  Dog's happiness
    Aymar, B. and Sagarin, E. eds. The
    personality of the dog

Kurosaka, Bob
  Those who can, do
    Merril, J. ed. 11th annual edition, the
    year's best S-F

Kurtz, M. R.
  Waxing wroth
    Prize stories 1967: The O. Henry Awards

Kuttner, Henry   ← *Author listing*
  Don't look now
    Janifer, L. M. ed. Masters' choice
  Happy ending
    Knight, D. ed. Beyond tomorrow
  Jesting pilot
    Knight, D. ed. Cities of wonder
  Those among us
    Nolan, W. F. ed. The pseudo-people
  We guard the Black Planet!
    Moskowitz, S. ed. Modern masterpieces
    of science fiction
     For other stories by this author see
    Padgett, Lewis

KUZARS. See Chazars

Kyrie. Anderson, P.

L

L As in loot. Treat, L.

LSD. See Lysergic acid diethylamide

The label. Allen, E.   ← *Title listing*

LABOR AND LABORING CLASSES   ← *Subject listing*
  Bergelson, D. In a backwoods town
  Čapek, J. and Čapek, K. System
  Chekhov, A. P. My life
  Conrad, E. The feasibility plan
  Dorn, E. C.B. & Q.
  Edmunds, M. Carry me back to old Vir-
    ginny
  Edmunds, M. Prelude
  Hudson, H. The hungry eye
  London, J. South of the Slot
  Raboy, I. Solomon
  Somerlott, R. Eskimo Pies
  Walrond, E. The wharf rats
    See also Agricultural laborers; Labor
    unions; Migrant labor

LABOR CAMPS
  Gallant, M. My heart is broken

LABOR DEMONSTRATIONS. See Strikes
  and lockouts

LABOR UNIONS
  London, J. The Dream
  Reisin, A. The trial
    See also Labor and
    Strikes and lockouts

LABORATORY ANIMALS
  Vivante, A. The rats

LABORERS. See Labor
  classes; Labor union

LACROSSE
  Strong, P. Land Torped

Lacy, Ed
  Death by the numbers
    Mystery Writers of A
    malice toward all

Lacy, Mary Lou
  The pullers of the star
    Robinson, M. V. ed.
    mas

Lacy, Robert
  Win a few, lose a few
    Tibbets, A. B. ed. Let's

The ladies of Catsmeat Yard.

Ladies with a past. McGerr, P

The lady from Portugal. Mu

Lady from the Cape of Goo
  H.

The lady in the capital. P

The Lady of Great Occasion

The Lady of Little Fishing.

The Lady of the Green Jade
  Ibañez, F.

The lady or the tiger? Sto

The lady over the wall. V

Lady Penny goes too far.

The lady, Roku-no-miya. Ak

The lady walks. Powell, J.

The Lady who was a beggar
  Stories from a Ming colle

The lady with the little dog.

Lady, you started somethin

"The Lady Yü-nu: a beg
  ter"
    Chai, Ch'u, and Chai,
    treasury of Chinese li

Ladyhood. Hughes, L.

The lady's maid's bell. Wharto

La Farge, Oliver
  The ancient strength
    La Farge, O. The doo
  Caviar remembered
    La Farge, O. The doo
  The creation of John Man
    La Farge, O. The door
  The door in the wall
    La Farge, O. The door in
  Independent research
    La Farge, O. The door
  Journey in remembering
    La Farge, O. The d
  The little stone man
    La Farge, O. The door
  No Rosetta Stone
    La Farge, O. The door in
  The pot and the cup
    La Farge, O. The door

LASERS, Gas—*Continued*

Scaling laws for CW 337-um HCN waveguide lasers. P. Belland and others. bibl App Opt 15:3047-53 D '76

Temperature coefficients of the indices of refraction and of the birefringence in cadmium sulphide. R. Weil and D. Neshmit. bibl diag Opt Soc Am J 67:190-5 F '77

Theory of modes in a loaded strip confocal unstable resonator. G. T. Moore and R. J. McCarthy. bibl Opt Soc Am J 67:228-41 F '77

Use of perfluoropolyether fluids in HV sparkgaps. A. Luches and L. Provenzano. diags App Phys 10:339-41 F 21 '77

H_2O, NO, and N_2O infrared lasers pumped directly and indirectly by electronic-vibrational energy transfer. A. B. Petersen and others. bibl J App Phys 48:230-3 Ja '77

X-ray measurements of electron temperatures in CO_2-laser-heated magnetoplasmas. W. Halverson and C. V. Karmendy. bibl diags J App Phys 48:99-103 Ja '77

Control

CO_2 laser beam shaping with computer generated holograms. D. W. Sweeney and others. bibl il diag App Opt 15:2959-61 D '76

HF laser spectral analysis using nearfield holography. C. R. Pond and others. bibl diags App Opt 16:67-9 Ja '77

Injection tuning of a pulsed TEA CO_2 laser. D. P. Hutchinson and K. L. Vander Sluis. bibl diag App Opt 16:293-4 F '77

Resonance absorption measurements of NO with a line-tunable CO laser; spectroscopic data for pollution monitoring. B. K. Garside and others. bibl diag App Opt 16:398-402 F '77

Tunable linearly polarized TEM_{oo} operation of CO_2 laser with a concave diffraction grating. E. Bernal G. and R. McClellan. bibl il App Opt 15:2956-8 D '76

Testing

Atomic absorption of thermally dissociated iodine for laser applications. D. R. Gray and others. bibl diag App Phys 10:169-77 F 1 '77

LASERS, Liquid

Axial mode structure of a copper vapor pumped dye laser. A. A. Pease and W. M. Pearson. bibl il diags App Opt 16:57-60 Ja '77

Effect of pH on dye-laser output power. Y. Matsunaga and others. diag J App Phys 48:842-4 F '77

Electrochemical pumping of laser dyes. C. A. Heller and J. L. Jernigan. bibl il App Opt 16:61-6 Ja '77

Fringe formation in two-wavelength contour holography. A. A. Friesem and U. Levy. bibl il diags App Opt 15:3009-20 D '76

Near-resonant dye laser scattering and twophoton absorption in a sodium neon plasma. L. Vriens. bibl diags J App Phys 48:653-61 F '77

Quantitative detection of atomic absorption by intracavity dye-laser quenching. M. Maeda and others. bibl il diag App Opt 16:403-6 F '77

Resonance flame atomic fluorescence spectrometry with continuous wave dye laser excitation. R. B. Green and others. bibl diag Anal Chem 48:1954-9 N '76

Soft X-ray gain in the alkali earths. E. J. McGuire and M. A. Duguay. bibl App Opt 16:83-8 Ja '77

Ultrafast gating and amplification of broadband optical signals. G. L. Olson and G. E. Busch. bibl il J App Phys 48:678-80 F '77

Control

Sum frequency mixing in potassium pentaborate as a source of tunable coherent radiation at wavelengths below 217 nm. F. B. Dunning and R. E. Stickel, jr. bibl App Opt 15:3131-4 D '76

LASERS, X ray

Shortest wavelength laser from harmonic generation. H. R. Leuchtag. bibl Phys Today 29:17-19 D '76

LATERITE

Genesis of low iron bauxite, northeastern Cape York, Queensland, Australia. A. H. White. bibl map diags Econ Geol 71:1526-32 D '76

Process for recovery of nickel, cobalt and copper from domestic laterites. R. E. Siemens and J. D. Corrick. bibl diags Min Cong J 63:29-34 Ja '77

LATHES

Acoustic emission of a cutting process. I. Grabec and P. Leskovar. bibl diag Ultrasonics 15:17-20 Ja '77

Extra fast boring and turning lathe is cut above the others; Poreba lathe. J. Hollingum. il Engineer 243:21 D 9 '76

Loud bar feed lathes are muffled by tubes of plastic and steel. J. Hollingum. il Engineer 243:26 D 2 '76

Multi-tool skiving block method doubles productivity. il Cutting Tool Eng 29:14 Ja '77

Parting tool reduces cut-off time 65%. A. Yakamazich. il Cutting Tool Eng 29:10 Ja '77

Rapid fire tool changing, and a different approach to edge geometry. il diags Manuf Eng 78:37 Ja '77

Trends in lathe tooling. il Tooling & Prod 42:54-8 F '77

Turret on a turret aids the drive for productivity. il diag Manuf Eng 78:38 Ja '77

See also
Turning

LATIN AMERICA

See also
Chemical industry—Latin America

LATITUDE

Space-time spectral analysis of mid-latitude disturbances appearing in a GFDL general circulation model. Y. Hayashi and D. G. Golder. maps J Atmos Sci 34:237-62 bibl(p259-62) F '77

LATTICE theory

Theorem concerning the integer lattice. D. E. Bell. Studies App Math 56:187-8 Ap '77

LAUMONTITE

Low-temperature serpentinization of peridotite fanglomerate on the west margin of the Chiwaukum graben, Washington. S. M. Cashman and J. T. Whetten. bibl il map Geol Soc Bull 87:1773-6 D '76

LAUNDRIES

Equipment

Case study; savings from energy recovery. il diags Heating-Piping 48:60-2 N '76

LAUNDRY

Colorimetric determination of laundering effects. R. Griesser. Soap/Cosmet/Chem Spec 53:54+ Ja; 39-40+ F '77

LAVA

Abyssal pahoehoe with lava coils at the Galapagos rift. P. Lonsdale. bibl il diags Geology 5:147-52 Mr '77

Evolution of Santa Maria volcano, Guatemala. W. I. Rose, jr and others. il map diags J Geol 85:63-87 bibl(p86-7) Ja '77

Petrology of McKinney basalt, Snake River Plain, Idaho. W. P. Leeman and C. J. Vitaliano. bibl il map diags Geol Soc Bull 87:1777-92 D '76

LAW

Encroachment. P. W. Robinson. Surv & Mapp 37:33-8 Mr '77

Engineer and the law. Published in monthly numbers of PE-Professional engineer

Legal exchange. J. H. Heckman. Published in monthly numbers of Modern plastics
See also
Contracts
Expert evidence
Labor laws and regulations
Liability
Maritime law

LAW offices. See Offices

LAWNS

Flow resistance in broad shallow grassed channels. C. Chem. bibl Am Soc C E Proc 102 [HY 3 no 11994]:307-22 Mr '76; Discussion. O. N. Wakhlu. 103 [HY 1 no 12651]:90-1 Ja '77
See also
Grasses, Artificial

LAYOFF systems

ACS committee gives details of 13 layoffs. Chem & Eng N 55:21-3+ F 7 '77

ACS committee reports on 12 more layoffs. Chem & Eng N 54:19-24 N 1 '76

Layoff investigations; a progress report. M. Heylin. Chem & Eng N 54:57-9 O 25 '76

LEACHING

Cyanidation studies at the S.A. Lands gold mine. M. I. Brittan and others. bibl CIM Bull 70:100-4 F '77

Leaching Duluth Complex concentrates, mattes, and roasted mattes with H_2SO_4. L. A. Haas and others. bibl Eng & Min J 178:80-2 Ap '77

Leaching of oxadiazon and phosalone in soils. D. Ambrosi and C. Helling. bibl J Agr & Food Chem 25:2 '77
also

GENERAL REFERENCES

The secret to using a library effectively is in knowing what kind of material will have the information you need in the most available form. We all know that if someone wanted to fill a sandbox on the playground, a wheelbarrow or a bucket rather than a five-ton truck should be used. And a swatter does a better job of getting rid of the unwanted fly than does a baseball bat. There are times, of course, when only the truck or the bat will serve, but you have to choose the equipment best fitted for the job.

When you search for information in the library, there are times when neither ordinary books nor magazines are best fitted to answer your question. For an overview of a large topic, it is often better to look in a reference book because the information is more conveniently arranged and, therefore, easier to find. For example, suppose you were going to write a paper on the Civil War in the United States. You could probably find a ten-foot shelf of books about the Civil War, but where should you begin? A condensed encyclopedia article on the Civil War would give you an idea of some of the different aspects of your topic that you could deal with in your paper. Then you would be better prepared to select from your array of regular books.

Reference books are also more convenient when you need certain kinds of specific information. For example, suppose you had to find out who holds the Major League record for runs batted in or to learn the names of the present two Senators from Tennessee or to find out who fought at Wounded Knee. You might find the answers from regular books or magazine articles, but it would be much faster to look in reference books.

For both answers to specific questions and overviews of a general subject, you will find reference books extremely useful. They are shortcuts; they collect information for you on thousands of subjects that could be found only by searching through countless separate books, magazines and newspapers. They condense this information and arrange it so you can find it quickly. For this reason they are usually well indexed.

Since reference books are meant to be quickly consulted for a small amount of specific information, rather than to be read through, they are often kept in the library for people to use there. Often reference books are arranged together in a special area which may be one shelf or a whole room, depending on the size of the library.

There are *general* reference books and *special* reference books. General reference books, such as general encyclopedias, almanacs, and dictionaries, contain condensed information about a broad range of subjects. Special references, such as the *Space Encyclopedia*, *Oxford Companion to English Literature*, or *Documents of American History*, focus on a narrower range of subject matter and often include more specific detail.

There is no magic way to select and use an appropriate reference book. There is no abracadabra to reveal the answers to your questions. You have to take time to look at the reference books available and to learn how to use them. If you do this, if you will learn to use reference books efficiently, you can save yourself many hours of work, and that is a kind of magic.

Part II of this Guide is designed to help you achieve that kind of magic. First, we list over one hundred different reference books to give you an idea of the range of references that exist. Of course your library probably will not have them all, but it will have some of the major ones. Second, we give a short description of the kinds of information contained in each of these books. Third, in order to help you be sure that you understand how this information is organized and how you can retrieve it, we have designed Search Questions and Clues.

A good way to use Part II on References is to work with one section at a time. After reading the introduction to the section, look at the list of reference books that section includes to get an idea of the books discussed. Pick out the reference books you think you already know and quickly try some of the Search Questions for these. That way you can eliminate the references you really know and concentrate on others.

Much of the information about references you will not want to memorize, but you will want to become familiar with the basic kinds of references. You can then refer to the appropriate section again when you need some specific information about references. The page numbers for each of these sections and for the lists of books in each are given in the table of contents.

ENCYCLOPEDIAS

A reference librarian in a large metropolitan library once told me she could answer over half of the questions asked her by using either an encyclopedia or an almanac.

Our word *encyclopedia* comes from an old Greek word meaning a circle of knowledge or a well-rounded education. Our encyclopedias do indeed contain information about all fields of knowledge. They are probably our most important single reference.

The number of volumes in a set of encyclopedias may vary from one to fifty or more depending on how detailed or general they are.

We are not going to tell you how to choose the right volume in a set of encyclopedias, how to use the guide words at the tops of the pages, nor how to use the cross-references to related articles. We are assuming that you already have these skills.

There are two important parts of encyclopedias, however, that are often overlooked — the index and the yearbook. We will briefly discuss these before going on to describe the different encyclopedias.

Using the index. If you are looking in the encyclopedia for information on a specific subject, for example "dog," it is usually quicker to look it up directly in the *D* volume of the set of encyclopedias where you will find the word *dog* listed alphabetically. The article often will give you cross-references, which are other places to look for information on the same subject. But if you are looking for information on a broader or more abstract subject, for example "marriage," "atomic energy," or "law enforcement," use the index.

The index is an alphabetical list of the subjects included in the encyclopedia. Each entry shows all of the places in the encyclopedia where a subject is discussed. Some sets of encyclopedias have the index for the whole set in one separate volume. In other cases there is an index in each volume. In any case using the index is particularly helpful when you have a broad or abstract topic since all of the information will not be found in a single article, but may be scattered about under different headings.

Suppose you were interested in finding information about cave men. The *Encyclopaedia Britannica's* index refers you to "man, evolution of." The *Americana Encyclopedia* uses the headings "cave dwellers" and "man, prehistoric types of"; in addition the index refers you to eight other articles which contain information on the subject. *Collier's* index under "prehistoric man" refers you to "evolution of man and archeology," while the *World Book* uses "cave dwellers" and "prehistoric man." So, if you had looked only under "cave men" you would not have found much information of value to you.

To give another example, suppose you were interested in information about the Saturn V rocket. The *Encyclopaedia Britannica* does not use

It is important to check the index of an encyclopedia.

All of these articles include information about rockets.

Look also under these headings in the index for other information about rockets.

There are rocket diagrams.

Bibliographies list sources for more reading.

CKAWAY, N.J. 20–117b
—Map 17–New Jersey
Rockaway, Oreg.: Map 18–Oregon
Rockaway, pen., N.Y. 19–571d
Rockaway Beach, Mo.: Map 16–Missouri
Rock bass (fish): Ill. 10–Fish pl. I (10)
Rock Bay, B.C., Can.: Map 4–British Columbia
Rock bee 3–762b
Rock Bluff, Fla.: Map 10–Florida
Rock bolting (mining) 16–308d
ckbridge, O.: Map 18–Ohio
ckbridge, co., Va.: Map 23–Virginia
astle, co., Ky.: Map 14–Kentucky
ckcastle, riv., Ky. 7–559c
—Map 14–Kentucky
ock Cave (W. Va.): Map 23–West Virginia
Rockcliffe Park, Ont.: Map 18–Ontario
Rockcod (zool.): see Rockfish
ROCK CRAB 20–117b; 7–415a
Rock cranberry: see Mountain cranberry
Rock Creek, B.C., Can.: Map 4–British Columbia
Rock Creek, Kans.: Map 13–Kansas
Rock Creek, O.: Map 18–Ohio
ck Creek, butte, Oreg.: Map 18–Oregon
Creek Park (Wash., D.C.) 17–203a
crystal (min.) 10–604c, 608c, 612c; 19–554b
ck cuy (zool.) 11–534d
ockdale, co., Ga.: Map 10–Georgia
Rockdale, Ill.: Map 12–Illinois
Rockdale, Tenn.: Map 22–Tenn.
Rockdale, Tex.: Map 22–Texas
Rock dormouse (zool.) 8–354d
Rock dove: see Rock pigeon
Rock drill (sculp., Epstein): Ill. 9–281
Rock Eagle, mound, Ga.: Map 10–Georgia
Rock eel (zool.): see Gunnel
OCKEFELLER (Amer. fam.) 20–117c
kefeller, David (Amer. bus.) 20–119d
20–119c
kefeller, John Davison (Amer. fin.) 20–117c; 5–25a; 10–230b; 22–722b
Chicago, Univ. of 6–214d
Grand Teton National Park 11–309a
Williamsburg 23–497d
—Ill. 20–117c
—Bib. 24–43: 1,428
Rockefeller, John Davison, Jr. (Amer. philan.) 20–118a
Great Smoky Mountains National Park 11–386c
Williamsburg 23–497d
—Ill. 20–119c
ckefeller, John Davison, III (Amer. philan.) 20–118b
20–119c
kefeller, Laurance Spelman (Amer. philan.) 20–119b; 17–184b
—Ill. 20–119c
Rockefeller, Nelson Aldrich (Amer. pol.) 20–118b, 16c; 17–483d, 491b, 568b
—Ill. 20–118c, 119c
Rockefeller, Winthrop (Amer. bus.) 2–650b, 650c; 20–119b
—Ill. 20–119c
Rockefeller, plat., Antarc. 19–208a; 5–56d
—Map 19–Polar Regions
ckefeller Brothers Fund, Inc.

Rockefeller Park (Cleveland) 6–626b
Rockefeller University (N.Y.C.) 20–117d; 10–52a, 230b; 18–221a
Rock elm (bot.) 9–105d
Rocker, Mont.: Map 16–Montana
Rocker (art instr.) 11–317Gc
Rocket (locomotive) 12–773b; 19–633b, 634c
ROCKET (mach.) 20–120b; 1–351b; 13–197a
ceramics 5–662c
fireworks 9–752d
Goddard, Robert H. 11–185d
International Years of the Quiet Sun 13–179a
Oberth, Hermann 18–41c
space exploration 21–343a fol.
warfare 23–262b, 625b; 2–722b, 726b, 731c; 20–696a
see also Ballistic missiles; Guided missiles; Rocket engines; Rocket fuels; Rocket propellants; Satellites, Artificial; Space vehicle; and individual rocket weapons or missiles, such as Bazooka, Honest John, Nike-Ajax
—Diag. 20–122 fol.; 2–722a
—Bib. 24–175 fol.: 99–114; 24–177: 170; 24–180: 170–173
Rocket candytuft (bot.) 5–348a
Rocket engines 20–121a; 1–346d, 350d
see also Liquid-propellant rockets; Rocket; Solid-propellant rockets
—Diag. 20–123 fol.
—Ill. 1–345d
—Table 21–370
Rocket fuels 5–180d
space exploration 21–343b fol.
Tsiolkovsky, K. E. 21–380a
see also Liquid fuels; Rocket propellants; Solid fuels
—Diag. 21–380
—Table 21–370
Rocket into Interplanetary Space (bk., Oberth) 20–121a
Rocket larkspur (bot.) 14–325c
Rocket launcher (mil.) 2–733b
Rocket propellants 10–102b; 20–120b, 122b
space exploration 21–343b fol.
Tsiolkovsky, K. E. 21–380a
see also Liquid propellants; Rocket fuels; Solid propellants
—Diag. 21–380
—Table 21–370
Rocketry and Space Exploration, the International Story (bk., Haley) 20–121a
Rockets (mach.): see Rocket
Rockets, Missiles, and Space Travel (bk., Ley) 20–120c
Rocketsonde (meteor. instr.) 16–65c
Rocket torpedo (weapon) 22–368d
Rocket to the Moon (play, Odets) 2–37a
Rockfall, Conn.: Map 7–Connecticut
Rockfield, Ind.: Map 12–Indiana
Rockfield, Ky.: Map 14–Kentucky
Rockfield, Wis.: Map 23–Wisconsin
Rock-fill dams 7–672d
ROCKFISH (Sebastodes)

Rockford, O.: Map 18–Ohio
Rockford, Tenn.: Map 22–Tennessee
Rockford, Wash.: Map 23–Washington
Rockford College (Rockford, Ill.) 6–723a
Rockglen, Sask.: Map 20–Saskatchewan
Rock Hall, Md.: Map 15–Maryland
Rockham, S.D.: Map 21–South Dakota
ROCKHAMPTON, Austl. 20–130a; 3–255d
—Maps 3–Australia; 18–Pacific Ocean
Rock Harbor, Fla.: Map 10–Florida
Rock hare 11–653a
Rockhaven, Sask.: Map 20–Saskatchewan
Rockhill, William W. (Amer. dipl.) 3–45a
ROCK HILL, S.C. 20–130b; 21–300d
—Maps 21–South Carolina; 22–United States (Eastern)
Rockholds, Ky.: Map 14–Kentucky
Rockhopper penguin 18–542d
—Ill. 18–543
Rockhurst College (Kansas City, Mo.) 6–723a
Rock hyrax (zool.) 12–446d
Rockies, The, mt., Wash.: Map 23–Washington
Rockies, The: see Rocky Mountains, mts.
Rocking Chair and Other Poems, The (poems, Klein) 5–316c
ROCKINGHAM, 2ND MARQUIS OF (Charles Watson-Wentworth) (Eng. states.) 20–130c; 4–745d; 11–372; 22–706a
Rockingham, co., N.H.: Map 17–New Hampshire
Rockingham, co., N.C. 7–398c
—Map 17–North Carolina
Rockingham, Vt.: Map 23–Vermont
Rockingham, co., Va.: Map 23–Virginia
Rockingham (historic site, N.J.) 17–416c
—Map 17–New Jersey
Rockingham ware 5–654Xd
Rock Island, co., Ill.: Map 12–Illinois
ROCK ISLAND, Ill. 20–130d; 12–503d, 684b; 16–404c
—Maps 12–Illinois; 22–United States (Eastern)
economy 12–501
Rock Island, Okla.: Map 18–Oklahoma
Rock Island, P.Q.: Map 19–Quebec
Rock Island, Wash.: Map 23–Washington
Rock Island, Treaty of (1832) 12–510d
Rock Island Dam (Wash.): Ill. salmon ladder 10–6a
Rock kangaroo: see Wallaroo
Rocklake, N.D.: Map 17–North Dakota
Rockland, Del.: Map 8–Delaware
Rockland, Ida.: Map 12–Idaho
ROCKLAND (East Thomaston), Me. 20–130d; 15–247b
—Map 15–Maine
ROCKLAND, Mass. 20–131a
—Map 15–Massachusetts
Rockland, Mich.: Map 16–Michigan
Rockland, co., N.Y. 17–484a
—Map 17–New York
Rockland, Ont.: Map 18–Ontario
Rockledge, Fla.: Map 10–

Excerpt from *Collier's Encyclopedia* index.
Reprinted with permission from the *Index Volume of Collier's Encyclopedia.* © 1972 Cromwell-Collier Educational Corporation.

that heading, but the index refers you to the article on "rockets and guided missiles." The *Americana* index sends you to "rockets" and "space exploration" plus five other related articles. *Collier's* has information under the heading of "rocket" and "space exploration" as well as some information under "Von Braun." The *World Book* uses the headings of "space travel" and "rocket." Without using the index you probably could not have found the information on the Saturn V.

Often when you think that your encyclopedia doesn't have some information, it is simply that you haven't tracked down the proper heading. Using the index is the only way to be sure you have found all the information that an encyclopedia has on a specific subject. Proper use of the index will help avoid a lot of fruitless jumping here and there through mountains of encyclopedia volumes.

Using the yearbook. Most encyclopedias publish *yearbooks.* These valuable single volumes deal with the current events of that year in most of the areas of information covered by the encyclopedia. If, for example, you are looking for recent discoveries in medicine, use a current yearbook. Or, if you want information on political affairs of the last year in Chile, use the current yearbook. Remember that each yearbook has its own index to help you locate all the information on a particular subject contained in that yearbook.

IMPORTANT GENERAL ENCYCLOPEDIAS

Each encyclopedia handles the information in its articles differently. There are differences in the content they tend to emphasize, differences in the length of articles, and differences in style. The following descriptions provide an introduction to some of the more widely used encyclopedias. After you have read the descriptions, try to use the encyclopedias to find the information to answer the set of Search Questions.[1] If

you need help, look at the Clues that follow each set of questions.

Encyclopedia yearbooks chronicle important events of the past year.

ENCYCLOPEDIA AMERICANA

Encyclopedia Americana. New York: Encyclopedia Americana Corp., 30 vol. This is continuously revised, so there is an edition each year.

The *Encyclopedia Americana* has articles that are concise, reliable, and up-to-date. The language is easily understood. Despite the title it deals with things other than American, although it has articles on American towns and cities. There are articles on major operas, books, musical compositions, and works of art. The articles by centuries, e.g., Nineteenth century, summarize the social conditions, important events, political history, and technological advances of the century. There is a subject index and a yearbook, the *Americana Annual.*

Problem 5

SEARCH QUESTIONS[1]

1. What were the social conditions of the 15th century?

2. What is the plot of the *Aeneid?*

3. Find as much information as you can on penicillin.

4. Describe the world of art in 1972.

CLUES

1. Remember fifteenth has to be spelled out, so look under *f.*

2. Look under the name of the book, *A.*

3. Here you would find information under Penicillin, but if you checked the index, you would find 27 other references to articles that had information on penicillin. (It is sufficient to give only the page number of the index entry.)

4. Look in the 1973 yearbook (the year following the date you want) under Art.

---

[1]Teacher: If this is a class assignment, you might want the students to write the numbers of the pages on which they find the answers to each question.

---

[1]Check with your teacher to see whether you should give only the page number where the answer is found or give the answer itself.

energy

Energy developments in 1974 are reviewed in this article under the following headings: (1) Survey; (2) Coal; (3) Electricity; (4) Gas; (5) Nuclear Energy; and (6) Petroleum.

Survey

The United States and much of the rest of the world faced a number of serious problems associated with the so-called energy crisis. Heading the list of energy-related problems is the high cost of petroleum sold by the oil-rich nations that form the Organization of Petroleum Exporting Countries (OPEC).

Impact of Oil Costs. The continued high cost of OPEC oil was seen by Western industrialized nations as being one of the prime reasons for inflation, which remained unchecked. Poor nations, which are attempting to industrialize to improve the lives of their citizens, viewed the high oil prices as constituting an almost insurmountable obstacle to their development plans because without energy a nation cannot build an industrial base.

To make matters worse, much of the agricultural activities in both the Western industrialized nations and the poor developing countries depend on chemical fertilizers, many of which are derived from petroleum. Thus, the cost of oil resulted in increased prices for fertilizer. While U. S. farmers generally could pay higher prices, farmers in the poor nations often could not. This situation was particularly serious because many poor nations depend on hybrid crops to produce the large yields necessary to feed growing populations, and such crops produce well only with heavy applications of chemical fertilizers.

Another basic problem occasioned by the price paid for oil to the OPEC nations was the fear by the Western industrialized nations that the revenues earned by the oil nations would seriously undercut international monetary stability if caution and restraint were not used in their investment. In 1974 alone, it was estimated that the consuming nations paid $60 billion for oil.

Oil-Fed Arms Buildup. A special problem related to the high price of oil is the amount of oil revenues that are earmarked or spent by the Arab petroleum nations as they continue their confrontation with Israel. In October an Arab summit conference in Rabat, Morocco, concluded with a pledge to the Arab neighbors of Israel that more than $2 billion will be provided from oil revenues to finance the anti-Israel campaign. Most of the funding will go to Egypt and Syria, with lesser amounts for Jordan and the Palestine Liberation Organization. The immediate objective of the Arab states is to establish an independent Palestinian state on the west bank of the Jordan River. The area has been held by Israel since it was occupied during the 1967 war.

As the Arab states used their oil wealth to arm for another conflict with Israel, fears were expressed in the West that the Arabs might again cut off oil shipments to pressure Western nations to cease selling military equipment to Israel. With the increasing dependence of Western countries on Arab oil such action could

223

Excerpt from *Americana Annual*, 1975, p. 223.

Reprinted with permission of *The Encyclopedia Americana*, © 1975, The Americana Corporation.

ENCYCLOPAEDIA BRITANNICA

Encyclopaedia Britannica. Chicago: Encyclopaedia Britannica, Inc., 1973, 24 vols.

The *Encyclopaedia Britannica* is a comprehensive reference. Its articles vary in length, but they tend to be long. The contributors are authorities in their respective fields. For the most effective use of this reference, the index should be consulted first. There is a yearbook, *Britannica Book of the Year.*

The new 15th edition (1974) of the *Encyclopaedia Britannica* is organized on a very different pattern. It has three parts. There is a 10-volume *Micropaedia* which contains brief articles about all the subjects treated in the encyclopedia. These articles give the basic facts about each subject. Many of these refer to longer relevant articles in the *Macropaedia.* For example, Napoleon would be identified in the *Micropaedia,* but to find out more about his effect on French history, you would have to read the in-depth article in the *Macropaedia.*

The *Macropaedia* is subtitled *Knowledge in Depth.* Its 19 volumes contain much longer articles which are written by experts in the fields. The third part is the one-volume *Propaedia: Outline of Knowledge — Guide to the Britannica* which is a topical outline of knowledge by ten subject fields with references to related *Macropaedia* articles. If you wanted to know what comprises the field of music, you would probably begin with the *Propaedia.*

Trinidad and the coast of Paria. Returning to Spain imbued with the project of making an expedition to the new country in search of treasure, he secured the royal permission to sail once more, one fifth of the proceeds to be the share of the king. Thus, during 1499–1500, he was the companion of Cristobal Guerra in the first successful commercial voyage to America. He obtained much treasure from the Indians, but was accused of withholding the share belonging to the king; he died before his trial was concluded.

NINON DE LENCLOS. See LENCLOS, ANNE.

NINTH CENTURY. During the 9th century, three comparatively new civilizations occupied the old Graeco-Roman Mediterranean world and its hinterlands: (1) western Europe, centering on Italy, France, Germany, and England; (2) the Byzantine Empire, including Asia Minor and the Balkans; and (3) the Moslem world, extending from Spain across North Africa to India. Despite some military, economic, and cultural contacts, the history of each civilization was relatively self-contained. Each civilization was under attack from the barbarians on its borders—Vikings and Magyars in western Europe, Slavs and Asiatic nomads in the Byzantine Empire, and Turks in the Moslem world—but all eventually maintained themselves, and by the end of the century each had made progress in the conversion of its heathen.

Of these civilizations, only the Moslem world had significant direct contacts with Asia, but the 9th century Abbasid caliphate was no longer strong enough to continue the expansion of the previous period. The Chinese Empire, under the feeble rulers of the later T'ang dynasty (618–907 A.D.), labored under political anarchy, although the cultural level remained high. Meanwhile, the various Turkish tribes of the Asian steppe profited by Chinese and Moslem weakness. They raided and conquered outlying portions of China, and they penetrated the Moslem world as mercenaries who often remained as masters. In India, the Moslems in the 7th and 8th centuries had conquered portions of Sind and the Punjab, and the boundary changed little in the 9th century. The Moslems lacked strength to continue the conquest, and a politically disunited India could not expel the invaders. Despite this political disunity, 9th century India laid many of the bases of Hindu culture of the medieval period.

WESTERN EUROPE

The unity of western Europe at the beginning of the 9th century was symbolized by the coronation of Charlemagne by Pope Leo III at Rome on Christmas Day 800 A.D.: "To Charles, Augustus, crowned of God, the great and peace-bringing emperor of the Romans, long life and victory!" The coronation reflected the west European fusion of three originally separate traditions: Germanic, Graeco-Roman, and Christian. Charlemagne came to Rome as king of the Germanic Franks; he was invested with the Graeco-Roman imperial power of the Caesars; and Pope Leo III acted as the religious leader of Western Christendom.

The *Encyclopedia Americana* contains articles by centuries. *Encyclopedia Americana*, Vol. 20, 1973.

Reprinted with permission of The *Encyclopedia Americana.* © 1973, The Americana Corporation.

Problem 6

SEARCH QUESTIONS

1. Discuss entertainment in the Middle Ages.

2. What is an air-to-air missile?

3. Discuss the development of French literature.

CLUES

1. Use the index! Check under *Middle Ages – Entertainment*.

2. Again, check the index first under *a*. It refers you to a page of the article on rockets and guided missiles which you have to scan to find the information you need.

3. There is an article under *F*, but if you forgot to check the index you missed 38 other references to other articles like criticism and short story. It is sufficient to report only the page of the index where the references are found.

COLLIER'S ENCYCLOPEDIA

Collier's Encyclopedia. New York, Crowell-Collier, 24 vol. This is continuously revised, so there is an edition each year.

The *Collier's Encyclopedia* has articles which are written clearly and in a popular style. These articles vary in length and contain numerous illustrations. There is an index and a yearbook, *Collier's Yearbook.*

Problem 7

SEARCH QUESTIONS

1. How do banks create money?

2. Find information on parabolas.

CLUES

1. With luck you could find this under Banking, commercial by going directly to the article, but it is much simpler to check the index under either *money* or *banking*. These both refer you to the article Banking, commercial.

2. There is no article on parabolas; you must check the index under *parabola*. This refers you to three separate sections of other articles (Conics, Analytic geometry, and Calculus) that contain information.

COMPTON'S PICTURED ENCYCLOPEDIA

Compton's Pictured Encyclopedia and Fact-Index. Chicago: F.E. Compton and Company, 15 vol. This is continuously revised, so there is an edition each year.

This is a clearly written encyclopedia. There are pictures and illustrations on almost every page. The articles vary in length according to the size of the subject, and they range from a short paragraph to several pages. Instead of one general index, there is a "fact-index" at the end of each volume which is a guide to subjects beginning with the letter of that volume. The fact-index also defines terms and gives important facts about people, places, or things that need only brief information to understand. There is also a yearbook, *The Compton Yearbook*.

Problem 8

SEARCH QUESTIONS

1. Find how rabbits can run as fast as they do.
2. Why did Eric the Red leave Ireland?
3. Who was Alessandro Scarlatti?

CLUES

For all of these you need to choose the correct volume covering the letter of the subject and then check the fact index at the end.

1. Check the fact index for *R – rabbit*; there are several subtopics. Find the one about speed, and turn to the right page and scan.
2. Check the fact index in the *E* volume. You will then have to scan the article it refers to.
3. Check the fact index in the *S* volume. You will find enough information given here to answer the question without looking any further. Notice, though, that this is one time when you

could not have turned directly to the place in the encyclopedia where you would expect to find Scarlatti because he is discussed in the article on opera, volume *O*.

WORLD BOOK

World Book Encyclopedia. Chicago: Field Enterprises, 22 vol. This is continuously revised, so there is an edition each year.

The style is easy to read, and there are many illustrations. The articles vary in length, depending on the subject. Many articles are short. The longer ones become more complex as they progress. In other words, you can read the introduction of the longer article and have a good summary, or you can read the whole article and get more detailed information. Earlier editions of the World Book have the Reading and Study Guide. Beginning with the 1972 edition, there is a comprehensive index. There is also a *World Book Yearbook*.

Problem 9

SEARCH QUESTIONS

1. What was Shakespeare's influence on the English language?
2. Find all the information you can on Robin Hood.
3. What does training to be an RN include?

CLUES

1. You can go directly to the article on Shakespeare for this, but scan the article to find the appropriate subhead.
2. There is an article under Robin Hood, but to find all the information the encyclopedia has, you must check *Robin Hood* in the index. There you'll find four other references.
3. *RN* in the index sends you to Registered nurse which refers you to two articles: Hospital (Professional Services Staff) and Nursing (Professional Nurses). This means you have to look at these sections of these two articles to see which has the information you need. You will find the article on

Nursing has a subheading, *Nursing as a Career*, with a sub-subheading *Professional Nursing* which includes the information you need.

LINCOLN LIBRARY

Lincoln Library of Essential Information. Buffalo: The Frontier Press, 1 or 2 vol. This is frequently revised to keep it up to date.

This is a one- or two-volume encyclopedia which was originally intended for self-study; therefore, it is arranged by large subject fields. These subject fields range from literature and the English language to fine arts, economics, and science. There is a section of biographies of famous historical and living people. Each major subject section begins with a subject guide to the material in that section. At the end of each section there are review questions with page references showing where you can find the answers, and a bibliography for further study. There is an excellent general alphabetical index in the back which helps you locate specific information.

Problem 10

SEARCH QUESTIONS

1. Find a copy of the periodic table of elements.
2. What were the draft riots of 1863?
3. Who is James Baldwin?
4. Find some information on architecture.

CLUES

Use the index to find all of these.

1. Check *periodic* or *elements*.
2. Check *draft*.
3. See *Baldwin*. Since you know this is a person, you could turn directly to the large section on biography and find him in alphabetical order.
4. Check *architecture*.

COLUMBIA ENCYCLOPEDIA

Columbia Encyclopedia. New York: Columbia University Press, 3rd ed., 1963.

The *Columbia Encyclopedia* is a one-volume encyclopedia. One-volume encyclopedias are useful for very condensed information on many of the subjects covered in the larger encyclopedias. The *Columbia Encyclopedia* is particularly good for identifying names of people, places, and events.

Problem 11

SEARCH QUESTIONS

1. Name three inventions of Thomas Edison.
2. What was the South Sea Bubble?
3. What is pi?
4. Where is the Bay of Fundy?

CLUES

There is no index so the problem is picking out the main word in the subject you are looking for.

1. See *Edison*
2. See *South*
3. See *pi*
4. See *Fundy*

Now that you have used several general encyclopedias, it would be worthwhile to compare how they treat the same topic. Look up some of the following topics in three different encyclopedias to compare their treatment of the same subject:

allergy
cartoons
Chicago, Illinois
short story
algebra
rockets
cats
American Revolution

In addition to these general encyclopedias there are some encyclopedias that are general in the sense that they cover many fields of knowledge, yet are special in that they emphasize one ethnic group or subculture. The following entries describe some of these important general, yet special, encyclopedias.

NEW CATHOLIC ENCYCLOPEDIA

New Catholic Encyclopedia. New York: McGraw-Hill, 1967. 15 vol.

This encyclopedia was prepared by Catholic University of America. It includes articles on arts and sciences as well as on religion and church history. The articles are readable and concise. There is a separate index volume. There is an older 15-volume *Catholic Encyclopedia* (1907-1922) which focuses more on medieval history and philosophy and church doctrine and history. The *New Catholic Encyclopedia* has a more current focus.

Problem 12

SEARCH QUESTIONS

1. What Europeans first explored Arkansas? Is there currently a bishopric in the state?

2. What kind of music did Corelli write?

3. What does a DNA molecule look like?

4. Who are the mendicants?

5. Why is it that after his election, a pope usually assumes a new name?

CLUES

1. Look directly for the article under Arkansas, or look under *A* in the index.

2. Again look directly under Corelli, or check the index.

3. You must look in the index for this. Under *DNA* the index tells you to look under a different entry where you will find subtopics which will give you the information.

4. You could go directly to the article on Mendicant Orders, or look in the index under *M*.

5. Check the index under *popes, names of.*

ENCYCLOPEDIA JUDAICA

Cecil Roth, ed. *Encyclopedia Judaica.* New York: Macmillan Co., 1972, 16 vol.

This encyclopedia was prepared by *Encyclopedia Judaica* in Jerusalem. It is worldwide in

Almagest is that on quadrilaterals inscribed in circles. This theorem contained the kernel of some of the fundamental trigonometrical relations, but these did not become evident until much later. Most of Heron's writings are on the practical uses of mathematics as applied to surveying and to elementary physics. Heron had no scruples about representing line lengths, areas, and volumes as numbers. His remarkable formula for the area of a triangle in terms of the lengths of its three sides would not have been acceptable to the earlier Greeks.

The only Greek mathematics of an algebraic nature was produced by Diophantus, who was interested also in number theory. Much of his work is lost, but fragments of his number theory were responsible for the revival of interest in the subject in the 17th century. Babylonian and Egyptian problems, which are now solved by algebraic equations, were originally expressed in full "rhetorical" form and solved arithmetically, usually by the rule of false position. Diophantus's contribution to algebra consisted in syncopating the "rhetorical" form by means of abbreviations for the unknowns and their powers, and special symbols for subtraction and equality. Along with such problems as would now be solved by simple linear and quadratic equations, many of Diophantus's problems led to indeterminate equations. Diophantus picked his coefficients in such a way that the required solutions were positive whole numbers or fractions, since he recognized no others. What are known today as Diophantine equations are indeterminate equations requiring integral solutions.

The last important member of the Alexandrian school of Greek mathematicians was Pappus (fl. *c.* A.D. 300). His *Mathematical Collection* is one of the chief sources on the development of Greek mathematics; it also contains much original material, some of which inspired later geometric developments.

CENTURIES OF DOUBT: A.D. 500 TO 1500

Most of the innovations developed within the realm of mathematics during this millenium were non-European in origin. The mathematical legacy of Rome to the nations that emerged slowly after the downfall of the empire consisted of nothing more than elementary arithmetic and a minimum of practical geometry. Because of this and because of the unsettled state of Europe until the beginning of the 9th century, nothing significant in the way of mathematical development took place.

Hindu Mathematics. The next important advances in mathematics occurred in the East. Because of complete lack of source materials, the beginnings of mathematics in India remain unknown. The earliest well-authenticated mathematical document of India is the *Surya-Siddhanta.* This primarily astronomical text (*c.* A.D. 350) bears evidence of Babylonian and Greek influences. Its most remarkable feature is that Ptolemy's table of chords is replaced by a table of sines, or half-chords, in sexagesimal notation. The Indians completed the decimal position numeration by introducing a zero

---

Sample excerpt from the *New Catholic Encyclopedia,* vol. 9. This encyclopedia contains articles on arts and sciences as well as on religion and church history.

scope and covers ancient as well as current information on politics, culture, science, and art. In the entries for a field of knowledge like art or medicine, there are lists of outstanding Jews who have made contributions to that field. It is clearly written and well illustrated. The first volume serves as a thorough index. An *Encyclopedia Judaica* yearbook will be published. There is an older, 10-volume, *Universal Jewish Encyclopedia* (1939-43) which focuses on American Jewish history.

Problem 13

SEARCH QUESTIONS

1. Who was Sholom Aleichem?

2. What is the kibbutz movement in Israel?

3. Who are some modern Jews who have made important contributions to biology?

4. Describe the "illegal" immigration of Jews from 1918 to 1938.

5. What has been the picture of the Jew in Russian literature?

CLUES

1. You can go directly to the article or to the index under *A*.

2. Go directly to the article or look in the index under *k*.

3. Look in the index under *biology* and then the subheading *modern biology*. Turn to the page listed to find the names of important Jews in the field. The asterisk by a name shows there is an article about that person in the Encyclopedia. You could find this by turning directly to the article on Biology; then by following the outline at the beginning of the article, you could find the section on modern biology and the list.

4. Look in the index under *"illegal" immigration*. If you look under *immigration*, you find a cross-reference which sends you to the right entry.

5. Use the index to find *Russian literature*, and look for the proper subheading, *the image of the Jew*.

INTERNATIONAL LIBRARY OF NEGRO LIFE AND HISTORY

International Library of Negro Life and History. New York: Publishers Company. 10 vol. The volumes are revised individually.

This encyclopedia was prepared by the Association for the Study of Negro Life and History. Each of its volumes deals in detail with an aspect of the historical or current information concerning black Americans. The titles of these volumes show the areas they include:

Anthology of the American Negro in the Theatre
Historical Negro Biographies
The History of the Negro in Medicine
I, Too, Am American – Documents from 1619 to the Present
Negro Americans in the Civil War
An Introduction to Black Literature in America
The Negro in Music and Art
The Black Athlete – Emergence and Arrival
In Freedom's Footsteps – From the African Background to the Civil War
The Quest for Equality – From Civil War to Civil Rights

Some of the earlier volumes of this series have slightly different titles, but they deal with the same areas. Each volume has its own table of contents and its own index. If you are looking for information about a general area, look at the table of contents. If you want information about a particular person or event, look in the index. For example, if you were trying to find something on black literature of the 1960s, you should look in the table of contents. If you wanted to know about James Baldwin, you should look in the index.

An attractive series which also includes information on both the historical and current aspects of black Americans is *The Negro Heritage Library*, Educational Heritage, 1966.

Problem 14

SEARCH QUESTIONS

1. What important contribution to medicine was made by Dr. Charles R. Drew?

2. How did the Harlem Globetrotters basketball team get its name?

3. Who are the main subjects of John T. Biggers paintings?

4. How did the Black Power movement start?

CLUES

1. In *The History of the Negro in Medicine*, look in the index under *Drew*. You will find several pages listed, but choose the longer, main article.

2. In *The Black Athlete*, look in the index under *H*. Several pages are listed, but look at the longer entry first.

3. Look in the index under *Biggers* in *The Negro in Music and Art*.

4. In *The Quest for Equality – From Civil War to Civil Rights*, look in the index under *Black Power, origin of movement*.

THE AMERICAN NEGRO REFERENCE BOOK

John P. David, ed. *The American Negro Reference Book*, Englewood Cliffs, N.J.: Prentice Hall, Inc., 1966.

The preface of this one-volume encyclopedia states that its purpose is "to bring together in a single volume a reliable summary of current aspects of Negro life in America . . . in sufficient historical depth to provide the reader with a true perspective." This reference includes sections on all phases of Negro life in America. There are long articles written by experts; these include many tables full of information. These articles cover a variety of topics such as The Negro in American Agriculture, The Negro in American Religious Life, The Negro Scholar and Professional, and The Negro in Sports. Since these articles are broad, you must look in the index to find a specific bit of information.

Problem 15

SEARCH QUESTIONS

1. Find some information about the African Company, an early black Shakespeare company.

2. Describe the slave trade of the 17th and 18th centuries.

3. Discuss Negroes in the field of law.

4. Find out something about the composer William Grant Still.

CLUES

Since the articles are long, it is necessary to use the index to find a specific bit of information.

1. Look in the index under either *African Company* or *Shakespearean drama, Negro*.

2. See the index under *slave trade*. There is a subheading for the *17th and 18th centuries*.

3. Look under *lawyers, Negro* in the index.

4. Under *Still* in the index you will find at least five different references.

ENCYCLOPEDIA OF INDIANS OF THE AMERICAS

Encyclopedia of Indians of the Americas. St. Clacr Shores, Mich.: Scholarly Press.

Volume 1 of this encyclopedia is a conspectus and chronology of Indian life and history. This helpful reference surveys and summarizes important areas in Indian life and history and discusses these in considerable length. This section includes topics such as art, the image of the Indian, society and culture, geography, science and technology, and religion and philosophy.

There is a chronology of Indian history from 25,000 B.C. to 1975. This chronology is about 280 pages long, and each event is described or explained in a short paragraph.

There is a good index of both sections of this volume. This is the first of a projected 20-volume set. The subsequent volumes are to have specific topics arranged alphabetically.

Problem 16

SEARCH QUESTIONS

1. Describe the pottery of the San Augustin Indians.

2. What was the dream of Tecumseh?

3. What scientific knowledge did the American Indian have?

CLUES

1. Look in the index under *pottery, San Augustin.*

2. Find *Tecumseh* in the index. Reference is made to two places which you have to scan to answer the question.

3. For a topic this broad you would probably check the table of contents for the chapter on science and technology, although you can look for *science* in the index.

THE AMERICAN INDIAN 1942-1970

Henry C. Dennis. *The American Indian 1942-1970.* Dobbs Ferry, N.Y.: Oceana Publications, Inc. 1971.

This useful one-volume reference includes a chronology of important events in Indian history, statisticalninformation such as population figures, and biographies of famous Indians both historic and contemporary. There is an index which is good for locating people and groups, but the table of contents must be used to find topics like chronology, population, etc.

Problem 17

SEARCH QUESTIONS

1. What is Jim Thorpe famous for?

2. What was Geronimo's real name?

3. Are there any Indian newspapers?

4. What happened in 1875 that affected the Indian?

CLUES

1. Look in the index under *T.*

2. Again, check the index under *G.* You could find this by turning to the section Indians of the Past and looking under *G.*

3. Look in the table of contents which lists a section Some Indian Publications.

4. Look in the table of contents for the section on Chronology. Then turn to that section and look for 1875. (The dates are listed chronologically.)

REFERENCE ENCYCLOPEDIA OF THE AMERICAN INDIAN

Bernard Klein and Daniel Icolari, eds. *Reference Encyclopedia of the American Indian,* 2nd ed. New York: Klein, 1973.

This one-volume encyclopedia includes lists of government agencies and schools associated with American Indians, and a Who's Who section on current American Indians prominent in business, the arts, and professions, as well as on non-Indians active in fields related to Indians.

Remember, an encyclopedia is invaluable as a source of answers to specific questions or as a starting point for a larger project, but it should not be your only source of information for in-depth reference work.

ALMANACS

Originally, *almanacs* were calendars of information for farmers and sailors. They included information about the rising and setting of the sun, the phases of the moon, and the time of the high and low tides. Later they added humorous sayings, or recipes and first-aid advice for housewives. Now the modern almanac contains information on almost any subject.

Today almanacs are books of facts usually published yearly. They have short articles on events of special interest that happened during the year that just ended. For example, if you want the details of the Olympic Games of 1956 or the platforms of the Democratic or Republican parties for the same year, look in the almanac for 1957. If you don't have almanacs that far back, use the lateft one available which might have a summary of these topics.

Almanacs contain statistics on population, sports, schools, industries, crops, and many other things. There is also a chronology of important events during the year. Information can be located by looking up the subject in the index. The index of an almanac may be at the back, in the front, or even in the middle, but it is always there!

Suppose you wanted to find out who was baseball rookie of the year in 1968. Turn to the index, find *baseball* and then look under the subheading *rookie of the year*.

Turn to the page shown in the index after the subheading. In this case the page is 917.

(1974 SPORTS CHAMPIONS AND RECORDS BEGIN ON PAGE 925)   **917**

heading ──── (Baseball, 740, 908–22, 952–57)

subheading ──── Rookie of Year, 917

MOST VALUABLE PLAYERS
(Baseball Writers Association selections)

1962	Mickey Mantle, New York	1945	Phil Cavarretta, Chicago
1963	Elston Howard, New York	1946	Stan Musial, St. Louis
1964	Brooks Robinson, Baltimore	1947	Bob Elliott, Boston
1965	Zoilo Versalles, Minnesota	1948	Stan Musial, St. Louis
1966	Frank Robinson, Baltimore	1949	Jackie Robinson, Brooklyn
1967	Carl Yastrzemski, Boston	1950	Jim Konstanty, Philadelphia
1968	Dennis McLain, Detroit	1951	Roy Campanella, Brooklyn
1969	Harmon Killebrew, Minnesota	1952	Hank Sauer, Chicago
1970	John (Boog) Powell, Baltimore	1953	Roy Campanella, Brooklyn
1971	Vida Blue, Oakland	1954	Willie Mays, New York
1972	Dick Allen, Chicago	1955	Roy Campanella, Brooklyn
1973	Reggie Jackson, Oakland	1956	Don Newcombe, Brooklyn
		1957	Henry Aaron, Milwaukee
		1958–59	Ernie Banks, Chicago

National League

1931	Frank Frisch, St. Louis	1960	Dick Groat, Pittsburgh
1932	Chuck Klein, Philadelphia	1961	Frank Robinson, Cincinnati
1933	Carl Hubbell, New York	1962	Maury Wills, Los Angeles
1934	Dizzy Dean, St. Louis	1963	Sandy Koufax, Los Angeles
1935	Gabby Hartnett, Chicago	1964	Ken Boyer, St. Louis
1936	Carl Hubbell, New York	1965	Willie Mays, San Francisco
1937	Joe Medwick, St. Louis	1966	Roberto Clemente, Pittsburgh
1938	Ernie Lombardi, Cincinnati	1967	Orlando Cepeda, St. Louis
1939	Bucky Walters, Cincinnati	1968	Bob Gibson, St. Louis
1940	Frank McCormick, Cincinnati	1969	Willie McCovey, San Francisco
1941	Dolph Camilli, Brooklyn	1970	Johnny Bench, Cincinnati
1942	Mort Cooper, St. Louis	1971	Joe Torre, St. Louis
1943	Stan Musial, St. Louis	1972	Johnny Bench, Cincinnati
1944	Marty Marion, St. Louis	1973	Pete Rose, Cincinnati

CY YOUNG AWARD

1965	Sandy Koufax, Los Angeles N. L.		Dennis McLain, Detroit, tied in A. L.; Tom Seaver, N. Y. N. L.
1966	Sandy Koufax, Los Angeles N. L.	1970	Jim Perry, Minnesota A. L.; Bob Gibson, St. Louis N. L.
1967	Jim Lonborg, Boston A. L. and Mike McCormick, San Francisco N. L.	1971	Vida Blue, Oakland A. L.; Ferguson Jenkins, Chi. N. L.
1968	Dennis McLain, Detroit A. L. and Bob Gibson, St. Louis N. L.	1972	Gaylord Perry, Cleveland A.L. Steve Carlton, Phila. N.L.
1969	Mike Cuellar, Baltimore, and	1973	Jim Palmer, Baltimore A.L. Tom Seaver, New York N.L.

▶ ROOKIE OF THE YEAR
(Baseball Writers Association selections)

1965	Curt Blefary, Baltimore	1957	Jack Sanford, Philadelphia
1966	Tommy Agee, Chicago	1958	Orlando Cepeda, San Francisco
1967	Rod Carew, Minnesota	1959	Willie McCovey, San Francisco
1968	Stan Bahnsen, New York	1960	Frank Howard, Los Angeles
1969	Lou Piniella, Kansas City	1961	Billy Williams, Chicago
1970	Thurman Munson, New York	1962	Ken Hubbs, Chicago
1971	Chris Chambliss, Cleveland	1963	Pete Rose, Cincinnati
1972	Carlton Fisk, Boston	1964	Richie Allen, Philadelphia
1973	Alonzo Bumbry, Baltimore	1965	Jim Lefebvre, Los Angeles
	National League	1966	Tommy Helms, Cincinnati
1949	Don Newcombe, Brooklyn	1967	Tom Seaver, New York
1950	Sam Jethroe, Boston	1968	John Bench, Cincinnati
1951	Willie Mays, New York	1969	Ted Sizemore, Los Angeles
1952	Joe Black, Brooklyn	1970	Carl Morton, Montreal
1953	Jim Gilliam, Brooklyn	1971	Earl Williams, Atlanta
1954	Wally Moon, St. Louis	1972	Jon Matlack, New York
1955	Bill Virdon, St. Louis	1973	Gary Matthews, San Francisco
1956	Frank Robinson, Cincinnati		

──── **subheading**

---

heading ──── Index entries:

Bahrain, 156
   See also Countries
Baikal, Lake, 342
Baikonur launch site, 412–14
Bakelite, 441
Baker Island, 647
Balance of payments, 93
Balaton, Lake, 206
Bale (weight), 434
Balearic Islands, 261
Balfour Declaration, 215, 361
Balkan Wars, 200, 356
Ballistic missiles, 429
Balloons:
   Flights, 449, 450
   Invention, 441
Baltic Sea, 180, 337
Baltimore, Md., 633, 650
   See also Cities (U.S.)
Baluchaung plant, 163
Bangkok, Thailand, 268
Bangladesh, 156–57, 279, 347
   See also Countries
Bank, holiday (1933), 361
Bank, International, 99
Bank of America, 79, 627
Bank of North America, 585
Banks & banking:
   Firsts, 585
   Largest banks, 79, 627
   Legislation, 582–84
Banks (island), 343
Baptist chs., 124–25, 129–30
Barbados, 148, 157, 279, 347
   See also Countries
Barbary pirates, 150
Bare-knuckle champions, 872–73
Barley:
   Economic statistics, 32
Barometer, 441
Barrel (measure), 435
heading ──── Baseball, 740, 908–22, 952–57
   Aaron's home run record, 957
   All-Star Games, 918
   Amateur, 960
   American League Averages, 953
   Attendance records, 921
   Batting statistics, 912, 922, 953, 954
   Club standings (1974), 952
   Commissioner, 908
   Cy Young Award, 917
   Franchise shifts & additions, 921
   Government, 908
   Greatest players, 918
   Hall of Fame, 675, 908, 916
   History, 908
   Home run statistics, 911–12, 919, 920, 957
   Individual all-time records, 919
   Koufax's pitching record, 914
   Larsen's perfect game, 911
   Little League World Series, 922
   Longest games, 908
   Mantle's batting record, 922
   Minor League, 956–57
   Most Valuable Players, 917
   Musial's batting record, 916
   Nicknames for clubs, 921
   No-hit games, 915
   Pennant winners, 914, 915
   Pitching statistics, 915, 919, 920
   Records, 909–12
   Records 1974, 952–57
subheading ──── Rookie of Year, 917

The *World Almanac* and the *Information Please Almanac* are two of the best known general almanacs, although there are many others. If you learn to use these two, you will be able to use any almanac.

Sample index excerpt from the *Information Please Almanac*, 1975. © 1975; Reprinted with permission.

Sample excerpt from the *Information Please Almanac*, 1975. © 1975; Reprinted with permission.

WORLD ALMANAC

World Almanac, and Book of Facts. New York: World Telegram. Published since 1868. There is an edition each year.

This annual book of facts is filled with information on almost any subject and with statistics on population, sports, schools, industries, crops, etc. A chronology of important events of the preceding year is included. The alphabetical index in front is by subject. Using the index is the only way to locate information unless you are lucky enough to drop the book downstairs and have it land open at the right page.

Problem 18

SEARCH QUESTIONS

1. What motion picture got the Academy Award in 1971?

2. Are more males or females arrested as runaways?

3. What is the net per farm income in Utah?

4. What is the population of the Republic of Ireland? Do children have to go to school?

5. What were the headline news stories of 1962?

6. What are the months in the Chinese lunar calendar?

7. Who have been some of the leading passers in professional football?

CLUES

These clues were made using the 1973 *World Almanac.* Other editions may have slight variations in indexing.
For all of these questions you must use the index. If you have tried that unsuccessfully, perhaps you haven't used the right subject. You need detective-like imagination.

1. Look under *Academy Awards.*

2. Check *crime* and the subtopic under that, *arrests.*

3. See *agriculture;* if you look under *farms, U.S.,* there is a note |that refers you to *agriculture.*

4. See *Ireland, Republic of.*

5. Find the memorable dates section, and then check chronologically for 1962.

6. See *Calendars – Chinese lunar.*

7. Check *Football, professional – all-time records.*

INFORMATION PLEASE ALMANAC

Information Please Almanac. Supervised by Dan Golenpaul Associates. New York. The publisher varies, but this has been published since 1947. There is an edition each year.

The *Information Please Almanac* includes much of the information found in the *World Almanac* plus occasional articles on the developments during the year in fields like space flights, sports, music, or the year in Washington. The table of contents in the front provides an outline of the material in the book, and there is a detailed alphabetical subject index in the back.

Problem 19

SEARCH QUESTIONS

1. What is the Colombo Plan?

2. In which U.S. cities have reported narcotics addicts increased or decreased between 1960 and 1970?

3. Which of the major TV networks has the most affiliated stations?

4. What team was the first all-professional baseball team in the U.S.?

CLUES

These clues were made using the 1973 *Information Please Almanac.* Other editions may have slight variations in the indexing.

The main clue is to *use the index.*

1. Check *Colombo Plan.*

2. If you looked under *narcotics,* there is a note to "see drugs." Check under *drugs (narcotics) – addicts.*

3. Look under *television – networks.*

4. See *baseball – history.*

THE NEGRO ALMANAC

Harry A. Ploski and R.C. Brown. *The Negro Almanac.* New York: Bellwether Publishing Co., 1971, 2nd ed.

The Negro Almanac is general in the sense that it covers many fields, yet it is specialized in the sense that it is concerned with only black Americans. This almanac contains 32 sections dealing with the scope of history and culture of black Americans in such areas as art, science, politics, religion, mass media, employment, education, and athletics. There is a biographical section of famous black Americans and a section on black firsts. Considerable statistical information is included, and the detailed index makes this information easily located. There is a table of contents that serves as an outline of major topics.

Problem 20

SEARCH QUESTIONS

1. Who is Wilt Chamberlain?
2. What is the Germantown Mennonite Resolution?
3. When was the first postage stamp issued honoring a Negro?
4. Name three prominent black artists in the United States.
5. Give a chronology of the violence leading to the black power movement.

CLUES

These clues were made using the 2nd edition of *The Negro Almanac* (1971). Other editions may have slight variations in indexing.

1. Check *Chamberlain.*
2. Look under *Germantown.*
3. The index lists *firsts* alphabetically, so look under *first postage stamp.*
4. This topic could be found in the table of contents since it is one of the large sections in the book. The index also uses the subject *black artists.*
5. Look under *black power.*

DICTIONARIES

A *dictionary* is a book most people know about, many people own, and too few use. There are many kinds of dictionaries: dictionaries for languages and dictionaries for special subjects like music, science, biography, or geography. Geography dictionaries are often called *gazetteers.* The dictionaries for special subjects we will discuss under special references and focus here on the dictionaries of the English language.

There are two kinds of dictionaries based on their size or the number of words they contain: *abridged* dictionaries which include the most common words in a language and *unabridged* dictionaries which try to include all the words in the language. For example, an unabridged dictionary might contain more than 400,000 words while an abridged dictionary might contain one-tenth of that number. Unabridged dictionaries also have more detailed information on each word. They try to give all the various meanings of a word. Sometimes they give examples of these in sentences and often they give some history of the word.

We will assume that you already know how to find words in an alphabetical list, how to use the guide words at the top margin, and how to use the pronunciation key. However, the dictionary often has many extras that you should remember:

- *Biographical information* — The names and a few facts about well-known people are sometimes mixed in with all the regular words or sometimes listed in a special section.
- *Geographical information* — The names of cities, countries, rivers, etc., are at times mixed in with the words or sometimes listed in a special gazetteer section. This is particularly helpful to learn the correct pronunciation of places we are not familiar with.
- *Synonyms and antonyms* — Some dictionaries include synonyms within the definition of the words. Others list both synonyms and antonyms separately after the definition of the word.
- *Prefixes and suffixes* — These are usually included in the alphabetical listing of regular words, and the number that is included increafes with the difficulty-level of the dictionary.

43

- *Foreign words and phrases commonly heard* — These may be found either in a separate section or within the other words.
- *Abbreviations* — Common abbreviations are often mixed in with other words while a more inclusive set of abbreviations is often listed separately.
- *Miscellaneous lists* — Dictionaries often include lists of first names for people, tables of measurements, and lists of colleges and universities.

Take a minute to look at the dictionary you commonly use to see what extra aids it includes.

There is a growing variety of dictionaries to serve different age groups. There are preschool picture dictionaries, beginning dictionaries for the early reader, elementary dictionaries for young readers, junior dictionaries for junior high or middle school students, and adult dictionaries for high school and older students.

Many words will appear in most of these dictionaries, but as the level of the dictionary advances, more complex or more specialized meanings will be added. For example, if you want the meaning of the word *medium* as it is used in science and it is not included in the dictionary you are using, you need a more advanced dictionary. Or, if the needed definition is not clear in the dictionary you are using, perhaps a less advanced dictionary with examples might help. Your needs as a student change and so must the dictionary you use.

In addition to these abridged and unabridged dictionaries, there are some specialized dictionaries for the English language you will find to be time-savers. There are dictionaries of usage of synonyms and of rhyming words.

DICTIONARY OF CONTEMPORARY AMERICAN USAGE

Bergen and Cornelia Evans. *Dictionary of Contemporary American Usage*. New York: Random House, 1957.

This dictionary deals with word preferences, style, grammar, and punctuation in one alphabet. It is concerned with both American and British usage but from the American point of view. It is clear and readable.

Problem 21

SEARCH QUESTIONS

1. Do I say, "These scissors are sharp" or "This scissors is sharp"?
2. Should I say, "He forbade her to go" or "He forbid her to go"?
3. What is the difference between *elemental* and *elementary*?
4. Is *up to scratch* in good usage?
5. When are ellipsis marks used?
6. What are adverbs and how many uses do they have?

CLUES

The Search Questions for dictionaries are more to illustrate the kinds of information that the dictionary contains than to show how to find material. Since dictionaries are made up of one alphabetical list, all you need to do is to locate your key word in that list. Key words:

1. scissors
2. forbid
3. elemental
4. up to scratch
5. ellipsis marks
6. adverb

DICTIONARY OF MODERN ENGLISH USAGE

Henry Watson Fowler. *Dictionary of Modern English Usage*, 2nd ed. Oxford: Clarendon Press, 1965.

A scholarly dictionary which has become an authority on fine points in word usage, this book tells when to use what word. It goes beyond grammatical correctness to cover moot points, and it sometimes gives the background of words as an aid to understanding how they should be used.

A Dictionary of American-English Usage (New York, Oxford University Press, 1957) by Margaret Nicholson, is a simplified version of Fowler, and it has a more American emphasis.

radix. The plural is *radixes* or *radices*.

raft, as a colloquial term for a great quantity or a lot, especially of people (*There was a raft of folks crowding into town for the grand opening*), is now rustic and a little archaic.

rail, as short for railroad or railway, is standard American usage (*Ship by rail, I find it more convenient to go by air than by rail*). The objection of some English authorities to this usage is curious, since the English themselves are masters of the art of reducing syllables and often hold up their *tram* and *lift* in triumphant comparison to the American *streetcar* and *elevator*.

railroad; railway. In England *railroad* is seldom used. Since the beginning of the twentieth century *railway* has been the usual term there. In the United States *railroad* is the more common term, though *railway* also has its uses. In general, *railroad* is the term for a line for heavy traffic (*The Pennsylvania Railroad*), while *railway* describes a rail line with lighter weight equipment and roadbed (*The elevated railways are being replaced by buses and subways*).

As a verb, *railroad* has certain special American senses. It may mean to transport by means of a railroad, though this is now rarely heard, being replaced almost entirely by *ship* in relation to goods and *travel* or *go* in relation to persons. It may also mean to work on a railroad (*My husband and my two boys railroaded out in Kansas City for three years*), though this, too, is now rare. Colloquially, to *railroad* is to send or push forward with great or undue speed (*Jacksonians tried to railroad the Indian bill through Congress while Davy Crockett was off on a speaking tour*). As slang, but slang which is so old and so widespread that it might well be accepted as standard, *railroad* is to imprison on a false charge in order to be rid of (*Many people believe that Tom Mooney was railroaded*).

raining cats and dogs. Swift listed the phrase *rain cats and dogs* as a cliché in 1738 (in his *A complete collection of genteel and ingenious conversations*) but it remains in full use among those who seek to be original in an unoriginal way. Whoever first thought of the expression to describe a torrential downpour, with its suggestion of snarling and yelping tumult heard in the gurgle and drumming rush and splatter of the rain, had something so felicitous in its absurdity, so consonant in the violence of its own exaggeration with the violence it described, that he immediately captured all imaginations. But it is time to seek a fresher, newer image.

rain or shine, as a term for in any event, under any circumstance, positively, is hackneyed.

raise. This verb means "cause to rise." Historically, it does not mean *rise* even in speaking of dough, where we say *it is raising* and *set it to raise*. These are old passive uses of the *-ing* form and the infinitive, comparable to *supper is cooking* and *wait for it to cook*. Some people also say *the drawbridge raised*, rather than *the drawbridge rose*, because they are conscious of the fact that this is a passive act, something that is being done to the drawbridge. This use

of an active form with passive meaning is frequent in English and is seen in such familiar sentences as *the boat upset, the cup broke, the color washes well*. See **passive voice** and **transitive verbs**.

The same distinction holds between the nouns *raise* and *rise*. A salary increase is called *a pay raise* by those who feel that someone is responsible for the size of their salary. *A pay rise* carries the implication that these things happen of themselves, like a rise in the temperature. *Pay raise* is the preferred form in the United States, where *pay rise* was unknown before the 1930's. *Pay rise* is the preferred form in Great Britain. (For the difference between *raise* and *rear*, see **rear**.)

raise one's sights. One of the commonest metaphors of college presidents and others in charge of large funds or large hopes when they seek to arouse those who beg for them to even wilder frenzies of solicitation is to say that *we must raise our sights*. The metaphor, drawn from artillery, would be most unfortunate were it not that those who analyze metaphors form an inconsiderable portion of those upon whom the fund-raiser has his eye. Its naïve admission that the donor is something to be shot down and the fund-raiser one who carefully adjusts his weapon is so alien to the general tenor of the language of solicitation that one assumes it would be avoided if it were understood.

raison d'être, a French expression meaning the reason for being or existence, is an affectation when employed in English speech or writing for *reason* and an error when employed for *explanation*.

rake-off is an exclusively American slang term to describe a share or portion, as of a sum involved or of profits. Often the implication is that it is a share or amount taken or received illicitly, as in connection with a public enterprise (*Are you a man of business or a philanthropic distributor of rake-offs? Some estimate the alderman's rake-off at ten percent*).

rally has the special meaning in America of a coming together of persons, as for common action, political or religious or—in the colleges—sporting, which the British would call a mass meeting or a demonstration (*When they attended Montana political rallies, Mrs. Wheeler knitted with calm absorption. There will be a football rally for freshmen in the meadow tomorrow afternoon at five*).

ran. See **run**.

rancor. See **malice**.

rang. See **ring**.

rank and file. In the strictest sense a *rank* of soldiers is a number drawn up in line abreast. (*When the ranks are broken you have to fight singly*) and the *file* is the number of men constituting the depth from front to rear of a formation in line. Taken together, the two mean the body of an army, apart from officers or leaders. Used figuratively for ordinary people, the expression is a cliché.

rap. Formerly a slang term meaning to censure or criticize, *rap* is used so consistently in the head-

Sample page from Bergen and Cornelia Evans, *Dictionary of Contemporary American Usage*, New York, Random House, Inc. © 1957. Used with permission.

Problem 22

SEARCH QUESTIONS

1. Which is preferred — *lengthwise* or *lengthways?*

2. What are the shades of difference for *sensible, sensitive,* and *susceptible?*

3. What are the rules governing the use of *O* and *Oh?*

CLUES

1. *Lengthwise* refers you to the entry under *wise, ways* which discusses these suffixes in any combination.

2. See *sensible.*

3. See *O.*

ROGET'S THESAURUS

P. M. Roget. *International Thesaurus of English Words and Phrases.* New York: Crowell. There are various editions of this thesaurus.

Some editions of *Roget's Thesaurus* are arranged like any dictionary of synonyms and antonyms. The words, listed alphabetically, are each followed by their synonyms, grouped according to meaning. The original *Roget's Thesaurus* and many current editions group words and phrases by idea rather than by alphabetical order. In these you look up the word you want in the index.

The introduction to the *Thesaurus* tells that we look in a dictionary when we have a word but want to be sure of its meaning and that we look in a thesaurus when we have a meaning for which we want to find the word. The *Thesaurus* has over 1,000 categories of meanings, and these all have subcategories. All the words in the thesaurus are in the index which gives you the category number of the word you want. For example, if you look up *cajole,* you find 646.14. The category number 646 is used for all words referring to the idea of motivation or inducement. The subcategory .14 includes *cajole* and its synonyms. In the *Thesaurus* these numbers appear in the page corners as guide numbers, like guide words in a dictionary. Using these guide numbers, you turn to the proper page to find your category of words.

If you want to find some words which describe or are synonyms for *green,* look under *green* in the index. You will find the category number 370 listed for all words referring to green. Turn to the page which includes the category number 370. This is not the page number!

Problem 23

SEARCH QUESTIONS

Try to use a *Thesaurus* arranged by idea rather than by alphabetical order.

1. Find some words conveying the idea of *tiny.*

2. Find some words which mean to *outdo* in the sense of to defeat.

CLUES

1. Check *tiny* in the index and turn to the section indicated.

2. Look under *outdo* in the index. You will find three shades of meaning: *excel, defeat, outwit.* Since *defeat* is the meaning we want, look under that number.

SOULE'S DICTIONARY OF ENGLISH SYNONYMS

A.D. Sheffield, ed. *Soule's Dictionary of English Synonyms.* Boston: Little, Brown & Co., 1959.

In this dictionary the words are arranged alphabetically. Each word is followed by groups of synonyms. This grouping helps to make the shades of meaning clear.

Problem 24

SEARCH QUESTIONS

1. What could be substituted for *irresolute* in the following?
   His was an irresolute mind.

2. In each of the following, what could be substituted for *express?*

a. I would like to express my desire to help.
b. His speech expressed the wishes of most people there.
c. That was his express desire.

CLUES

1. Check *irresolute*.

2. Check *express*. I would probably select one of these:
   a. speak or declare
   b. represented
   c. explicit or positive

WEBSTER'S NEW DICTIONARY OF SYNONYMS

Webster's New Dictionary of Synonyms. Springfield, Mass.: Merriam Co., 1973.

This synonym dictionary is arranged in alphabetical order and, therefore, it is very easy to find any word you need. It also includes analogous words, words that are almost synonyms, as well as contrasted words.

Problem 25

SEARCH QUESTIONS

1. Find some synonyms for *happy*.

2. Is there any word that means the same as the verb *to quarrel?*

3. How many different kinds of meanings are there for *gain?*

CLUES

1. Look under *h*.

2. This is under *quarrel;* just be sure you have the meaning for the verb.

3. Under *gain* you will find several numbered groups of meanings.

STANDARD HANDBOOK OF ANTONYMS

Funk and Wagnalls Standard Handbook of Synonyms, Antonyms and Prepositions. N.Y.: Funk & Wagnalls.

This is another dictionary of antonyms which you might find very useful. This dictionary has key words arranged in alphabetical order with associated synonyms listed under each and discussed. To find a specific word, it is usually fastest to use the index at the back, which will refer you to the right group. The discussion helps to make distinctions between similar words.

Rhyming dictionaries can also be helpful. One old but useful rhyming dictionary is by Burges Johnson, *New Rhyming Dictionary and the Poets' Handbook*, N.Y., Harpers, 1931. This contains a section on English verse forms and a rhyming dictionary which includes rhymes for one, two, and three syllable words.

Part Two — Reference Books

wood—*Frost*⟩ ⟨heel nails *bit* on the frozen ruts—*Hemingway*⟩ ⟨a summer *bitten* into Joan's memory—*H. G. Wells*⟩ **Gnaw**, on the other hand, implies an effort to bite something hard or tough: it implies repeated action and a slow wearing away, sometimes stressing one in preference to the other ⟨the dog *gnaws* a bone⟩ ⟨rats have *gnawed* the rope into shreds⟩ ⟨*gnaw* at a crust of bread⟩ ⟨life goes on forever like the *gnawing* of a mouse—*Millay*⟩ Therefore *gnaw* is used of what eats, frets, or corrodes something that is strong, resistant, or not easily affected ⟨old pains keep on *gnawing* at your heart—*Conrad*⟩ ⟨they were both . . . *gnawed* with anxiety—*D. H. Lawrence*⟩ **Champ** implies vigorous and noisy action of the teeth and jaws as they attempt to penetrate something hard or, sometimes, inedible. The word usually is associated with animals (as horses) and connotes impatience or extreme hunger, but it is also used of men who avidly apply themselves to the task of biting with their teeth and crushing with their jaws: often it suggests the flow and foaming of saliva ⟨the horse *champed* at its bit until its mouth was covered with foam⟩ ⟨he ate in a ruthless manner, *champing* his food—*Waugh*⟩ ⟨others, devoted themselves to the sodden and lee-dyed pieces of the cask, licking, and even *champing* the moister wine-rotted fragments with eager relish—*Dickens*⟩ **Gnash** usually implies the striking of the teeth against each other or a grinding of them (as in anguish, despair, or extreme rage): it often emphasizes this action as the visible sign of an overpowering emotion or distress ⟨but the children of the kingdom shall be cast out into outer darkness: there shall be weeping and *gnashing* of teeth—*Mt 8:12*⟩ Sometimes, however, it implies a savage biting that rends a thing in two or tears it apart ⟨I strove . . . to rend and *gnash* my bonds in twain—*Byron*⟩ ⟨the tiger *gnashed* the fox, the ermine and the sloth—*Landor*⟩
Ana *eat, consume, devour

biting cutting, crisp, trenchant, *incisive, clear-cut
Ana *caustic, mordant, acrid: *pungent, poignant, piquant, racy

bitter, acrid are applied to things with an unpleasant taste (also smell, in the case of *acrid*) that is neither sweet nor bland yet seldom distinctly sour or really sickening. **Bitter** is traditionally associated with the repellent taste of wormwood, quinine, and aloes, but it is also used to describe the taste of beer, unsweetened chocolate, and the rind of citrus fruits. Something *bitter* usually lacks the pleasant tang and freshness of an acid flavor (as of lemon juice) and has a penetrating and persistent quality difficult to mask. **Acrid** implies a bitterness in taste that has an astringent or irritating effect (as the taste of chokecherries, various unripe fruits, or alum). It is also applied to something both bitter and salty (as sweat). An *acrid* smell is a penetrating, suffocating, repugnant odor. It is especially associated with certain fumes (as from burning sulphur) or with certain noxious vapors (as of a heavy city fog).
Ana *sour, acid, acidulous, tart: *pungent, piquant
Ant delicious —*Con* delectable, luscious, *delightful

bizarre grotesque, *fantastic, antic
Ana outlandish, erratic, eccentric, *strange, singular, odd, queer, curious: extravagant, extreme (see EXCESSIVE)
Ant chaste: subdued

blab tattle, *gossip
Ana babble, gabble, chatter, prate, *chat: divulge, dis-

scamp, rapscallion, miscreant

blame *vb* reprehend, reprobate, condemn, denounce, censure, *criticize
Ana *accuse, charge, indict, impeach: impute, attribute, *ascribe: implicate, *involve
Con exonerate, vindicate, *exculpate, absolve, acquit: *excuse, remit, forgive

blame *n* Blame, culpability, guilt, fault are comparable when they mean responsibility for misdeed or delinquency. **Blame** is a term of shifting denotations, sometimes meaning the reprehension, criticism, or censure of those who find fault or judge one's work or acts ⟨I have never desired praise . . . I have been indifferent to, if not indeed contemptuous of, *blame*—*Ellis*⟩ or sometimes a charge or accusation of some fault, misdeed, or delinquency ⟨fear of incurring *blame* in Wiltstoken for wantonly opposing her daughter's obvious interests—*Shaw*⟩ When the term denotes responsibility for wrongdoing or delinquency, it also implies the meriting of reproof, censure, or the appropriate penalty ⟨he took on himself all the *blame* for the project's failure⟩ ⟨they tried to shift the *blame* for their defeat⟩ Often the term means ultimate rather than immediate responsibility ⟨the *blame* [for backwardness in American education] has sometimes been put, and with some justice, upon our migratory habits and upon the heterogeneous character of our population—*Grandgent*⟩ **Culpability** usually means little more or no more than the fact or the state of being responsible for an act or condition that may be described as wrong, harmful, or injurious ⟨they could not prove his *culpability* for the accident⟩ ⟨as if the estrangement between them had come of any *culpability* of hers—*Dickens*⟩ ⟨an inescapable responsibility rests upon this country to conduct an inquiry . . . into the *culpability* of those whom there is probable cause to accuse of atrocities and other crimes—*R. H. Jackson*⟩ **Guilt** usually carries an implication of a connection with misdeeds of a grave or serious character from the moral and social points of view. Also it usually implies a deserving of severe punishment (as condemnation, loss of freedom, or, in the case of sin, loss of salvation) or of a definite legal penalty (as a fine, imprisonment, or death). Therefore, when the term denotes responsibility for a crime or sin, it also carries implications of need of proof before punishment can be determined or forgiveness granted ⟨though she was strongly suspected of murder, her *guilt* was not established until after her death⟩ ⟨since he admitted his *guilt*, he saved the state the cost of a trial⟩ ⟨to confess one's sins is to acknowledge one's *guilt* for those sins⟩ **Fault** (see also FAULT 2) is often used in place of *culpability* as a simpler word ⟨the *fault* is her parents', not the child's⟩ ⟨the *fault*, dear Brutus, is not in our stars, but in ourselves, that we are underlings—*Shak.*⟩
Ana responsibility, accountability, answerability (see corresponding adjectives at RESPONSIBLE): censure, condemnation, denunciation, reprehension (see corresponding verbs at CRITICIZE)
Con commendation, compliment (see corresponding verbs at COMMEND): *applause, acclaim, plaudits, acclamation

blameworthy, guilty, culpable are comparable when they mean deserving reproach and punishment for a wrong, sinful, or criminal act, practice, or condition. One (as a person or his act or work) is **blameworthy** that deserves blame or criticism and must suffer or receive reproach, censure,

From *Webster's New Dictionary of Synonyms,* © 1973 by G. & C. Merriam Co., Publishers of the Merriam-Webster Dictionaries. Used with permission.

SPECIALIZED REFERENCE BOOKS

If you wanted some help with a science problem, you wouldn't ask just any friend. You would find someone who was good in science. Some friends are good at one thing and others excel in another area. The same is true of reference books. If you want help with a science question, you don't go to any reference book; you use one that specializes in science. For such a question, a general encyclopedia might not help you, but a science dictionary or encyclopedia probably could. General references are broad and cover many subjects. Specialized reference books, on the other hand, focus on a specific area such as literature, art, or science.

Knowing which special reference to use for information is like knowing which friend to ask for help. You need to know which references are available and which are likely to have the information you need. We will introduce you to some of the most important specialized reference books. Regardless of whether they are encyclopedias, almanacs, dictionaries, or some other form, we will group them by the four most common areas of specialization, which are *biography*, *government – history*, *literature*, and *science – mathematics*.

You may want only to browse through the lists of titles of the reference books under each specialization. It may be enough for you to know that such reference aids exist. If you want to get an idea of what these books contain, you can read the descriptions of the books in any field that interests you. If you want to be sure you know how to use these references to find information,

try to answer the Search Questions. If you need help, read the Clues.

Remember that no one library will have all the references we are describing, but it will have some of these specialized reference books. So trade in your general reference magnifying glass for a specialized reference microscope and zero in on your target. We begin with descriptions of biographical references.

BIOGRAPHY[1]

Biographical references are fascinating. They give us a chance to look in on the real lives of other people. Where else could you find answers to questions like the following?

What is Harold Pinter's hobby?[2]
What is Elizabeth Peabody remembered for?[3]
Did Barbara Walters to go college?[4]
How tall is Goldie Hawn?[5]
What is Joe Frazier's childhood nickname?[6]

---

[1]Biographical references to people in a specialized field are described under that field. For example, Kunitz's *Twentieth Century Authors* is given under the *literature* section of specialized references rather than under biography.

[2]Harold Pinter's hobby is sailing. *Who's Who*, New York: St. Martin's Press, 1973-74, p. 2562.

[3]Elizabeth Peabody opened the first American kindergarten. *Webster's Biographical Dictionary*, Springfield, Mass.: Merriam, 1961, p. 1156.

[4]Barbara Walters has a B.A. degree in English from Sarah Lawrence College. *Current Biography*, New York: Wilson Co., 1971, p. 432.

[5]Goldie Hawn is five feet six inches tall. *Current Biography*, 1971, p. 184.

[6]Joe Frazier's childhood nickname was Billy. *Current Biography*, 1971, p. 143.

Not many of us have such details at our fingertips, but special references on biography contain all of this information and more. Of course there are many general sources of biographical information about famous characters in history. You can find biographies in the subject section of the card catalog. The *Readers' Guide* or the *Biography Index* will tell you where to find information about people written up in magazines. Also, encyclopedias contain articles about outstanding people.

But if we want to know about people who are not important historical characters, we need to consult reference books specialized in biography. These biographical references that are brief and easy to use can be scholastic lifesavers, and it is worthwhile and interesting to become familiar with some of them.

WHO'S WHO

Who's Who. London: Black. Published annually since 1849. The publisher in the United States varies.

WHO'S WHO IN AMERICA

Who's Who in America. Chicago: Marquis. Published every other year beginning 1899/1900.

Who's Who is an annual handbook of biographies of prominent men and women who are *living*. This book includes *mainly British* people. Other nationalities are represented by a few names. The biographies are brief. They include main facts about the person, his address, and lists of his works. The people are listed alphabetically by last name.

When these famous people die, their biographies are taken out of these books and from time to time are printed in *Who Was Who* (6 volumes cover 1897 to 1970) and *Who Was Who in America* (an historical volume covers 1607-1896 and four other volumes cover 1897-1968).

Problem 26

SEARCH QUESTIONS

These questions are from *Who's Who in America*, 1972-73.

1. How old is Charles Schultz?

2. What are some things Leonard Bernstein is noted for?

3. Where did Judge John Sirica go to law school?

CLUES

In each case, merely look in alphabetical order for the person's last name: *Schultz, Bernstein,* and *Sirica.*

You would have to know that they are living Americans to choose the right volume. A question about Queen Elizabeth II would have required that you check *Who's Who,* and for a question about George Washington you would need the historical volume for *Who Was Who in America.*

WEBSTER'S BIOGRAPHICAL DICTIONARY

Webster's Biographical Dictionary. Springfield, Mass.: Merriam, 1974.

This dictionary includes both living and historical figures of all periods, nationalities, races, religions, and occupations. Each entry is brief, factual, and tells very clearly how to pronounce the names. In the back are tables of high government officials in the United States, Britain, and some other countries.

Problem 27

SEARCH QUESTIONS

1. What was the highest rank Benedict Arnold obtained?

2. Who was Barbara Fritchie? What works tell her story?

3. Did John Witherspoon sign the United States Declaration of Independence?

4. How many Caesars ruled in ancient Rome?

5. Who was the first British diplomat to the U.S.?

6. Who was the first U.S. Secretary of Agriculture?

CLUES

For questions 1 and 2 look under the last names (Arnold and Fritchie) in alphabetical order.

Strachan, John. 1862–1907. British classical and Celtic scholar, b. in Banffshire, Scotland; professor of Greek, Owens Coll., Manchester (1885–1907); with Kuno Meyer, founded Summer School of Irish Learning at Dublin (1903); with Whitley Stokes, produced *Thesaurus Palaeohibernicus* (2 vols., 1901–03). Author of memoirs on Irish philology and *Introduction to Early Welsh* (pub. 1909).

Stra′chey (strā′chǐ), **John St. Loe**. 1860–1927. English journalist; editor of *Cornhill Magazine* (1896–97), and proprietor and editor of *Spectator* (1898–1925). Among his books are *The Manufacture of Paupers, Problems and Perils of Socialism, A New Way of Life* (1909), and *The Adventure of Living* (1922). His son **Evelyn John St. Loe** (1901–1963), Socialist writer and politician; author of *Revolution by Reason* (1925), *The Menace of Fascism* (1933), *The Nature of Capitalist Crisis* (1935), *The Theory and Practice of Socialism* (1936), *The Economics of Progress* (1939); minister of food (from 1946).

Strachey, Lytton, *in full* **Giles Lytton.** 1880–1932. English writer; educ. Cambridge; among his books are *Landmarks in French Literature* (1912), *Eminent Victorians* (1918), *Queen Victoria* (1921), *Books and Characters* (1922), *Pope* (1925), and *Elizabeth and Essex* (1928).

Strachey, Sir Richard. 1817–1908. Anglo-Indian administrator, b. in Somersetshire; member, Council of India (1875–89); fellow of Royal Society (1854) for his investigations in Indian geology, botany, and meteorology. His older brother, **Sir Edward** (1812–1901), was student of Oriental languages and Biblical criticism; author of *Jewish History and Politics* (1874) and *Miracles and Science* (1854). Their younger brother, **Sir John** (1823–1907), Anglo-Indian administrator, was chief commissioner of Oudh (1866); lieutenant governor of North-West Provinces (1874–76); member of Council of India (1885–95).

Strachey, William. An English colonist in Virginia; secretary and recorder of Virginia under Lord De La Warr (1610–11); author of *The Historie of Travaile into Virginia Britannia*...(first publ. by Hakluyt Society, 1849), etc.

Strack (shträk), **Hermann.** 1848–1922. German Protestant theologian and Orientalist.

Stra·del′la (strä-děl′lä), **Alessandro.** 1645?–1682. Italian singer and composer, a master of the aria; composer of operas, oratorios, cantatas, and sonatas, all still in manuscript. He figured in a love affair which served as subject of Flotow's opera *Alessandro Stradella.*

Stra′di·va′ri (strä′dĕ·vä′rē), **Antonio.** *Lat.* **Antonius Strad′i·var′i·us** (străd′ĭ·vâr′ĭ·ŭs). 1644–1737. Italian violinmaker, b. Cremona; pupil and associate of Nicolò Amati; worked independently (1669 ff.); made Cremonas, violas, and violoncellos; assisted in later work by his sons **Francesco** (1671–1743), who carried on father's art, and **Omobono** (1679–1742), known esp. for skill in repairing stringed instruments.

Stradonitz, Kekule von. See KEKULE VON STRADONITZ.

Straf′ford (străf′ẽrd), **1st Earl of.** Sir **Thomas Went′worth** (wĕnt′wûrth; -wẽrth). 1st Baron **Ra′by** (rā′bǐ). 1593–1641. English statesman; M.P. (1614); opposed agitation for war against Spain (1625); anti-Puritan and supporter of royal prerogative; imprisoned for failure to contribute to forced loan (1627); virtual leader of House of Commons, introduced bill for securing liberties of subjects from forced loans, billeting of soldiers, arbitrary imprisonment, but on its nonacceptance by Charles, relinquished leadership to Eliot and Coke (1628); did not oppose Petition of Right, which replaced his moderate bill. Taken into court favor; made president of council of the north (Dec. 25, 1628) and as royal executive checked insubordination; privy councilor (1629). As lord deputy of Ireland (1632–38), adopted "Thorough" policy, coerced country into obedience and order. Chief adviser to Charles I (1639); created Baron Raby and earl of Strafford (1640); lord lieutenant of Ireland (1640); advocated invasion of Scotland to crush Presbyterian insurgents and force adoption of the English liturgy; obtained £180,000 in subsidies from Irish parliament and prepared to lead Irish troops against Scots (1640); urged Charles to various despotic actions; commanded forces in Yorkshire against invading Scots. Impeached for treason by Pym and followers in Commons, who accused him of subverting the law of the kingdom by plotting to coerce parliament with a northern army; imprisoned, tried (1641) under a bill of attainder, substituted for impeachment and passed by commons and lords, and unwillingly assented to by Charles I; beheaded on Tower Hill. His grandnephew **Thomas Wentworth** (1672–1739), 3d Baron Raby and 3d Earl of Strafford, diplomatist, was ambassador at Berlin (1703–11), at The Hague (1711–14); one of negotiators of the peace of Utrecht (1711–13).

Straight (strāt), **Willard Dickerman.** 1880–1918. American diplomat and financier; in Chinese customs service (1901–04); U.S. vice-consul at Seoul, Korea (1905); U.S. consul general at Mukden (1906). Acting chief, division of Far Eastern Affairs, U.S. Department of State (1908–09). Again in China (1909–12), acting for American business and financial interests. Volunteered at entrance of U.S. into World War; died of pneumonia contracted in line of duty, Paris (Dec. 1, 1918).

Stran′a·han (străn′á·hăn), **James Samuel Thomas.** 1808–1898. American civic leader, b. Peterboro, N.Y.; moved to Brooklyn, N.Y. (1844); identified himself with municipal development of Brooklyn, as in building of harbor improvements, docks and piers, and in East River ferry lines; president, Brooklyn park board (1860–82) and largely responsible for development of Prospect Park; supported project for East River Bridge (opened 1883); advocated consolidation of Brooklyn with New York City (accomplished 1898). A statue of him by Frederick William MacMonnies is in Prospect Park.

Strand′berg′ (strånd′bär′y), **Carl Vilhelm August.** *Pseudonym* **Ta′lis Qua′lis** (tä′lǐs kvä′lǐs). 1818–1877. Swedish poet and journalist; published *Poems of Passion* (1845), *Wild Roses* (1848), etc.

Strand′man (strånd′mån), **Otto.** 1875– . Estonian statesman; prime minister of Estonia (1919); president of parliament (1920–22); minister of foreign affairs and of finance (1924); minister to Poland (1927–29); chief of state and prime minister (1929–31); minister to France (1933 ff.).

Strang (străng), **William.** 1859–1921. Scottish painter and etcher.

Strange (strānj), **Earl.** See 4th duke of ATHOLL.

Strange, Sir Robert. 1721–1792. Scottish line engraver; executed historical engravings in London (from 1751), chiefly after Italian masters; knighted by George III for engraving of West's *Apotheosis of the Royal Children* (1786).

Strangford, Viscounts. See under Sir Thomas SMYTHE (1558?–1625).

Stra′pa·ro′la (strä′pä·rô′lä), **Giovanni Francesco.** d. about 1557. Italian writer, b. in Caravaggio; known for his collection of 73 novelle and tales *Tredici Piacevoli Notti* (vol. 1, 1550; vol. 2, 1553; called in Eng. *Facetious Nights*), notable as source material for Shakespeare, Molière, et al., and containing such tales as *Beauty and the Beast* and *Puss in Boots.*

āle, chåotic, câre (7), ădd, ăccount, ärm, åsk (11), sofá; ēve, hẹre (18), ĕvent, ĕnd, silĕnt, makẽr; īce, ĭll, charĭty; ōld, ȯbey, ôrb, ŏdd (40), sȯft (41), cȯnnect; fo͞od, fo͝ot; out, oil; cūbe, ŭnite, ûrn, ŭp, circŭs, ü = u in Fr. menu;

For questions 3 through 6 look in the table of contents for the page number of the appropriate table; e.g., for 4 look for Roman emperors or Caesars, for 5, British diplomats to the U.S., and for 6 look for the table of signers of the Declaration of Independence.

CHAMBER'S BIOGRAPHICAL DICTIONARY

J.O. Thorne, ed. *Chamber's Biographical Dictionary.* New York: St. Martin's Press, 1962.

This is another useful one-volume biographical dictionary which gives a brief assessment of the person. Names are listed in alphabetical order.

Problem 28

SEARCH QUESTIONS

1. When was George Telemann's music rediscovered?

2. Where was Marc Chagall born?

3. How might John Hersey have become interested in the Orient?

CLUES

Look for the last names in their alphabetical place: *Telemann, Chagall, Hersey.*

DICTIONARY OF AMERICAN BIOGRAPHY

Dictionary of American Biography. Prepared by the American Council of Learned Societies. New York: Scribner's Sons, 1928-present. 20 vol. with index and supplements. A later edition of this work is printed in 10 vol. with index and supplements.

J. G. E. Hopkins, ed. *Concise Dictionary of American Biography.* New York: Scribner's Sons, 1964.

The *Dictionary of American Biography* includes important Americans no longer living. Their contributions may be in any field — athletics, industry, literature, politics, religion. The articles on each person are well-written, usually by experts in the same field. The biographies are alphabetically arranged. The supplementary volumes contain biographies of famous Americans who have died since the original dictionary was published.

The index volume is a valuable addition to this set. There is an index of people included in the set and an index of the biographers with their subjects. Another index is by state of the subject's birth. There is also an index by occupation with such categories as humorist, industrialist, and map makers. Another useful index is by topic such as the gold rush, labor movement, and naval oil reserves. This way you can find lists of people associated with an occupation or with a certain topic.

The Concise Dictionary of American Biography is a one-volume condensation of the larger work and is very handy for quick identification. It has no indexes, however.

Problem 29

SEARCH QUESTIONS

These questions are from the *Dictionary of American Biography*.

1. Who was Sylvester Malone? Was he active in politics?

2. What church did Mary Morse Baker Eddy start?

3. How did Nathaniel Hawthorne come to spend so much time alone?

4. Name three people involved with starting the U.S. Postal Savings system.

CLUES

1.-3. Find the last names of these people in their proper alphabetical sequence. Look under *Malone, Eddy,* and *Hawthorne.*

4. In the index volume find the topic index section. Here look under *Postal Savings System.* This entry will give you two references. Each reference has a roman and an arabic numeral. The roman numeral tells you the volume to look in, and the arabic numeral tells you the page in that volume.

Volck, Adalbert John
Wales, James Albert
CATERER (See RESTAURANTEUR)
CATTLEMAN (See also DAIRY
  HUSBANDMAN, RANCHER)
Chisum, John Simpson
Goodnight, Charles
Lasater, Edward Cunningham
Littlefield, George Washington
McCoy, Joseph Geating
Renick, Felix
Strawn, Jacob
CENSUS DIRECTOR
Kennedy, Joseph Camp Griffith
Merriam, William Rush
CHANCELLOR (STATE)
Livingston, Robert R., 1746–1813
Walworth, Reuben Hyde
Harrington, Samuel Maxwell
Saulsbury, Willard, 1820–1892
CHANDLER
Jackson, William, 1783–1855
CHAPLAIN (For related occupa-
  tions, see RELIGIOUS LEADER)
Hunter, Andrew
Jones, David
Jones, George
Munro, Henry
CHEMIST (See also BIO-CHEMIST)
Austen, Peter Townsend
Babcock, James Francis
Bache, Franklin
Bailey, Jacob Whitman
Barker, George Frederick
Baskerville, Charles
Beck, Lewis Caleb
Bolton, Henry Carrington
Boltwood, Bertram Borden
Booth, James Curtis
Boyé, Martin Hans
Burnett, Joseph
Chandler, Charles Frederick
Cooke, Josiah Parsons
Crafts, James Mason
Cutbush, James
Dana, James Freeman
Dana, Samuel Luther
Day, David Talbot
Doremus, Robert Ogden
Draper, John William
Drown, Thomas Messinger
Dudley, Charles Benjamin
Duncan, Robert Kennedy
Freas, Thomas Bruce
Genth, Frederick Augustus
Gibbs, Oliver Wolcott
Goessmann, Charles Anthony
Gorham, John
Grasselli, Caesar Augustin
Green, Jacob
Griscom, John
Guthrie, Samuel
Hall, Charles Martin
Hare, Robert
Hayes, Augustus Allen
Hendrick, Ellwood
Hill, Henry Barker
Hillebrand, William Francis
Horsford, Eben Norton
Hunt, Thomas Sterry
Jackson, Charles Thomas
James, Charles
Jarves, Deming

Jones, Harry Clary
Keating, William Hypolitus
Kedzie, Robert Clark
Kinnicutt, Leonard Parker
Koenig, George Augustus
Ladd, Edwin Fremont
Langley, John Williams
Lea, Mathew Carey
Leffmann, Henry
Levy, Louis Edward
Loeb, Morris
Long, John Harper
Mabery, Charles Frederic
Maclean, John
McMurtrie, William
Mallet, John William
Matheson, William John
Matthews, Joseph Merritt
Merrill, Joshua
Metcalfe, Samuel Lytler
Mitchell, John Kearsley
Moore, Richard Bishop
Morfit, Campbell
Morley, Edward Williams
Nef, John Ulric
Nichols, James Robinson
Norton, John Pitkin
Parr, Samuel Wilson
Peckham, Stephen Farnum
Pendleton, Edmund Monroe
Peter, Robert
Phillips, Francis Clifford
Porter, John Addison
Power, Frederick Belding
Prescott, Albert Benjamin
Pugh, Evan
Randall, Wyatt William
Reid, David Boswell
Remsen, Ira
Rice, Charles
Richards, Ellen Henrietta Swal-
  low
Richards, Theodore William
Rogers, James Blythe
Rogers, Robert Empie
Sadtler, Samuel Philip
Sanger, Charles Robert
Scovell, Melville Amasa
Seabury, George John
Shepard, James Henry
Silliman, Benjamin, 1816–1885
Slosson, Edwin Emery
Smith, Alexander
Smith, Edgar Fahs
Smith, John Lawrence
Squibb, Edward Robinson
Stillman, Thomas Bliss
Stoddard, John Tappan
Storer, Francis Humphreys
Takamine, Jokichi
Talbot, Henry Paul
Tilghman, Richard Albert
Torrey, John
Vaughan, Daniel
Warren, Cyrus Moors
Washburn, Edward Wight
Weber, Henry Adam
Weightman, William
Wetherill, Charles Mayer
White, Henry Clay
Whitney, Josiah Dwight
Wiechmann, Ferdinand Gerhard
Wiley, Harvey Washington

Witthaus, Rudolph August
Wood, Edward Stickney
Woodhouse, James
Wurtz, Henry
CHESS PLAYER
Loyd, Samuel
Mackenzie, George Henry
Morphy, Paul Charles
Pillsbury, Harry Nelson
Rice, Isaac Leopold
Steinitz, William
CHIEF-JUSTICE (STATE) (See also
  JUDGE, JURIST, LAWYER, SU-
  PREME COURT JUSTICE)
De Lancey, James
Gaines, Reuben Reid
Horsmanden, Daniel
Livermore, Arthur
Lloyd, David
Lowe, Ralph Phillips
Lumpkin, Joseph Henry
Mellen, Prentiss
More, Nicholas
Morris, Lewis, 1671–1746
Morris, Robert Hunter
Morton, Marcus, 1819–1891
Nicholls, Francis Redding Tillon
Read, George
Rusk, Thomas Jefferson
Shippen, Edward, 1728–1806
Simpson, William Dunlap
CHOIRMASTER (See also CONDUC-
  TOR)
Tuckey, William
CHRISTIAN SCIENCE LEADER (For
  related occupations, see RELI-
  GIOUS LEADER)
Stetson, Augusta Emma Sim-
  mons
CHRONICLER (See also HISTORIAN)
Clyman, James
Johnson, Edward
CHURCH HISTORIAN (See also
  HISTORIAN)
Dubbs, Joseph Henry
Edwards, Morgan
Jackson, Samuel Macauley
Perry, William Stevens
Schaff, Philip
Walker, Williston
Whitsitt, William Heth
CIRCUS CLOWN (See CLOWN)
CIRCUS PROPRIETOR (See SHOW-
  MAN)
CITY-PLANNER
Brunner, Arnold William
Robinson, Charles Mulford
Wacker, Charles Henry
CIVIC LEADER
Adams, Charles Francis
Fallows, Samuel
Fortier, Alcée
Hay, Mary Garrett
Hirsch, Emil Gustav
Loring, Charles Morgridge
Mosher, Eliza Maria
Ochs, Julius
O'Connor, William Douglas
Seligman, Isaac Newton
Seligman, Joseph
Spaulding, Oliver Lyman
Stranahan, James Samuel
  Thomas

DICTIONARY OF NATIONAL BIOGRAPHY

Leslie Stephen and Sidney Lee, eds. *Dictionary of National Biography*. London: Smith, Elder and Co., 1885-1901. Supplements since 1912 published by Oxford University Press.

Concise Dictionary of National Biography. London: Oxford University Press, 1961. 2 vol.

The *Dictionary of National Biography* is a scholarly work similar to the *Dictionary of American Biography*. The *Dictionary of National Biography*, however, concerns itself with famous British people who are no longer living.

This longer reference has been condensed into a two-part *Concise Dictionary of National Biography* which is convenient to use for quick identification.

WHO WAS WHEN?

Mariam Allen DeFord. *Who Was When?* New York: Wilson Co., 2nd ed., 1950.

This is a less-known but handy reference for placing people in their times and for showing who their contemporaries were. Each page is laid out in 12 columns headed: Year; Government and Law; Military and Naval Affairs; Industry, Commerce, Economics, Finance, Invention, Labor; Travel and Exploration; Philosophy and Religion; Science and Medicine; Education, Scholarship, History; Literature; Painting and Sculpture; Music; and Miscellaneous. The information runs from 500 B.C. to 1950 A.D. An alphabetical index of people is at the back of the book.

Problem 30

SEARCH QUESTIONS

1. Darius the Great of Persia died in 486 B.C. What two great religious leaders lived until just a few years later?

2. When Kublai Khan was born, who was ruling England?

3. James Joyce was born in 1882. What other famous writers were born that year?

4. Who was the famous actor born that same year (1882)?

CLUES

1. Locate 486 chronologically — remember it is B.C. — then scan the philosophy and religion column.

2. Find the year Kublai Khan was born from the index under *Khan*. Locate that year chronologically, and scan the government column.

3. Turn to 1882 chronologically, then scan the literature column.

4. Again for the year 1882, scan the miscellaneous column.

CURRENT BIOGRAPHY

Current Biography. New York: H.W. Wilson Co. This has been published since 1940.

Current Biography is one of the most interesting biographical sources. It contains feature-length biographical sketches, often three pages long, of people currently in the news, in fields such as entertainment, government, sports, literature, and music. These interesting sketches focus on the personality of the person as well as on facts about his or her life. Each article includes facts about the person, a biographical sketch, and often a picture. *Current Biography* comes out monthly (except August). There is a *Yearbook* each year which includes the biographies for that year in one volume. The biographies are listed alphabetically in the *Yearbook*, and each volume includes a cumulative index to the preceding volumes of the decade. (There are separate index volumes for the decades 1951-60 and 1961-70). Each yearbook also has a useful index of the biographies listed by profession.

Problem 31

SEARCH QUESTIONS

These questions are from the *Current Biography Yearbooks*.

Schuster. He is also gestating a novel about the exploits of an enterprising "rock 'n' roll newsman" not too unlike himself. "I think that my life goal is to look back on the day before I die and say to myself, well, I achieved something significant," the reporter told Carol Burton. "It may be the Geraldo Rivera method of caring for the mentally retarded, you know, something like that."

References

Biog N 941+ Ag '74 por
Esquire 83:88+ Ap '75
[MORE] 4:11+ S '74 pors
N Y Sunday News Mag p20+ S 10 '72
    pors
New York 5:56+ Ag 7 '72 por
Who's Who in America, 1974-75

PETE ROSE

ROSE, PETE

Apr. 14, 1942-   Baseball player
Address: b. Cincinnati Reds, 100 Riverfront Stadium, Cincinnati, O. 45202

Pete Rose is the field leader of the Cincinnati Reds, a team known as the Big Red Machine, because of its potent offense. On a club famous for its home run hitters, Rose hits mostly singles and doubles—but enough of them to win three National League batting titles. En route to his third title, in 1973, he collected more than two hundred hits for the sixth time in his career, and ten days before the season ended he broke the club record for the most hits in a single season, the mark of 219 set by Cy Seymour in 1905. Rose is the only active major leaguer to hit .300 for nine consecutive seasons, beginning with 1965. As of July 1975, his career average was .309. Rose was named Most Valuable Player of the 1975 World Series after his team defeated the Boston Red Sox, 4-3.

Rose's value to Cincinnati goes beyond his ability at the plate, however. He is the team's spark plug, the type of player who runs into outfield walls to catch a fly ball, slides into a base headfirst, and runs full-tilt to first base when he draws a walk; who can jar a lazy teammate with a few caustic words or push a less talented one to the limits of his ability with some judicious praise. It is with good reason that Rose is known around the National League as "Charlie Hustle," and that he can refer to himself as baseball's "only $100,000 singles hitter." Rose, formerly an outfielder, has been moved to third base, a change that should contribute to the lengthening of his athletic career.

Peter Edward Rose was born on April 14, 1942, in Cincinnati, Ohio. One of four children—two boys and two girls—he was raised in a comfortable middle-class atmosphere. He was drawn to sports early in his childhood, primarily because of his father, the late Harry F. Rose, whom he calls "the most important guy" in his life. Before becoming chief cashier at the Union Trust Company in Cincinnati, the father was a semi-pro football player of some note, an active participant in the game until the age of forty-two. "The first clear memory I have of Dad involves sports," Rose told Dick Kaplan of *Sport* (April, 1971). "I can still remember carrying the water bucket for his football team when I was only a little shaver. I could hardly handle the bucket, but I remember how proud I was that I was able to share such an important part of Dad's life."

"I guess I must have been about two when he started playing catch with me," Rose recalls. "He wanted me to share his love of sports, and I did. So help me, he never pushed me, never made me play when I didn't want to play, never forced me. He wasn't that kind of man. But like I say, everything was sports. Every Christmas I would get a new glove or a new basketball. Once, Mom sent Dad downtown to buy a pair of shoes for my sister. Instead, he came back with a pair of boxing gloves for me."

When he was nine Rose played organized baseball for the first time in the Knot Hole League, Cincinnati's equivalent of Little League. "Dad went up to my manager and struck a bargain with him," Rose told Bill Libby, author of *Pete Rose, They Call Him Charlie Hustle* (1974). "The only way Dad would let me play," he said, "was if the manager let me switch-hit." The manager agreed, with the ultimate result that Rose became the most accomplished switch-hitter in baseball. (While throwing only right, he bats both right and left.) The advantage of switch-hitting is that it gives one the ability to bat left-handed against a right-handed pitcher and right-handed against a left-handed pitcher.

In his formative years Rose was aided by instruction from his uncle, Buddy Bloebaum, a minor league player who later became a scout for the Reds. At Western Hills High School Rose played football as well as baseball, even though he weighed less than one hundred fifty pounds by the time he graduated. His father later recalled: "Pete was a great all-around athlete for a boy his size. Although he was short, he could dunk a basketball. And although he was not nearly the

CURRENT BIOGRAPHY 1975   361

1. What unusual "team" did Sylvia Mead lead?

2. For what was Richard Hatcher famous?

3. What did Roberto Clemente want to do for kids in Puerto Rico?

4. What did Carroll O'Connor do after he graduated from high school?

5. What positions has Johnny Bench played?

6. Name five contemporary scientists.

CLUES

1.-5. Use the latest *Yearbook* you have available. Check the index for the last name of the person you are looking for. The index will tell you the year which has an article about him. (If he is not listed in the index, you know there is no article about him in the 1970s). Get the volume for the proper year, and look in alphabetical order for the person's last name.

6. Use the profession index which is in the back of each *Yearbook*. Look under *scientists*.

GOVERNMENT AND HISTORY

You have probably already discovered that there is a lot of information about government and history in general references such as encyclopedias and almanacs. Often, however, you need more specific information or more detail than these general sources contain. For example, where would you look to find the answers to the following questions?

> Did more freight travel the Mississippi River in 1970 or 1950?[1]

> The Bureau of Indian Affairs is part of the Department of Interior, but which was created first?[2]

> How large is the army of Costa Rica?[3]

For these and thousands of other questions, a well-indexed special reference dealing with history or government would provide you a short-cut to the answers. Some of these questions might have been answered with information from a general reference like an encyclopedia, but it would take you much longer.

When we begin to explore the specialized reference books we find that the topics of government and history are intertwined so that it is impossible to separate them. We have tried to divide these government-history references into four kinds. First are those that specialize in statistical facts and figures about countries, including such things as population, education, economics, agriculture, or industry. Second are the handbooks which give details of the political organization of countries. Third are references that clearly deal with the subject of history; these may take many different forms such as dictionaries, atlases, and encyclopedias. Fourth, we had to include a few books under miscellaneous. For a direct route to specific information you need about government or history, you should know some of these special references, and they can provide interesting background for your pleasure reading.

Quantitative summaries. Some special references focus on quantitative summaries of political, social, and economic information.

STATISTICAL ABSTRACT OF THE UNITED STATES

> U.S. Bureau of the Census. *Statistical Abstract of the United States.* Washington: Government Printing Office, 1878 to the present.

This book is a yearly digest of statistical data about the United States. It includes information about areas such as population, immigration, education, finance, railroads, trade, geography, and public facilities. It is arranged by 33 topical sections with an alphabetical index. Each of these sections is preceded by a brief introduction. Most information is arranged in tables which cover several years to show trends. There is a good alphabetical index at the end.

Problem 32

SEARCH QUESTIONS

1. How did the sizes of farms (in acres) compare between the years 1950 and 1959?

---

[1]About three times as much freight was carried in 1970 as in 1950. *Statistical Abstracts of the U.S.*, 1972, p. 573.

[2]The Bureau of Indian Affairs is 25 years older than the Department of Interior. *U.S. Government Organization Manual*, 1973-74, p. 272.

[3]Costa Rica abolished its army in 1948 and has a 1,200 man Civil Guard. *Statesman's Yearbook*, 1972-73, p. 838.

vi   **Contents**

CONTENTS

[Numbers following subjects are page numbers]

Part of table of contents from *Statistical Abstract of the United States* (1974) shows range of material covered.

57

2. In 1968 how many people were eligible to vote for President? How many did? How does this compare with 1920?

3. What was the illiteracy rate in 1969? Is this larger or smaller than 1959?

4. How many dollars worth of tea did the U.S. import in 1971?

CLUES

The *index must be used* for all of these. It is almost impossible to use a statistical reference without using the index.

1. Look in the index under *farms*, then look under the subheading *acreage*.

2. Check the index under *voting age, population* or under *population* and then the subheading *voting age.* Either will lead you to the right page.

3. Check *illiteracy* in the index.

4. If you look in the index under *imports*, you are told "see foreign trade." Under *foreign trade*, find the subhead *(coffee, tea, cocoa)* which will refer you to the right page.
Or, you might begin by checking the index under *tea*, subhead *foreign trade*. Here several pages are listed, and you have to look at them to see which has the information you need. Either approach will lead you to the information.

HISTORICAL STATISTICS OF THE UNITED STATES

> U.S. Bureau of Census. *Historical Statistics of the United States, Colonial Times to 1957.* Washington: Government Printing Office. There is a supplement which continues to 1962.

This book contains historical statistics on the political, social, industrial, and economic aspects of the United States. Tables cover several years, some going back to the mid-eighteenth century. The tables are similar to those found in the *Statistical Abstracts* and include the kinds of things covered by the census. A section of explanation, telling where and how the information was obtained, precedes each section. The table of contents outlines general areas such as Social Conditions, and the index lists material by more specific subjects.

Problem 33

SEARCH QUESTIONS

1. What was the percentage of the civilian labor force employed in 1947? 1957?

2. How many institutions of higher education were there in 1880?

CLUES

Since the table of contents is by general area, you could look there for these question areas, or you could check the index for the specific thing you are seeking. The index seems the quicker route, but either way works.

1. Look under *labor* in the table of contents or in the index under *unemployment – labor force.*

2. Look in the table of contents for *social Statistics – education* or in the index under *education – institutions of higher education – number.*

YEARBOOK OF THE UNITED NATIONS

> *Yearbook of the United Nations.* New York: United Nations, Office of Public Information, 1947 to the present.

Each year the *Yearbook of the United Nations* summarizes the happenings at the U.N. The activities, discussions, and decisions of the U.N. are organized by subject. These subjects are arranged by subtopic and include full texts of U.N. resolutions and bibliographic references to U.N. documents. Appendices include a roster of U.N. members, a list of delegations, the U.N. charter, and the U.N. structure. There is an index arranged by subject and an index of names.

Problem 34

SEARCH QUESTIONS

1. Did the U.N. deal with the peaceful uses of the sea bed in 1970?

2. Find something about the Food and Agriculture Organization's freedom from hunger campaign.

CLUES

1. Remember that all of these books take time to compile, so material dealing with a particular date won't be included until a year or two after that date. The volume for 1972 includes material on the sea bed discussed in 1970. Check the index *sea bed and ocean floor, peaceful uses of.* This happens to have been a large topic for the year, and therefore it is also listed in the table of contents, but the index is generally easier to use.

2. Look in the index under *Food and Agriculture Organization,* subheading *act.* (stands for activities). Freedom from hunger is listed under activities.

Political organization handbooks. Some references focus on the political organization of countries and on the people currently holding important offices. These handbooks often also give some description of the current social and economic characteristics of the country.

U.S. GOVERNMENT ORGANIZATION MANUAL

U.S. Government Organization Manual. Washington: Government Printing Office, 1935 to present.

This is a valuable source of information on the U.S. federal government. It gives the date of creation, organization, activities, and chief officials of each branch and agency. The appendices include descriptions of some international organizations, a list of commonly used abbreviations for agencies, and an alphabetical list of prominent men in the federal government. There is a good index of the subjects included in the *Manual.*

Problem 35

SEARCH QUESTIONS

These questions are from the 1973-74 *Manual.*

1. In what department is Stanley Goldberg a prominent official?

2. The Agricultural Adjustment Agency was a part of Franklin D. Roosevelt's New Deal. What happened to it?

3. How is the ACTION program organized?

4. Who is the Chaplain of the House of Representatives?

CLUES

1. Check the index of names under *Goldberg, Stanley.*

2. Look under *Agricultural Adjustment Act* in Appendix A which deals with federal agencies no longer existing.

3. Look in the main index under *Action.*

4. Look in the index under *House of Representatives,* subheading *officers. Chaplain* is listed under that.

U.S. CONGRESSIONAL DIRECTORY

U.S. Congressional Directory. Washington: Government Printing Office, 1809 to present.

This is an annual directory of the U.S. Congress. It is published to help members of Congress find their way around. Biographical information about all members is presented alphabetically according to the state they represent. Individuals are indexed at the back of the *Directory.* There is an important and detailed table of contents in the front which serves as a subject index.

Problem 36

SEARCH QUESTIONS

These questions are from the 1973 *Congressional Directory.*

1. When was the late Hubert Humphrey, the senator from Minnesota, born?

2. What is the address of the President's Council on Physical Fitness and Sports?

3. Find a diagram of the seating plan of the Senate.

4. How is your state divided into Congressional districts?

CLUES

1. Since you know the state Senator Humphrey represented, you can look directly in the text

WISCONSIN

(Population, 1970 census, 4,417,933)

SENATORS

WILLIAM PROXMIRE, Wisconsin.

GAYLORD NELSON, Democrat, of Madison, Wis.; born June 4, 1916, in Clear Lake, a village in northwestern Wisconsin, son of Dr. Anton Nelson; attended San Jose State College in California, graduating in 1939; received law degree from the University of Wisconsin in 1942; in the U.S. Army for 46 months during World War II, serving in the Okinawa campaign; married Carrie Lee Dotson in 1947; three children: Gaylord Nelson, Jr.; Cynthia Lee Nelson; and Jeffrey Nelson; elected to the Wisconsin Legislature in 1948; elected Governor of Wisconsin in 1958 and reelected in 1960; elected to the U.S. Senate November 6, 1962; reelected November 5, 1968, and November 5, 1974.

REPRESENTATIVES

FIRST DISTRICT.—COUNTIES: Kenosha, Racine, Rock, and Walworth. GREEN COUNTY: City of Brodhead; towns of Albany and Spring Grove; and village of Albany. JEFFERSON COUNTY: That part constituting a part of the city of Whitewater. Population (1970), 490,817.

LES ASPIN, Democrat, of Racine, Wis.; born in Milwaukee, Wis., July 21, 1938; attended the public schools in Milwaukee, Wis.; graduated from Yale University, 1960; Oxford University, England, M.A. in a combined major, politics, philosophy, and economics, 1962; Massachusetts Institute of Technology, Ph. D. in economics, 1965; assistant professor of economics, Marquette University, Milwaukee, Wis., 1969–70; while serving in the U.S. Army, 1966–68, was an economist working in Systems Analysis in the Pentagon under Secretary of Defense Robert McNamara; entered military service as a second lieutenant, completed tour of duty with rank of captain; staff member of Senator Proxmire in 1960, staff assistant to Walter Heller, chairman, President Kennedy's Council of Economic Advisers, 1963; married Maureen Shea, 1969; elected to the 92d Congress, November 3, 1970; reelected to the 93d and 94th Congresses.

SECOND DISTRICT.—COUNTIES: Columbia, Dane, Iowa, Lafayette, and Sauk. DODGE COUNTY: Cities of Beaver Dam, Fox Lake, Horicon, Juneau, Mayville, and that part of the city of Waupun in the county; towns of Beaver Dam, Burnett, Calamus, Chester, Clyman, Elba, Fox Lake, Herman, Hubbard, Hustisford, Leroy, Lomira, Lowell, Oak Grove, Portland, Shields, Theresa, Trenton, Westford, and Williamstown; villages of Brownsville, Clyman, Hustisford, Iron Ridge, Kekoskee, Lomira, Lowell, Reeseville, Theresa, and that part of the village of Randolph in the county. FOND DU LAC COUNTY: Town of Waupun; that part of the city of Waupun in the county. GREEN COUNTY: All except city of Brodhead, towns of Albany and Spring Grove, and village of Albany. Population (1970), 490,941.

ROBERT WILLIAM KASTENMEIER, Democrat, of Sun Prairie, Wis.; born at Beaver Dam, Wis., January 24, 1924; educated in the public schools of Beaver Dam, and the University of Wisconsin, LL.B., 1952; entered United States Army as a private in February 1943; served in the Philippines; discharged August 15, 1946, as a first lieutenant; War Department branch office director, claims service, in the Philippines, 1946 to 1948; practiced law in Watertown, Wis., from September 1952 to December 1958; member of Wisconsin Bar Associations; married to the former Dorothy Chambers of Nacogdoches, Tex.; three sons; justice of the peace for Jefferson and Dodge Counties 1955–58; served as Jefferson County Democratic Party chairman from 1953 to 1956; chairman, House Judiciary Subcommittee on Courts, Civil Liberties and the Administration of Justice; member, State Democratic Central Committee in 1956; National Commission for the Review of Wiretapping and Electronic Surveillance; elected to the 86th Congress, November 4, 1958; reelected to the 87th, 88th, 89th, 90th, 91st, 92d, 93d, and 94th Congresses; member, House Committee on the Judiciary and House Committee on Interior and Insular Affairs.

Sample page from *U.S. Congressional Directory*, Washington: U.S. Government Printing Office, 1975.

under Minnesota. Or you could look under *Humphrey* in the individual index in the back which would refer you to the page in the text.

2. Check the table of contents (subject index) in the front under *President's*.

3. Again, use the table of contents in the front, but this takes some imagination. You have to look under *Capitol*, subheading *diagram of the* and under that, *seating plan of the Senate Chamber*.

4. Look under the subject in the index (table of contents) in the front: *Congressional: Districts, maps* of. Then look alphabetically for the name of your state.

POLITICAL HANDBOOK AND ATLAS OF THE WORLD

Political Handbook and Atlas of the World: Parliaments, Parties, and Press. Published for the Council on Foreign Relations, 1927 to date. New York: Simon & Schuster, 1970.

This excellent reference presents a short summary of the basic economic and political facts about nations, including information on geography, political parties, foreign relations, current issues, and news media. The countries are arranged alphabetically. There is also an alphabetically arranged section on intergovernmental organizations. The last section of the book is an atlas of the world. The index is between the text and the atlas, and it refers to both the text and map pages. Beginning in 1971 an annual supplement, *The World This Year*, has been printed to keep the information in the *Political Handbook* up to date. It is organized similarly, but has no atlas.

Problem 37

SEARCH QUESTIONS

1. In what languages are the newspapers of Burma written?

2. What is the program of the Independence Party in Iceland?

3. What is the political history of Colombia?

4. What is the African name of Rhodesia?

5. Who are the members of the Arab League?

6. Find the Cayman Islands on a map.

CLUES

All of these can be found in the index, but remember that the index is after the text but before the atlas. In the case of simpler questions like 3 and 4, you could turn directly to the country since they are alphabetically arranged in the book. Usually it is easier and faster to use the index.

Using the index look under:

1. Burma — news media — press.

2. Iceland — political parties. You should also check the latest *The World This Year* to update this information.

3. Colombia.

4. Rhodesia.

5. Arab League. You could also find this by turning directly to the intergovernmental organization section and looking under *A*.

6. Cayman Islands.

STATESMAN'S YEAR-BOOK

Statesman's Year-Book. London: Macmillan Press, 1864 to the present.

This valuable yearbook gives concise, up-to-date information about the governments of the world. It usually has four sections: International Organizations (the U.N., NATO, the Arab League, etc.), the Commonwealth, the U.S., and Other Countries. The section on Other Countries is arranged alphabetically. For each country there is usually a brief description of its physical characteristics, government, social conditions, economic structure, and currency. Comparative statistical tables are found in the front of the book. You can look in the table of contents to find material, but the index is surer and faster.

Problem 38

SEARCH QUESTIONS

These questions are from the 1972-73 *Year-Book*.

1. Which country grows more maize, Romania or Venezuela?

2. Who is the Secretary-General of the OAS (Organization of American States)? What is his nationality?

3. What is the area of Togo? What livestock is raised there? Who is Togo's ambassador to the United States?

4. Describe the educational system in Costa Rica.

CLUES

1. Look in the index under *maize*. This will lead you to the proper comparative table.

2. Look in the index under *Organization of American States*. It sends you to two or three pages which you have to scan to find the list of officers.

3. These are listed in the article about Togo. Check the index.

4. Find the article on Costa Rica listed in the index, and scan for the education section.

History. There are many references dealing with history. Their titles usually provide enough of a guide to help you select the reference you need; they indicate whether that reference deals with U.S. or world history, with original documents, speeches, or facts about events.

DICTIONARY OF AMERICAN HISTORY

James Truslow Adams, ed. *Dictionary of American History*. New York: Scribner's Sons. Originally, in 1940, there were 5 volumes and the index. In 1961 Vol. 6 was published as a supplement which covered the period 1940-60.

The *Dictionary of American History* is a comprehensive reference, and the articles are well-written. They cover political, social, economic, and cultural history. There are no biographies included because this dictionary was designed to complement to *Dictionary of American Biography*.

The index is thorough and detailed. For example, if you were to look up *Indians*, there would be more than 40 references with over 100 subreferences. There would also be specific tribes index such as *Navajo* or *Sioux* and subheadings listed under these.

Problem 39

SEARCH QUESTIONS

These questions are from the *Dictionary of American History*.

1. What happened at the Battle of King's Mountain?

2. What were the main issues in the presidential campaigns of 1932 and 1952?

3. What is meant by a *single tax*?

CLUES

1. Check the index under *King's Mountain, battle of*.

2. Look under *campaign of 1932* and *campaign of 1952* listed in the index. If you checked under *presidential campaigns*, you found a cross-reference to "see campaigns of various years."

3. Indexed under *single tax*.

CONCISE DICTIONARY OF AMERICAN HISTORY

James Truslow Adams, ed. *Concise Dictionary of American History*. New York: Scribner's Sons. Later editions were prepared by Wayne Andrews.

The *Concise Dictionary of American History* is a useful, condensed version of the larger dictionary. It is arranged alphabetically. There is an index which helps locate material in complex topics, but usually the dictionary arrangement is clear.

Problem 40

SEARCH QUESTIONS

1. Describe the League of Nations.

2. What was the Bonus Army?

3. What were some of the provisions of the Federal Highway Act of 1956?

4. What was the Square Deal?

Japan, Italy and Germany were threatening international peace. The Democratic party was divided on foreign policy. The South, while not enthusiastic about all of Roosevelt's domestic policies, supported his program of resistance to aggression. The Middle West and West were in favor of his domestic reforms but tended to isolationism. The Northeast alone supported him in both. In the face of world conditions, especially after the Munich Crisis of September, 1938, the President felt compelled to subordinate his domestic reforms to keep southern support for his foreign policy. His failure actively to support an anti-lynching bill indicated a new outlook. Henceforth he would strive chiefly for party and domestic unity as the nations prepared for war.

NEW ENGLAND, DOMINION OF (June, 1686–April, 1689), represented the application of a principle which the English government had long had in mind, the consolidation of the American colonies into a few large provinces for the sake of better administration of defense, commerce and justice. The experiment in dominion government was first tried out in New England because of the necessity of replacing the old charter government of Massachusetts Bay Colony, after the annulment of the charter in 1684, with some form of royal control. The dominion was established in June, 1686, in temporary form, under the presidency of a native New Englander, Joseph Dudley, but was formally inaugurated in December, 1686, upon the arrival of Gov. Edmund Andros, under whose rule the former colonies or regions of Massachusetts, Plymouth, Rhode Island, Connecticut, New Hampshire, Maine, the County of Cornwall (northern Maine) and King's Province, a disputed region in southern New England, were consolidated into one province.

Governmental power was vested in the governor and a council, appointed by the king, but there was no representative assembly. Andros' strict administration of the Navigation Acts, his attempts to establish English land law, and above all the menace of taxation without representation (though taxation under him was not excessive in amount) drew all groups into opposition. To strengthen the line of defense against the French, New York and New Jersey were added to the dominion in 1688, making a unit too large for one man to administer well. Upon arrival of news that James II had abdicated, the Puritan leaders rose in revolt against Andros and overthrew him (April, 1689).

NEW ENGLAND COMPANY (1628–29) was the successor to the Dorchester Company which began settlement of the Massachusetts Bay region, and precursor to the Massachusetts Bay Company. The New England Company came into existence as an attempt to revive the dying Dorchester plantation, which had originated chiefly as a fishing venture, but which had failed to establish a strong settlement. A new group of men, interested primarily in making a plantation for religious purposes, took over the Dorchester enterprise, then applied to the Council for New England for a patent, which they are reputed to have received under date of March 19, 1628. The New England Company thus formed was an unincorporated, joint-stock affair, like so many which had attempted plantations under patents from trading companies but, under the leadership of John White, there was from the first a strong Puritan influence in the enterprise. With funds subscribed the company despatched a fleet with prospective settlers and supplies, and appointed John Endecott as governor of the tiny settlement already existing at Naumkeag (later Salem). Within the company doubts arose concerning the efficacy of their patent, which made the members decide to seek royal confirmation. Supported by important men at court, they succeeded in their endeavor and were able thenceforth to proceed in their project under the royal charter of March 4, 1629, which released them from further dependence upon the Council for New England.

NEW ENGLAND EMIGRANT AID COMPANY (1854–66), an important factor in the Kansas conflict and in the rise of the Republican Party, was first incorporated by Eli Thayer, April 26, 1854. Its plan of operations was to advertise Kansas, send emigrants in conducted parties at reduced transportation rates, and invest its capital in improvements in Kansas, from which it hoped to earn a profit. It sent to Kansas about 2000 settlers who founded all the important Free State towns. It established ten mills and two hotels, and assisted schools and churches. It aided the Free State party in various ways, and its officers sent the first Sharps rifles. It raised and spent, including rents and sales, about $190,000. Its activities furnished the pretext for the fraudulent voting by Missourians. It was blamed by President Pierce, Stephen A. Douglas, and the proslavery leaders for all the troubles in Kansas. Although the company failed financially, its friends believed it had saved Kansas from slavery. After the Civil War it undertook unsuccessful colonization projects in Oregon and Florida.

NEW-ENGLAND PRIMER, THE, first published about 1690, combined lessons in spelling with the Shorter Catechism and with versified injunctions to piety and to faith in Calvinistic fundamentals. Crude couplets and woodcut pictures illustrated the alphabet. Here first was published the child's prayer, "Now I lay me down to sleep." This eighty-page booklet, four and a half by three inches in size, was for a half century the only elementary textbook, and for a century more it held a central place in infant education. It is one of the most important colonial American cultural documents.

663

Sample page from James Truslow Adams, ed., *Concise Dictionary of American History*, New York: *Charles Scribner's Sons. Reprinted with permission.*

CLUES

In general I would look in the main part of the dictionary first. If what I need is not there, I would then look in the index. However, if you prefer, you can always begin with the index.

1. Look in the dictionary under *League*.

2. Look under *Bonus*.

3. There is nothing in the dictionary under Federal Highway Act of 1956, so you must look in the index under this heading. There is a page number given, and you will find the Act described there.

4. Look under *Square*.

ATLAS OF AMERICAN HISTORY

James Truslow Adams. *Atlas of American History*. New York: Scribner's Sons, 1943.

This is a companion volume to the set of the *Dictionary of American History*. As you study the events that make up our history, it is often important not only to know what happened, but also where. It is difficult to locate old maps, so this is a real time-saver. This one volume is arranged chronologically. For example, suppose you are interested in following the advance of the frontier as the pioneers pushed westward. From map to map you will see the falling back of the Indians, the establishment of trading posts, the growth of settlements, the formation of territories and the organization of states. The complete index in the back allows you to quickly locate any area.

Problem 41

SEARCH QUESTIONS

1. Daniel Boone went across Tennessee country. Where was Boone's Gap?

2. Canal traffic was important in the period from 1785 to 1850. There was also an important road during that period as the population moved westward. What and where were the canals and the road?

3. Between 1836 and 1848 the boundaries of Mexico were changed. Where were they originally and where did the treaty of Guadalupe-Hidalgo put them?

CLUES

1. Check the index under *Boone's Gap*.

2. Look in the index under *canals (1785-1850)*.

3. Look in the index under *Mexico, boundary*. You will find several dates listed chronologically. Keep going until you find 1836-1848. Or you could have found it by checking in the index for *Guadalupe-Hidalgo*.

ENCYCLOPEDIA OF AMERICAN HISTORY

R.B. Morris. *Encyclopedia of American History*. New York: Harper, 1965.

This is a useful single volume dealing with historical background of the U.S. The organization is both topical and chronological. Part I (the basic chronology) deals with major political and military events. Part II (topical chronology) includes sections on expansion, the Supreme Court, the economy, science and invention, and the arts. There is also a biographical section in which the names are alphabetically arranged. An index helps guide you to specific things.

Problem 42

SEARCH QUESTIONS

1. Who was Brigham Young?

2. What was the XYZ affair?

3. What was the Dred Scott case? How was it important?

CLUES

1. You could find this two ways. Either check the index or look under Y in the biographical section.

2. Check XYZ in the index.

3. Look up *Scott* in the index.

OXFORD COMPANION TO AMERICAN HISTORY

Thomas H. Johnson. *Oxford Companion to American History*. New York: Oxford Univ. Press, 1966.

The *Oxford Companion to American History* is another useful one-volume historical reference. It summarizes people, places, and events important in U.S. history. It is arranged in one alphabet like a dictionary, so there is no index.

DOCUMENTS OF AMERICAN HISTORY

Henry Steele Commager, ed. *Documents of American History*. Englewood Cliffs, N.J.: Prentice-Hall, Inc, 1963.

This collection of documents important to American history is arranged in chronological order. It is an excellent source book for history. Some of these documents, like colonial charters, illustrate typical historical documents; some, like the Missouri Compromise, made headlines; others reflect economic or social developments. An editorial comment about its background precedes each document. Since the organization is chronological, the index is necessary to locate a specific document.

Problem 43

SEARCH QUESTIONS

1. Compare the provisions for political freedom given in the First Charter of Virginia with those of the Pennsylvania Charter of Privileges.

2. What events lead to the passage of the Missouri Compromise?

CLUES

1. Check in the index under the titles of each of these charters.

2. Check the index under *Missouri Compromise* and read the comment preceding the document.

AN ENCYCLOPEDIA OF WORLD HISTORY

William L. Langer, ed. *An Encyclopedia of World History*. Boston: Houghton, 4th ed, 1968.

This one-volume *Encyclopedia of World History* briefly describes important events in the history of the world beginning with prehistoric man. It is arranged in chronological order. Each section which discusses a period of time begins with a brief outline of the period.

The table of contents is chronological. It serves as a comprehensive outline and helps locate material dealing with a time period. There are also maps and genealogical charts. Lists of these follow the table of contents.

The appendix in back includes lists such as rulers of the Roman, Byzantine, and Arab Empires; Popes; Holy Roman Emperors; Prime Ministers of Britain, France, and Italy; and Presidents of the U.S. The index is very good.

Problem 44

SEARCH QUESTIONS

1. Who was Hannibal?

2. Find a chart of the Norman and Plantagenet kings.

3. The year 1620 marked the beginning of an important era in U.S. history. At the same time, what was happening in England?

4. Find a map of the Mohammedan world of the 700s.

5. When was Neville Chamberlain's visit to Rome? What had been happening in England in the months before that?

CLUES

To use this reference you must be aware that there is an index, and also that there is a chronological table of contents and separate lists of maps and genealogical tables.

1. Check *Hannibal* in the index.

2. Remember the genealogical charts listed after the table of contents. Scan this for *Norman* and *Plantagenet* kings.

29. PENNSYLVANIA CHARTER OF PRIVILEGES
October 28, 1701

(F. N. Thorpe, ed. *Federal and State Constitutions*, Vol. V, p. 3076 ff.)

The Frame of Government of 1682, proving cumbersome and unsatisfactory in detail, was replaced by the Great Charter and Frame of April 2, 1683. The following year Penn returned to England. He soon fe'l ... William and in 1692 from him and place Governor Fletcher of it was restored to Pe to return to America affairs became thorou organized. Under t agreed the appoin the council and asser of government. This October 28, 1701, re Revolution. For refer

William Penn, nor of the Provir Territories thereunt whom these Prese Greeting. Whereas 1 by His Letters Pate of *England*, bearing *March*, in the Year *dred and Eighty-on* to give and grant un Assigns for ever, t *vania*, with divers g tions for the well C

KNOW YE THE further Well-being the said Province, a suance of the Rig mentioned, I the declare, grant and c men, Planters and Inhabitants of this these following Li

Privileges, so far as in me lieth, to be held, enjoyed and kept, by the Freemen, Planters and Adventurers, and other Inhabitants of and in the said Province and Territories

591. TRUMAN'S POINT FOUR PROGRAM
June 24, 1949

(81st Congress, 1st Session, *House Doc.* No. 240)

Following a proposal made in his inaugural address, President Truman sent a special message to Congress urging a program of technical assistance to underdeveloped areas. The President recommended a modest initial appropriation of $45 million to be expanded as future needs required. Congress enacted the President's proposal on June 5, 1950, and thus took another important step in the assumption of international responsibilities. See Doc. No. 580; W. A. Brown, *American Foreign Assistance;* R. T. Mack, *Raising the World's Standard of Living;* M. Curti and K. Beir, *Prelude to Point Four;* J. B. Bingham, *Shirt-Sleeve Diplomacy.*

To the Congress of the United States:

In order to enable the United States, in cooperation with other countries, to assist the peoples of economically underdeveloped areas to raise their standards of living, I recommended the enactment of legislation to authorize an expanded program of technical assistance for such areas, and an experimental program for encouraging the outflow of private investment beneficial to their economic development. These measures are the essential first steps in an undertaking which will call upon private enterprise and voluntary organizations in the United States, as well as the government, to take part in a constantly growing effort to improve economic conditions in the less developed regions of the world.

The grinding poverty and the lack of economic opportunity for many millions of people in the economically underdeveloped parts of Africa, the Near and Far East, and certain regions of Central and South America, constitute one of the greatest challenges of the world today. In spite of their age-old economic and social handicaps, the peoples in these areas have, in recent decades, been stirred and awakened. The spread of industrial civilization, the growing understanding of modern concepts of government, and the impact of two World Wars have changed

their lives and their outlook. They are eager to play a greater part in the community of nations.

All these areas have a common problem. They must create a firm economic base for the democratic aspirations of their citizens. Without such an economic base, they will be unable to meet the expectations which the modern world has aroused in their peoples. If they are frustrated and disappointed, they may turn to false doctrines which hold that the way of progress lies through tyranny. . . .

For these various reasons, assistance in the development of the economically underdeveloped areas has become one of the major elements of our foreign policy. In my inaugural address, I outlined a program to help the peoples of these areas to attain greater production as a way to prosperity and peace.

The major effort in such a program must be local in character; it must be made by the people of the underdeveloped areas themselves. It is essential, however, to the success of their effort that there be help from abroad. In some cases, the peoples of these areas will be unable to begin their part of this great enterprise without initial aid from other countries.

The aid that is needed falls roughly into two categories. The first is the technical, scientific, and managerial knowledge necessary to economic development. This category includes not only medical and educational knowledge, and assistance and advice in such basic fields as sanitation, communications, road building, and governmental services, but also, and perhaps most important, assistance in the survey of resources and in planning for long-range economic development.

The second category is production goods —machinery and equipment—and financial assistance in the creation of productive enterprises. The underdeveloped areas need capital for port and harbor development, roads and communications, irrigation and

Sample pages from Henry Steele Commager, *Documents of American History*, 7th ed., pp. 40, 558. © 1963, Prentice-Hall, Inc., Englewood Cliffs, N.J. Reprinted with permission.

3. Remember the chronological table of contents. Part IV is the *Early Modern Period 1500 to 1648*. Under that division find *Europe* and under that *England*.

4. Look in the list of maps following the table of contents.

5. Find *Chamberlain, Neville* in the index. There are three subtopics listed; find the right one. If you check the page listed, you will find other events current at that time discussed.

HISTORICAL ATLAS

William Robert Shepherd. *Historical Atlas.* New York: Barnes and Noble, 9th ed., 1964.

ATLAS OF WORLD HISTORY

Robert R. Palmer. *Atlas of World History.* Chicago: Rand McNally, 1957.

For more elaborate and detailed maps of historical events, you could consult a historical atlas. Rand McNally's *Atlas of World History* and William Robert Shepherd's *Historical Atlas* are both very good and well-indexed.

Other. Some books do not deal with what is traditionally called history, but yet they are very useful to find information on the total American scene. It may not be necessary to know that Abraham Lincoln could never have worked a crossword puzzle nor have drunk an ice-cream soda, but it's interesting.

These three references are some of the most useful and interesting in the miscellaneous category.

FAMOUS FIRST FACTS

Joseph Nathan Kane. *Famous First Facts.* New York: H.W. Wilson Co., 3rd ed., 1964.

Famous First Facts lists interesting and famous "firsts" in the United States. This useful book has five parts. Part 1, Famous First Facts, records first discoveries and inventions and events in the U.S. These are listed alphabetically by subject. You check under *a* for the first aquarium and under *f*

for the first flea laboratory, etc. This section has many cross-references so it is easy to use.

Part 2 is a chronological index by years to the first facts, so you can see what happened in a given year. Part 3 is an index by days (month and date) to the first facts, so if you want to know a famous first of February 21, look here. Part 4 is an index by people involved in the first facts. Part 5 is a geographical index by state, then town, to the famous first facts. Thus, this book helps you find "famous firsts" by subject, person involved, date it happened, and the place it happened.

Problem 45

SEARCH QUESTIONS

1. When was adhesive tape first patented?

2. When did the first crossword puzzle appear?

3. When was the first Japanese-American congressman elected?

4. When did the first comic books appear?

5. What are some of the famous firsts of 1871?

6. What happened for the first time on February 21? On your birthday?

7. What happened in Dayton, Ohio, for the first time?

8. What "famous first" is Laura Ingalls noted for?

CLUES

Questions 1 through 4 are from the first section of the book. Look for each subject in its alphabetical place.

1. Check *adhesive tape*.

2. Look under *crossword puzzle*.

3. If you check under *Japanese-American Congressmen*, you will be referred to *Congressman (US): Congressman of Japanese ancestry elected to the House of Representatives*. That entry under *Congressman (US)* will give you right page.

4. The entry under *comic books* will tell you to see *periodicals, comic books*. This will refer you to the right page.

5. Look in the chronological index by years under *1871*.

822   FAMOUS FIRST FACTS

FEBRUARY 20

1725 **Indians** — Indian scalping — by white men—New Hampshire colony

1768 **Insurance**—fire insurance company to receive a charter—Philadelphia, Pa.

1792 **Post Office**—Post Office Department of the United States—provided for by act of Congress

1792 **Postal Service**—postal service act—signed—George Washington

1794 **Congress (U.S.)—Senate** — contested election—A. A. A. Gallatin case started

1809 **Supreme Court (U.S.) Decision**—Supreme Court decision establishing the power of the United States—Chief Justice John Marshall

1862 **Ship**—iron-clad turreted vessel in the U.S. Navy—"Monitor"—delivered to U.S. Navy

1865 **Architectural School** — architectural school of collegiate character—established — Massachusetts Institute of Technology—Boston, Mass.

1867 **Insurance**—insurance rate standardization—National Board of Fire Underwriters — annual meeting — New York City

1872 **Elevator**—elevator patent, for a vertical-geared hydraulic electric elevator —C. W. Baldwin

1872 **Paper Bag Manufacturing Machine**—square-bottom paper bag machinery—patented—L. C. Crowell

1872 **Toothpick Manufacturing Machine Patent**—Silas Noble and J. P. Cooley —Granville, Mass.

1877 **Bridge**—cantilever bridge—completed —Kentucky River

1899 **Tunnel**—freight delivery tunnel system—Chicago, Ill.—franchise granted

1931 **Moving Picture**—moving picture of a complete grand opera—*Pagliacci*

1933 **Constitutional Amendment (U.S.)**—constitutional amendment submitted to the states for repeal—amendment submitted to the states

1937 **Automobile** — automobile-airplane combination—completed—Santa Monica, Calif.

1942 **Aviation — Aviator** — naval ace in World War II—E. H. O'Hare—in southwest Pacific

1952 **Baseball Umpire**—Negro umpire in organized baseball—E. L. Ashford

1962 **Astronauts** — American astronaut to orbit the earth—take-off—Cape Canaveral, Fla.—J. H. Glenn, Jr.

FEBRUARY 21

1828 **Newspaper**—Indian newspaper—*Cherokee Phoenix*—New Echota, Ga.

1842 **Sewing Machine** — sewing machine patent—J. J. Greenough

1846 **Woman** — woman telegrapher—S. G. Bagley—Lowell, Mass.

1853 **Money** — gold coinage — three-dollar gold pieces authorized

1858 **Burglar Alarm** — burglar alarm — installed—Boston, Mass.—E. T. Holmes

1862 **Execution** — execution (federal) for slave trading — Nathaniel Gordon—New York City

1864 **Catholic Church** — Catholic parish church for Negroes—dedicated—Baltimore, Md.

1866 **Dentist**—woman dentist to obtain a D.D.S. degree—L. B. Hobbs—graduated—Cincinnati, Ohio

1878 **Telephone Directory** — issued — New Haven, Conn.

1880 **Railroad**—municipal railroad—freight service between Cincinnati, Ohio, and Chattanooga, Tenn.—inaugurated

1885 **Monument** — monument to George Washington (national)—Washington, D.C.

1887 **Bacteriology Laboratory** — bacteriology laboratory—Hoagland Laboratory—Brooklyn, N.Y.—incorporated

1887 **Holiday**—Labor Day law (state)—enacted—Oregon

1903 **Army War College**—cornerstone laid —Washington, D.C.

1904 **Ski Club**—ski club association — National Ski Association—formed—Ishpeming, Mich.

1921 **Aviation—Flights (transcontinental)** —transcontinental flight within 24 hours flying time—W. D. Coney—San Diego, Calif. to Jacksonville, Fla.

1932 **Photography**—camera exposure meter —patent—W. N. Goodwin

1940 **Television—Telecast** — simulcast presented regularly by a sponsor—Lowell Thomas—New York City

1947 **Camera**—camera to take, develop and print pictures on photographic paper —demonstrated — E. H. Land—New York City

1949 **Degrees (academic and honorary)**—honorary degree awarded a Negro woman — M. M. Bethune — Winter Park, Fla.

FEBRUARY 22

1630 **Popcorn**—introduced to English colonists

1770 **Revolutionary War** — martyr in the Revolutionary War—Boston, Mass.—Christopher Snider killed

1784 **Ship**—trading ship sent to China — "Empress of China" — sailed — New York City

1836 **Whig Party**—state convention — Columbus, Ohio

1854 **Republican Party**—Republican Party meeting (local)

1855 **Agricultural School**—agricultural college (state) to be chartered—Farmers High School of Pennsylvania—reincorporated

1856 **Republican Party**—Republican Party meeting (national)—Pittsburgh, Pa.

1872 **Labor Party (political)**—Labor Party (national) — Labor Reform Party — formed—Columbus, Ohio

Sample page from Joseph N. Kane, *Famous First Facts*, 3rd ed., New York, The H.W. Wilson Company. © 1933, 1935, 1950, 1964 by Joseph Nathan Kane. Copyright renewed © 1961, 1963 by Joseph Nathan Kane. Reprinted by permission of the author.

6. Look in the index by month and date under *February* and then *21*. Again, for your birthday, check the same index by month and date.

7. Use the geographical index. Look under *Ohio*, then *Dayton*.

8. Use the index of people; look under *Ingalls*.

THE ENCYCLOPEDIA OF AMERICAN FACTS AND DATES

Gorton Carruth, ed. *The Encyclopedia of American Facts and Dates*. New York: Crowell. 4th ed., 1966.

The Encyclopedia of American Facts and Dates contains important and interesting dates beginning with the first explorations of America. The book is arranged chronologically. Pages are divided into four parallel columns, one for each of four fields of interest: politics and government, art and literature, science and industry, and sports and fashion. There is a good index, but notice that it refers you to the year, not the page.

Problem 46

SEARCH QUESTIONS

1. In 1810 a remedy for asthma was published. What was the remedy?

2. What was *The Portrait of a Lady*?

3. Did Horace Greeley write the famous line, "Go West, young man"?

CLUES

1. Since the book is organized chronologically and you know the date, turn directly to 1810 and scan.

2. Check *Portrait* in the index. This refers you to 1881, but remember this is the date, not the page, to look under.

3. Check *Greeley* in the index. Again, this refers you to the correct year.

THE AMERICAN BOOK OF DAYS

George William Douglas. *The American Book of Days*. New York: H.W. Wilson Co., 1948.

The American Book of Days is arranged day by day in calendar order. It gives holidays, celebrations, birthdays of famous Americans, and anniversaries of important events. There is an index by topic plus several useful appendices.

Problem 47

SEARCH QUESTIONS

1. What day is the Philadelphia Mummers' Parade?

2. When is Davy Crockett's birthday?

3. Find what happened on your birthday.

CLUES

1. Check index for *Philadelphia*.

2. Look under *Crockett, Davy* in the index.

3. Look up the month and day which are listed in order in the book.

LITERATURE

Early in this Library Guide, under the heading of using the card catalog, we showed you how to find books of fiction (novels), short stories, and poetry. Why do we again bring up the subject of literature, this time under the heading of specialized reference books? What sorts of books on literature are there that, unlike a novel, are not intended to be read from cover to cover?

There is much more to the field of literature than reading stories and poems. There are books which tell us about the authors' lives, books which analyze and criticize different works of literature, books which explain special vocabularies and allusions to fictional or mythical times, places, and people, and books which explain and illustrate different literary forms and styles. There are also books of quotations and indexes to poetry. These are all reference books because they are meant to be used for specific bits of information needed at the moment.

Even though general encyclopedias do include

articles about authors and literary works, they frequently do not include the particular information you need. For example, a general encyclopedia probably could not answer the following questions about the literary world:

> Who is "the old lady of Threadneedle Street"?[1]
>
> What are some of Margery Sharp's hobbies?[2]
>
> Who is Mrs. Malaprop?[3]

All of these questions can be answered quickly by consulting reference books specializing in literature. There are many kinds of these reference books. In some you can find the plots of long novels or plays boiled down to a few paragraphs. In others you can locate a poem even if you can remember only the first line or some of the phrases. There are reference books that talk about characters in fiction as well as about the plots and authors.

We have divided these references into six types: biographies of authors, poetry and quotations, digests, handbooks and encyclopedias, literary criticism, and miscellaneous. Most of the books we describe have Search Questions and Clues. Look at these Search Questions; you will be amazed at the things these references include. To help with your studying or to increase your enjoyment of reading, specialized literary references are worth knowing.

Biographies of authors. Bibliographical information about authors is easy to find. In addition to the general sources of biographical information such as encyclopedias and books of biographies about one person, there are collections of biographies especially about authors.

THE KUNITZ' AUTHORS SERIES AND THE JUNIOR AUTHORS SERIES

Stanley J. Kunitz and Howard Haycraft, eds. *American Authors: 1600-1900.* New York: Wilson, 1938 (7th printing 1969).

Stanley J. Kunitz and Vineta Colby, eds. *European Authors:* 1000-1900. New York: Wilson, 1967.

Stanley J. Kunitz and Howard Haycraft, eds. *British Authors Before 1800.* New York: Wilson, 1952 (4th printing 1965).

Stanley J. Kunitz and Howard Haycraft, eds. *British Authors of the Nineteenth Century.* New York: Wilson, 1936 (6th printing 1964).

Stanley J. Kunitz and Howard Haycraft, eds. *Twentieth Century Authors.* New York: Wilson, 1942. There is a *Twentieth Century Authors: First Supplement* written 1955, which somewhat up-dates this.

Stanley J. Kunitz and Howard Haycraft, eds. *The Junior Book of Authors.* New York: Wilson, 2nd ed., 1951.

Muriel Fuller, ed. *More Junior Authors.* New York: Wilson, 1963.

Doris de Montreville and Donna Hill, eds. *Third Book of Junior Authors.* New York: Wilson, 1972.

These books provide readable information on the lives of authors. The authors series focuses on writers for adults while the junior authors series includes information about writers and illustrators of books for young people. Often there is a portrait of the writer and a list of his writings as well as a short list of other sources of information for further study. The *Twentieth Century Authors* and the *Junior Book of Authors* often have interesting first-person accounts from people who knew the author personally.

In each of these books the authors are arranged alphabetically by last name, so your only problem is in selecting the correct volume. You need to know approximately when your author lived. And for authors who were prominent before the twentieth century, you need to know whether he or she was American, British, or European. Authors of all nationalities are included in the *Twentieth Century Authors.*

You would probably know enough about your author to select the correct book. If not, you can check a biographical dictionary to find his nationality and birth date.

---

[1]This is the Bank of England. *Brewer's Dictionary of Phrase and Fable,* 1963, p. 894.

[2]According to *Twentieth Century Authors* her hobbies are skating, painting, and sailing. 1966, p. 1268.

[3]Mrs. Malaprop is a character in *The Rivals* who is noted for her gross misuse of words such as "an allegory on the banks of the Nile." *Reader's Encyclopedia,* 1965, p. 677.

In actual fact she lived for several years after that, and died at fifty-eight of asthma, from which she had suffered for many years. She was a cheerful, equable person, fond of music and musically gifted, and in contrast to the vicissitudes of her heroines, she lived a peaceful, uneventful life. She received then unprecedented sums for her later novels —£500 for one, £800 for another. Even so, they made her publishers rich.

Nowadays it is difficult to understand why Scott admired her extravagantly, or why that exquisite poet, Christina Rossetti, wanted to write her biography. (She had to give the idea up, for lack of usable material.) Scott himself said that her prose was poetry and her poetry was prose. She was, indeed, a prose poet, in both the best and the worst senses of the phrase. The romantic landscape, the background, is the best thing in all her books; the characters are two dimensional, the plots far fetched and improbable, with "elaboration of means and futility of result."

The truth seems to be that Mrs. Radcliffe came at exactly the right time; in her hands the Gothic novels of her contemporaries, "Monk" Lewis and Horace Walpole, became wildly romantic, ancestors of a whole school, finding its culmination, perhaps, in America, in the supernatural and macabre stories of Poe and of Charles Brockden Brown. Schedoni, in *The Italian*, was the legitimate ancestor of the Byronic hero; her influence on both Byron and Scott was incalculable.

The best three of Mrs. Radcliffe's novels, by far, are *The Romance of the Forest, The Mysteries of Udolpho,* and *The Italian;* yet even in these there is the same dreary succession of trials of a persecuted heroine, conventionally represented, of dangers and terrors that peter out to nothing, and of final victory over the lady's enemies. Her one historical novel, published posthumously, is very bad. Nevertheless, Mrs. Radcliffe was a mistress of suspense, an ingenious weaver of intricate incident, and a real artist in the description of the wild scenery she loved. (Incidentally, she never saw Italy, scene of several of her books.) She introduced the "poetical landscape" into the modern novel. She is practically unreadable today, but she was a seminal influence in English fiction.

PRINCIPAL WORKS: The Castles of Athlin and Dunbayne, a Highland Story, 1789; A Sicilian Romance, 1790; The Romance of the Forest, 1791; The Mysteries of Udolpho, 1794; A Journey Made . . . through Holland and Germany, 1795; The Italian, or the Confessional of the Black Penitents, 1797; Poems, 1815; The Novels of Mrs. Ann Radcliffe, 1824; Gaston de Blondeville, or, the Court of Henry III, 1826.

ABOUT: Birkhead, E. The Tale of Terror; Hunt, L. Men, Women, and Books; Jeaffreson, J. C. Novels and Novelists from Elizabeth to Victoria; Lang, A. Adventures among Books; Le Fèvre-Deumier, J. Célébrités anglaises; MacIntyre, C. F. Ann Radcliffe in Relation to her Time; Scarborough, D. The Supernatural in Modern English Fiction; Scott, W. Memoir of the Life of the Author, *in* The Novels of Mrs. Ann Radcliffe.

RALEIGH, Sir WALTER (1552?-October 29, 1618), voyager, explorer, author of poems, history, and accounts of expeditions, was born in Hayes Barton, Budleigh, Devonshire, the son of Walter Raleigh, a country gentleman, and his third wife, Katharine (Champernown) Gilbert. The name was spelled in some seventy ways, and the one way Sir Walter never spelled it was "Raleigh," the common modern form! It was pronounced "Rawly." Raleigh was a true Devonshire man—he retained a broad Devon accent all his life—tall, handsome, dark, impetuous, full of energy, proud, quarrelsome, courageous, and an unconscionable liar. Not much is known of his early life; he spent three years from about 1566 at Oriel College, Oxford, but left without a degree; he was with the Huguenot army in France in 1569, and by 1576 he was in London, where he entered the Middle Temple but did not study law. He it was who first suggested the famous gatherings at the Mermaid Tavern (indeed, he is one of the many to whom Shakespeare's plays have been attributed); Ben Jonson called him his 'father' in literature; he was a close friend of Spenser and introduced him at court; he was even a member of the Society of Antiquaries. But his true forte was action. In 1578 he made a voyage with his half-brother, Sir Humphrey Gilbert, against the Spaniards, whom he always hated. In 1580 he was twice arrested for dueling. Later in 1580 he was a captain in Ireland, and was ruthless in suppressing the "rebels." Sent to court with dispatches in 1581, he caught Elizabeth's eye—perhaps, as alleged, by spreading his cloak over a puddle for her to walk on. He became one of her pets, and she kept him at 427

the ability to endure their own company. One is a criminologist and the other two are artists—realists in a rather unreal age.

My formal education included Augusta Military Academy, Hampden-Sydney College, and the University of Virginia. In each school I found one or two great teachers to whom I am forever grateful.

William H. Armstrong received his A.B. (*cum laude*) from Hampden-Sydney College in 1936. He married Martha Stone Street Williams in 1942 and their children are Christopher, David, and Mary.

In 1945 Armstrong became a history master at Kent School in Kent, Connecticut. He still lives in the house built entirely by his own hands and raises purebred Coniedale sheep. He received the National School Bell Award of the National Association of School Administrators in 1963 for distinguished service in the interpretation of education. *Sounder*, a story of a dog and his devotion to his master, a black sharecropper, won the Newbery Medal for 1970. *Sounder* also won a Lewis Carroll Shelf Award for 1970.

SELECTED WORKS: Study is Hard Work, 1956; Through Troubled Waters, 1957; The Peoples of the Ancient World (with Joseph Ward Swain) 1959; The Tools of Thinking; a Self-help Workbook for Students in Grades 5-9, 1969; Sounder, 1969; Barefoot in the Grass, 1970; Sour Land, 1971.

ABOUT: Contemporary Authors, Vol. 19-20; Horn Book August 1970; Publishers' Weekly August 17, 1970; Top of the News April 1970.

ISAAC ASIMOV

January 2, 1920-

AUTHOR OF the *Foundation* trilogy, etc.

Autobiographical sketch of Isaac Asimov who also writes under the pen name "Paul French":

I WAS born in the Soviet Union. However, I remember nothing of my foreign experiences since before I was three years old my family set out on the road to the United States, carrying with them me and my younger sister. We arrived in New York in February 1923 and by September 1928 we

all were American citizens. (My younger brother, born in 1929, was a citizen to begin with.)

We all set about learning English at once. It never occurred to my parents that it might be useful for me, someday, to know Russian. The result is that I now know approximately 40,000 different words of English and about 12 different words of Russian. (Of *course*, I'm sorry.)

My youth was divided between studying in various public schools in New York and working in my parents' various candy stores. At the age of fifteen I was inserted into a niche in Columbia University.

By 1939, I had received my bachelor's degree, having majored in chemistry. Not wanting to break up a winning combination, I decided to continue onward for more of the same. Same school, same major, same working in the store outside school hours, and by 1941 I had an M.A. and kept right on going.

However, we all know what happened at the end of 1941. I left both school and store to do what seemed useful. I was a chemist at the Naval Air Experimental Station in

Sample page from Doris de Montreville and Donna Hill, eds. *Third Book of Junior Authors*, New York: The H.W. Wilson Company. © 1972 by the H.W. Wilson Company. Reprinted by permission of the publisher.

Problem 48

SEARCH QUESTIONS

1. List several outstanding personal characteristics of the English author Emily Brontë and tell how they affected her writing.

2. Beatrix Potter used to write long letters. What important happened to one of them?

3. Helen MacInness writes suspense stories, some of them taking place in Europe. Has she ever seen the places she writes about?

4. Did Nathaniel Hawthorne want to go to college?

CLUES

Since all of these books arranged the authors alphabetically, your problem is selecting which volume to use. If you don't know enough about these people to choose the right book, look in a biographical dictionary

1. Emily Brontë lived in the 1800s in England, so check *British Authors of the Nineteenth Century*.

2. Beatrix Potter is known for her stories for children, so look in the *Junior Book of Authors*.

3. Since Helen MacInness is still writing, according to the question, look in *Twentieth Century Authors*. That's the first logical place to check, but you won't find her there since she is a more recent author. You need to check *Twentieth Century Authors, First Supplement*. Sometimes there is no guaranteed way to get the right source at first, but these are very quick references to check, so you don't use much time.

4. Hawthorne was an American writer of the 1800s, so check *American Authors: 1600-1900*.

SOMETHING ABOUT THE AUTHOR

Commire, Anne. *Something About the Author*. Detroit: Gale Research Co., 1971 and continuing.

These books give interesting biographical sketches of authors of books for young people. The series tries to help the young student who has been told by the teacher to tell "something about the author." A story is often more interesting if you know what the author is like, and these sketches contain personal information as well as facts about the writer's career. There are pictures of the author and often illustrations from their books. At present there are five volumes, each arranged alphabetically by the author's last name. Each volume (except the first) has an alphabetical index at the end which includes all the authors in it and all preceding volumes. So when you are looking for a specific person, look in the index of the latest volume you have under his or her last name. If the person is not listed, then there is no biography in the series. If he or she is listed, you will know in which volume and on which page to look.

Problem 49

SEARCH QUESTIONS

1. Where was Phyllis Whitney born?

2. What does Dr. Seuss look like?

3. Is it true that Jesse Jackson was once a carnival boxer?

4. Who is Edgar d'Aulaire's writing partner?

CLUES

1. Check the index in the latest volume under W.

2. The index in the latest volume under Seuss will tell you to see *Geisel, Theodor Seuss*. When you look under G, you will find the right volume and page.

3. Check *Jackson, Jesse*.

4. Look under *d'A*.

CONTEMPORARY NOVELISTS

James Vinson. *Contemporary Novelists*. New York: St. Martins Press, 1972.

Contemporary Novelists is a useful and interesting reference for information about contemporary authors. In addition to the biographical data, the articles contain comments and criticisms about the person's major writings as well as comments from the author about his or her writing. The authors are arranged alphabetically, so there is no need for an index.

Author Index

Ibbotson, M. C(hristine), *5:* 89
Ingraham, Leonard W(illiam),
    4: 129
Inyart, Gene, *6:* 119
Ipcar, Dahlov (Zorach), *1:* 125
Irving, Robert. *See* Adler, Irving,
    1: 2
Irwin, Constance, *6:* 119

Jackson, C. Paul, *6:* 120
Jackson, Caary. *See* Jackson, C.
    Paul, *6:* 120
Jackson, Jesse, *2:* 150
Jackson, O. B. *See* Jackson, C.
    Paul, *6:* 120
Jackson, Shirley, *2:* 152
Jacobs, Flora Gill, *5:* 90
Jacobs, Lou(is), Jr., *2:* 155

Kaufman, Mervyn D., *4:* 133
Kay, Helen. *See* Goldfrank, Helen
    Colodny, *6:* 89
Keane, Bil, *4:* 134
Keen, Martin L., *4:* 135
Keene, Carolyn. *See* Adams,
    Harriet S., *1:* 1
Keir, Christine. *See* Pullein-
    Thompson, Christine, *3:* 164
Keith, Carlton. *See* Robertson,
    Keith, *1:* 184
Keith, Harold (Verne), *2:* 159
Kellow, Kathleen. *See* Hibbert,
    Eleanor, *2:* 134
Kelly, Regina Z., *5:* 94
Kelsey, Alice Geer, *1:* 129
Kendall, Lace. *See* Stoutenburg,
    Adrien, *3:* 217
Kennell, Ruth E., *6:* 127
Kent, Margaret, *2:* 161

If we look in the Author Index for Carolyn Keene, we are told to go to volume 1, page 1 and see the article under the real name of the author, Harriet S. Adams.

ADAMS, Harriet S(tratemeyer)
(Victor Appleton II, May Hollis Barton, Franklin W. Dixon, Laura Lee Hope, Carolyn Keene)

PERSONAL: Born in New Jersey; daughter of Edward L. (an author) and Magdalene Stratemeyer; married Russell Vroom Adams (deceased); children: Russell Jr. (died in World War II), Patricia Adams Harr, Camilla Adams McClave, Edward Stratemeyer Adams. *Education:* Graduate of Wellesley College. *Office:* Stratemeyer Syndicate, 519 Main St., East Orange, N.J. 07018.

CAREER: Full-time professional writer. *Member:* League of American Pen Women, New Jersey Woman's Press Club, New Jersey Wellesley Club (founder and first president; class treasurer), Zonta, Business and Professional Women's Club, New York Wellesley Club.

WRITINGS: (All published under the pseudonym Carolyn Keene)—"Dana Girls" Series: *By the Light of the Study Lamp,* 1934, *In the Shadow of the Tower,* 1934, *Secret at Lone Tree Cottage,* 1934, *Three-Cornered Mystery,* 1935, *Secret at the Hermitage,* 1936, *Circle of Footprints,* 1937, *Mystery of the Locked Room,* 1938, *Clue in the Cobweb,* 1939, *Secret at the Gatehouse,* 1940, *Mysterious Fireplace,* 1941, *Clue of the Rusty Key,* 1942, *Portrait in the Sand,* 1943, *Secret in the Old Well,* 1944, *Clue in the Ivy,* 1952, *Secret of*

WORK IN PROGRESS: The Mystery as Mannequin (a new Nancy Drew story set in Turkey), for early 1970 publication. Also rewriting *The Whispering Statue* (Nancy Drew).

SIDELIGHTS: Mrs. Adams is a partner in the Stratemeyer Syndicate, producers of juvenile series books. Upon the death of her father Mrs. Adams took over his work in the Stratemeyer Syndicate, creating many hundreds of chapter-by-chapter book outlines for the syndicate's series. Scientists and other specialists wrote from these. In addition

Mrs. Adams has written over a hundred books herself. An outline is composed first, linking plot and subplot. The story is dictated into a recording machine. Secretaries transcribe the discs, then Mrs. Adams and her staff edit the manuscripts.

"In my childhood," says Mrs. Adams, "I was fortunate to have a father who could tell an original story at a moment's notice. I have followed his method, letting my young listeners choose topics around which I weave a story. Over the years the game has been enjoyed by my children, grandchildren, nieces, nephews, and their friends. They have been, and are, my best critics.

"I love animals, particularly dogs and cats, and own several. At college I majored in English literature, creative writing, religion, and music, and also had a great interest in science and archaeology. My stories contain exaggerated versions of incidents in my own childhood and teenage years, as well as my later adventures while traveling for pleasure and research, much of it with a camera. I like to entertain and find most people stimulating. They are often prototypes for my book characters."

Mrs. Adams has made extensive trips through the United States, Canada, Mexico, South America, Europe, Hawaii, the Orient and Africa, and has set many of her stories in these foreign locales. Her interests have included Sunday School teaching and writing, Red Cross and Girl Scout work. She founded the Maplewood New Jersey Woman's Club magazine and was chairman of its literature department; also, chairman of her college's fund-raising work and served two years as a Republican county committeewoman.

Films: "Nancy Drew and the Hidden Staircase," "Nancy Drew, Detective," "Nancy Drew, Reporter," "Nancy Drew, Trouble Shooter" (all Warner Bros., 1939).

Avocational interests: Doll collecting, running a farm, piano playing and traveling.

Sample pages from Anne Commire, ed., *Something About the Author,* Vol. 1. © 1971, Gale Research Company. Reprinted with permission.

Problem 50

SEARCH QUESTIONS

1. What does Conrad Aiken say his work is concerned with?

2. Has Christopher Isherwood written any plays?

CLUES

Turn directly to the author's last name in alphabetical order.

Poetry and quotations. Have you ever wanted to find a poem you once liked but now can remember only a few phrases of? You can't use the card catalog; even if you could remember the author, without the title, it would be hard to locate the poem. Or have you ever wanted to know who said a phrase like "'Tis strange what a man may do, and a woman yet think him an angel"? There are specialized references to help you answer questions like these.

GRANGER'S INDEX TO POETRY

William F. Bernhardt, ed. *Granger's Index to Poetry*. New York: Columbia University Press. 5th edition and Supplement 1960-65.

Granger's Index to Poetry is an ingenious guide for tracking down a poem, starting with only the sketchiest clue. If you know only the title, only the author, only the first line, or only the subject of the poem, *Granger's Index* will help you find the titles of books in which the poem appears. This poetry index has three sections: an author index, a subject index, and a title and first line index.

The *title and first line index* lists these in one alphabet. After each of these titles or first lines, one or more abbreviations is given. Each of these abbreviations stands for a book in which the particular poem can be found. A list in the front of the book spells out these abbreviations. For example, suppose you wanted to find the poem "Chicago." Locate it in the title and first line index, and you will find the first source is listed as AmPP. Now look in the key to symbols in the front of the book, and you will see that this means the poem is in the book *American Poetry and Prose*.

Suppose you wanted to find a poem which begins "I meant to do my work today." Look under *I* in the title and first line index, and you will see GoTP listed. By checking the key in the front, you find this poem can be found in Untermeyer's *Golden Treasury of Poetry*. You must use the key to find the book a poem is in. Once you know the title of the book your poem is in, you can go to the card catalog to see whether your library has the book and where it is located on the shelves.

If you know only the author's name, look in the *author index* which lists authors alphabetically by last names. The entry will give the author's full name and will list his or her peoms alphabetically by title. Once you have the title, you use the title and first line index which will tell you what collection the poem is in.

Sometimes you do not have a particular poem in mind; you just need a poem about a certain subject. Suppose, for instance, that you wanted a poem about dogs. Look under *D* in the subject index. Under the subject *dogs* find authors who have written about dogs and the titles of their poems. Again, once you have the title you want, look for it in the title and first line index to find where you can get the poem.

To summarize, if you know only the author of the poem you want, look at the author index which will give you the titles of poems written by that author. If you know only the subject of a poem you want, look in the subject index which will give you the authors and titles of many poems on that subject.

When you know the title of a poem, look at the title and first line index which will give you the author's full name and abbreviations for the names of the books in which you can find the poem. If you know only the first line, look at the title and first line index which will give you the title and author of the poem and the abbreviations for the names of the books in which you can find the poem. These abbreviations are spelled out in the key to symbols listed in the front of the *Index*.

Problem 51

SEARCH QUESTIONS

1. Where can I find a poem which begins "How do I love thee? Let me count the ways"? Who wrote this?

2. What poems did Stephen Crane write?

3. What are some poems that have been written about grandmothers?

4. What poems has Richard Wilbur written? Where can you find a copy of the last poem listed?

CLUES

These clues were taken from the 5th edition. Other editions may vary slightly.

1. Use the title and first line index under *How*. You will find *AnFE* is the first source listed. Check the table in the front to find what this means.

2. Check Crane in the author index.

3. Use the subject index and find *grandmother*.

4. Check the author index under Wilbur. "Years-end" is the last title listed. Now, find this in the title and first line index. There is a cross-reference to "At . . . ." Under "At Years-end" five sources are given. Check the key to the symbols in the front to translate LiTM.

BARTLETT'S FAMILIAR QUOTATIONS

John Bartlett. *Familiar Quotations*. Boston: Little, Brown, 14th ed., rev. and ed. by Emily M. Beck, 1968.

Familiar Quotations can be used to find a quotation by a particular person, to find the source of a quotation you know, or to find an appropriate quotation about a particular subject.

In the main section, the authors are arranged chronologically by the year they were born. This chronological arrangement of authors is useful to answer many questions like the following: Who were two writers contemporary with Shakespeare? What writers were important in 18th-century England? There is an alphabetical index by the authors' last names to help you locate any author in the chronology.

If you do not know the author but recall a few key words in the quotation, turn to the index by key words. This gives you phrases in which these key words are used and the page on which the quotation with the phrase can be found. This index has numerous entries for each quotation, so you can find a quotation even though you can remember only a few key words.

If you are looking for quotations about a certain topic, you can use the subject index to locate them.

Problem 52

SEARCH QUESTIONS

1. What are some famous quotations from Molière's *Le Misanthrope*?

2. Are there any quotations about "grumble" or "grumbling"?

3. What poem has the refrain "Stitch, stitch, stitch"?

CLUES

1. Check to find *Molière* in the index of authors. That will send you to the right page containing the quotations from Molière, and then you have to scan the page to find the right source, *Le Misanthrope*.

2. Check the subject index for *grumble*.

3. Check the index of key words for the phrases under *stitch*.

HOME BOOK OF QUOTATIONS

Burton E. Stevenson. *Home Book of Quotations, Classical and Modern*. New York: Dodd, Mead, 10th ed., 1967.

The *Home Book of Quotations* is another useful reference for finding quotations. The main part of the book is arranged alphabetically under subject headings. There are indexes for authors and key words.

Digests. There is some disagreement as to whether students should have access to plot summaries. I believe that, like so many things, digests of important literature can be either enriching or crippling. Plot digests can be used to avoid contact with good writing, or they can be used effectively to preview or review. Digests, especially those which include summaries of criticisms or critiques, can be used either after or before you read to sharpen your own awareness of what the author is doing.

It is perfectly legitimate to read the end of a whodunit first if your aim is to analyze plot manipulation and to see whether this author plays fair with the audience, both of which need to be done as you are reading the book rather than after. However, if you check to see "whodunit" and then put the book away, your reading becomes nothing more than a series of first and last chapters.

In addition to "Cliff's Notes" and similar paperback summaries, there are two sources of plot digests you should be familiar with.

MASTERPLOTS

Frank N. Magill. *Masterplots of World Literature in Digest Form*. New York: Salem Press, 1960.

This is a collection of summaries of important literary works. These summaries are arranged alphabetically by title. Each summary includes the author, type of plot, time, locale, publication date, a list of principal characters, a short critical analysis, and a two or three page plot summary. There is an author index arranged alphabetically.

Problem 53

SEARCH QUESTIONS

1. Thomas Hardy wrote *Return of the Native*. What type of plot did it have?

2. List the main characters of *The Hunchback of Notre Dame*.

3. What is the plot of *A Tale of Two Cities*?

CLUES

For each of these, find the title in its alphabetical place under *Return, Hunchback,* and *Tale.* For (1)

you could have checked the author index for Hardy, but since you already know the title, this is not necessary.

THESAURUS OF BOOK DIGESTS

Hiram Haydn and Edmund Fuller. *Thesaurus of Book Digests*. New York: Crown Publisher, 1949 (reprinted 1968).

This is a collection of digests of well-known writing. It contains brief summaries of important works and these summaries are presented alphabetically by title. Indexes by authors and characters help you find works they are associated with. The character index is especially useful.

Problem 54

SEARCH QUESTIONS

1. Is "Evangeline" a novel, a short story, or a poem?

2. Hotspur was a character in what story?

3. What is the story of Ivanhoe?

CLUES

For (1) and (3) look for the title in its alphabetical place in the book.
For (2) use the character index to find *Hotspur*. This will refer you to the proper plot summary.

Handbooks and encyclopedias. Perhaps the most widely used aid in studying literature is the encyclopedia or handbook for readers. A reader's encyclopedia usually contains brief articles on authors and their writing, summaries of plots, characters in literature, and literary terms and references. This is an excellent source for getting information quickly.

THE READER'S ENCYCLOPEDIA

William Rose Benét. *The Reader's Encyclopedia*. New York: Crowell. 2nd ed., 1965.

This encyclopedia includes brief articles, arranged alphabetically, about people in literature and the arts from all countries and all periods of time. It also includes brief articles about literary movements, plots and characters, allusions, and expressions. There are also some descriptions of musical compositions and works of art. It is a valuable reference book for anything connected with literature.

Problem 55

SEARCH QUESTIONS

1. What was the Bauhaus?
2. What is the story of Prometheus? What does Promethean mean?
3. Who was Salome? In what important literary works is she portrayed?
4. What is the Bay State?
5. What is meant by *Druid*?
6. What is a simile?
7. Who was Mrs. Malaprop?

CLUES

This Encyclopedia is arranged in alphabetical order, so you merely locate each entry as you would in any dictionary. The only one that might be a problem is (7). Here look under *Malaprop*.

NEW CENTURY CYCLOPEDIA OF NAMES

Clarence L. Barnhart, ed. *The New Century Cyclopedia of Names*. Englewood Cliffs, N.J.: Prentice-Hall, Inc., 1954.

This cyclopedia can be used to find information about proper names of importance. It includes names of people and places, events in history, characters in fiction and in art, and people and places in myth and legend. The appendix contains useful chronological tables and charts. This is a useful source of identifying and checking the pronunciation of proper names.

Problem 56

SEARCH QUESTIONS

1. Who were the Hyksos?
2. What is the Little Bighorn?
3. What is the Mona Lisa?
4. Was Amedeo Modigliani a real person?
5. Who lives in Valhalla?
6. Who was D'Artagnan?

CLUES

In each case merely look in alphabetical order for the proper name:

1. Hyksos
2. Little
3. Mona
4. Modigliani — since this is a person, you look under the last name.
5. Valhalla
6. When you look under D'Artagnan, you will be told to look under Artagnan, D', so this person will be identified in the *A*'s.

THE OXFORD COMPANION TO AMERICAN LITERATURE

James D. Hart, ed. *The Oxford Companion to American Literature*. New York: Oxford Press, 4th ed., 1965.

The *Oxford Companion* is a collection of articles about American authors and their writing. It contains short biographies of authors which give information about their style and the subjects of their works. There are summaries and descriptions of important American novels, essays, poems, and plays. Important characters in American fiction are also included. There are definitions and historical outlines of literary schools and movements. These articles are all in one alphabet.

In the back of the book is a chronological index giving in parallel columns the literary and social history of American authors from 1575 to 1965.

<table>
<tr><td>

La Forge, Frank

La Forge (lạ fôrzh'), **Frank.** b. at Rockford, Ill., Oct. 22, 1879; d. at New York, May 5, 1953. American pianist and composer, famous as an accompanist of such artists as Alda and Schumann-Heink, and as a voice teacher. Among his compositions are the songs *Before the Crucifix, Song of the Open, Retreat,* and *Supplication.*

Lafosse (là.fos), **Antoine de.** [Title, **Sieur d'Aubigny.**] b. at Paris, c1653; d. there, 1708. French poet. He wrote four plays, one of which, *Manlius Capitolinus* (1698), is worthy of note.

Lafosse or **La Fosse** (là.fos), **Charles de.** b. at Paris, c1636–40; d. there, Dec. 13, 1716. French historical painter, a pupil of Chauveau and Lebrun. He decorated the country house of Lord Montague in England, the cupola of the Church of the Invalides at Paris, the choir and dome of the Assumption, a part of the palace at Versailles, and other buildings, and his pictures are in many royal palaces and museums. Most of them have been reproduced in engravings.

Lafourche (là.försh'), **Bayou.** Bayou in SE Louisiana, formerly a distributary of the Mississippi, but now cut off by a dam at Donaldsonville. Length, ab. 150 mi.

La Fresnaye (la fre.nä), **Roger de.** b. at Le Mans, France, July 11, 1885; d. at Grasse, France, Nov. 25, 1925. French painter. He was strongly influenced by Cézanne and the cubists, but did not fully accept the theories of cubism. He illustrated André Gide's *Paludes,* Cocteau's *Tambour,* and La Fontaine's *Le Roman de Psyché.*

Lafuente or **La Fuente** (lä fwen'tä), **Modesto.** [Pseudonyms: **Fray Gerundio, Tirabeque.**] b. at Rabanal de los Caballeros, Palencia, Spain, 1806; d. Oct. 25, 1866. Spanish historian and, under his pseudonyms, satirist. His chief work is *Historia general de España* (30 vols., 1850–66).

Lafuente y Alcántara (là.fwen'tä ē äl.kän'tà.rä), **Miguel.** b. at Archidona, Málaga, Spain, July 10, 1817; d. at Havana, Cuba, in August, 1850. Spanish historian.

Lagado (lạ.gä'dō). In *Gulliver's Travels,* a city which figures in the voyage to the flying island of Laputa.

Lagae (lä.gä'), **Jules.** b. at Rousselaere, Belgium, March 15, 1862—. Belgian sculptor.

Lagamaru (lä.gä.mä'rö). Name of one of the deities of Elam in the cuneiform inscriptions. It appears in the name of the Elamite king Chedorlaomer (Assyrian, Kudur-Lagamar).

Lagan (lag'ạn). River in Northern Ireland, rising in County Down and flowing NE to Belfast Lough at Belfast. Length, ab. 40 mi.

La Gandara (là gän.dà.rà), **Antonio de.** b. at Paris, Dec. 16, 1861; d. there, June 30, 1917. French painter of portraits and landscapes, who had among his sitters Sarah Bernhardt and Verlaine. Aside from the portraits, his work includes *Luxembourg, Notre-Dame,* and *Place de la Concorde.*

Lagarde (lä.gärd'), **Paul Anton de.** [Original name, **Paul Anton Bötticher.**] b. at Berlin, Nov. 2, 1827; d. at Göttingen, Germany, Dec. 22, 1891. German Orientalist and Biblical scholar.

La Garenne-Colombes (là gà.ren.kọ.lôṅb). Town in N France, in the department of Seine, near the Seine River. It is a northwestern industrial and residential suburb of Paris. 24,080 (1946).

Lagaria (lạ.gãr'i.ạ). Ancient name of **Lauria.**

Lagash (lā'gash). [Also: **Shirpurla;** modern village, **Telloh.**] Ancient city-state of Sumeria, in Mesopotamia, N of Ur. It flourished in the 3rd millennium B.C. Many thousands of inscribed clay tablets have been unearthed on the site.

Lagenevais (làzh.nẹ.ve), **F. de.** See **Blaze de Bury.**

</td><td>

Problem 57

SEARCH QUESTIONS

1. Give a brief summary of the life of Sidney Lanier.

2. What were some of the outstanding characteristics of Herman Melville's style of writing?

3. Natty Bumppo was the main character in Cooper's *Leatherstocking Tales.* What was he like?

4. The Transcendentalism movement characterized literature of the 1830-1860 period. What was important about it?

5. *Member of the Wedding* is a novel by Carson McCullers. What is it about?

6. The 1880-1890 decade began a period of realism in American literature. At the same time, what main historical events were taking place in the U.S.?

CLUES

Look in the proper alphabetical spot for the main word:

1. Look under *Lanier.*

2. See *Melville.*

3. When you look under *Bumppo,* you are referred to *Leatherstocking.*

4. See *Transcendentalism.*

5. Look under *Member.* If you checked McCullers, you would find a little bit of information, but not much.

6. Look in the chronological index in the back under the period 1880-1890.

THE OXFORD COMPANION TO ENGLISH LITERATURE

Sir Paul Harvey, ed. *The Oxford Companion to English Literature.* New York: Oxford, 4th ed., revised by Dorothy Eagle, 1967.

The Oxford Companion to English Literature focuses on English writers and their works. It is similar in form and coverage to *The Oxford Companion to American Literature.*

</td></tr>
</table>

Sample entries from Clarence L. Barnhart, ed., *The New Century Cyclopedia of Names,* p. 2358. © 1954 by Prentice-Hall, Inc., Englewood Cliffs, N.J. Reprinted with permission.

THE OXFORD COMPANION TO CLASSICAL LITERATURE

Sir Paul Harvey, ed. *The Oxford Companion to Classical Literature.* Oxford: Clarendon Press, 1937.

The Oxford Companion to Classical Literature is a useful handbook for the study of Greek and Roman literature. It is similar in form to *The Oxford Companion to American Literature.* It has short articles which concern individual writers, literary works, institutions, and historical names and subjects. A date chart in the back of the book has Greek authors, Latin authors, and contemporary events in parallel columns. Also in the back are pictures and descriptions of armor and houses.

BREWER'S DICTIONARY OF PHRASE AND FABLE

Ebenezer Brewer. *Dictionary of Phrase and Fable.* New York: Harper. Revised by John Freeman, 1963.

This dictionary identifies famous names in fiction. It defines literary allusions and phrases, and tells about their possible origins. Included also are references to mythology. The entries are arranged alphabetically by key words. For example, "To lead a dog's life" would be under *dog,* so sometimes a bit of imagination is required to find the reference you want.

Problem 58

SEARCH QUESTIONS

1. What does it mean "to hit a nail on the head"?
2. What is the origin of the expression "Laugh and grow fat"?
3. Who was Cerberus?
4. What were the Sibylline Books?

CLUES

1. The key word here is *nail,* and you will find the meaning listed here. A small note is also under *head* and a cross-reference under *hit,* but the information is under nail.

2. Check *laugh.*
3. No choice here; look under *Cerberus.*
4. Check *Sibylline.*

A HANDBOOK TO LITERATURE

William F. Thrall and Addison Hibbard. *A Handbook to Literature.* New York: Odyssey Press. Revised by C.H. Holman, 1960.

This handbook gives an alphabetical list of terms in English and American literature. There are no biographies or plot outlines; only terms of literature are explained and defined. Here you can find such things as saga, irony, and scansion discussed and illustrated. These are listed in alphabetical order.

In the back of the book there is a chronological outline of English and American literature.

Problem 59

SEARCH QUESTIONS

1. What is a *nom de plume?*
2. Is a detective story different from a mystery story?
3. In 1863 Eliot wrote *Romola.* What else was written then?
4. What is alliteration?

CLUES

1. Look under *nom.*
2. Here you need to look under both *detective* and *mystery.*
3. Look in the outline of literary history at the back of the book.
4. Look under *alliteration.*

Literary Criticism. Some students may have occasion to refer to collections of literary criticism. There are several collections which give excerpts of critical writing about authors. These can be helpful to students analyzing or evaluating literature.

CONTEMPORARY NOVELISTS

James Vinson. *Contemporary Novelists.* New York: St. Martins Press, 1972.

This was described under biographies of authors since it does contain biographical data. It is also useful for its comments and criticisms of the author's work, and it is especially interesting for its comments from the author about his or her writing. (See Problem 50).

THE LIBRARY OF LITERARY CRITICISM

Charles Wells Moulton. *The Library of Literary Criticism of English and American Authors.* Buffalo, N.Y.: Moulton Publishing Co., 1901-05. 8 vo.s This has been reprinted.

This scholarly, older series includes long excerpts from critical writings and reviews of authors from the time of Beowulf through the 1800s. It deals primarily with British authors, but

---

PERCY BYSSHE SHELLEY
1792-1822

Born, at Field Place, near Horsham, Sussex
vately, 1798-1802; at a school at Brentford,
to 1809. Wrote poetry while at Eton. Matr
10 April 1810. Expelled (with Hogg) fro
The Necessity of Atheism, 25 March 1811
brook, 28 Aug. 1811. Lived for a few wee
then to Keswick, Nov. 1811. Friendship
Friendship with Godwin begun, Jan. 1812.
Lynmouth, June to Sept. 1812; in Carnarvon
in Ireland, Feb. to April 1913; to Londc
Bracknell, July 1813; in Edinburgh, winter
nell, spring of 1814. On account of his hav
as a minor, he remarried his wife in Londc
ment from his wife, and meeting with Mary
with Mary Godwin, 28 July 1814; returne
1814. Friendship with Byron begun, 1816.
of 1816. Mrs. Shelley committed suicide,
Mary Godwin, 30 Dec. 1816; settled with h
Friendship with Keats begun, 1817. Rem
Drowned, 8 July 1822. His body cremated
16 Aug. 1822. His ashes buried in old Prot
1822. WORKS: *Zastrozzi* (under initials: P.
by *Victor and Cazire* (no copy known (?)),
of *Margaret Nicholson,* 1810 (priv. ptd., e
St. Irvyne (anon.), 1811; *Poetical Essay on*
1811; *The Necessity of Atheism,* 1811; *An*
1812; *Proposals for an Association,* 1812;
Letters to Lord Ellenborough (1812); *The*
Mab, 1813; *A Vindication of Natural Diet*
of Deism (anon.), 1814; *Alastor,* 1816; *Pro*
Vote (anon.), 1817; *History of a Six We*
France (with his wife; anon.), 1817; *Laon a*
called; and reissued as *The Revolt of Islam,*
on the Death of Princess Charlotte (1818)
The Cenci, 1819; *Prometheus Unbound,* 182
1820; *Epipsychidion* (anon.), 1821; *Adona*
HUMOUS: *Posthumous Poems,* ed. by Mrs. S
Anarchy, ed. by Leigh Hunt, 1832; *The Shel*

---

548   PERCY BYSSHE SHELLEY

1833; *Essays, etc.,* by Mrs. Shelley, 1840; *The Dæmon of the World,* ed. by H. B. Forman (priv. ptd.), 1876; *Notes on Sculptures in Rome and Florence* (ed. by H. B. Forman; priv. ptd.), 1879. COLLECTED WORKS: ed. by H. Buxton Forman (8 vols.), 1880 (1876-80). LIFE: by Prof. Dowden, 1886.

R. Farquharson Sharp, 1897, *A Dictionary of English Authors,* p. 254

SEE: *Complete Works,* ed. Roger Ingpen and Walter F. Peck, 1927, 10 v.; *Complete Poetical Works,* ed. Thomas Hutchinson, 1905(OSA); *The Early Collected Editions of Shelley's Poems: A Study in the History and Transmission of the Printed Text,* ed. Lawrence John Zillman, 1958; *Shelley's "Prometheus Unbound": A Variorum Edition,* ed. Lawrence John Zillman, 1959; *The Essaile Notebook: A Volume of Early Poems,* ed. Kenneth Neill Cameron, 1964; *Notebooks,* ed. H. Buxton Forman, 1911, 3 v.; *Letters,* ed. Roger Ingpen, 1909, 2 v.; Newman Ivey White, *Shelley,* 1940, 2 v., rev. 1945 as *Portrait of Shelley,* one vol.; Kenneth Neill Cameron, *The Young Shelley: Genesis of a Radical,* 1951; Kenneth Neill Cameron, ed., *Shelley and His Circle, 1773-1822,* Vols. I, II, 1961; M. T. Solve, *Shelley: His Theory of Poetry,* 1927; Carl Henry Grabo, *The Magic Plant,* 1936; Carlos Baker, *Shelley's Major Poetry,* 1948; also see *Letters of Mary Shelley,* ed. F. L. Jones, 1944, 2 v.; *Mary Shelley's Journal,* ed. F. L. Jones, 1947; *New Shelley Letters,* ed. W. S. Scott, 1949.

PERSONAL

I went to Godwin's. Mr. Shelley was there. I had never seen him before. His youth and a resemblance to Southey, particularly in his voice, raised a pleasing impression, which was not altogether destroyed by his conversation, though it is vehement, and arrogant, and intolerant. He was very abusive towards Southey, whom he spoke of as having sold himself to the Court. And this he maintained with the usual party slang. . . . Shelley spoke of Wordsworth with less bitterness, but with an insinuation of his insincerity, etc.

Henry Crabb Robinson, 1817, *Diary,* Nov. 6

The author of *Prometheus Unbound,* has a fire in his eye, a fever in his blood, a maggot in his brain, a hectic flutter in his speech, which mark out the philosophic fanatic. He is sanguine-complexioned, and shrill-voiced. As is often observable in the case of religious enthusiasts, there is a slenderness of constitutional stamina, which renders the flesh no match for the spirit. His bending, flexible form appears to take no strong hold of things, does not grapple with the world about him, but slides from it like a river,—
"And in its liquid texture mortal wound
Receives no more than can the fluid air."

William Hazlett, 1821, "On Paradox and the Commonplace," *Table-Talk,* p. 355

Excerpts taken from *Moulton's Library of Literary Criticism of English and American Authors,* abridged, revised, and with additions by Martin Tucker. Used with permission of Frederick Ungar Publishing Co.

there are a few American writers included. This is somewhat difficult reading, but it is the only easily available source of criticism dealing with this period. The *Library of Literary Criticism* includes comments about the writer and his or her work by people who knew the writer.

There is a four-volume abridged version of the *Library of Literary Criticism* edited by Martin Tucker (New York: Unger Publishers, 1966).

A LIBRARY OF LITERARY CRITICISM: MODERN AMERICAN LITERATURE

Dorothy Nyrene Curley and Maurice Kramer: *A Library of Literary Criticism: Modern American Literature*. New York: Ungar Press, 1969. 3 vols.

This three-volume *Library of Literary Criticism* includes excerpts from critical writing about contemporary American authors. It contains information about more than 300 authors, arranged alphabetically by last name. There is an index to the critics at the end of volume 3. This is useful if you are studying the critical writings of a specific person. For example, this index would be helpful for a project like "Walter Kerr, Critic of Our Time."

Problem 60

SEARCH QUESTIONS

1. Have critics' views of Katherine Anne Porter changed since she began to write?

2. Find some criticisms of *The Great Gatsby* by F. Scott Fitzgerald.

3. What elements does John Ciardi stress in his criticisms of writers?

CLUES

1. Look under *Porter*. You will find about seven pages of criticism written between 1929 and 1966.

2. Turn to *Fitzgerald*. Find the subheading for *The Great Gatsby*; the criticisms follow.

3. Use the index to critics. Find *Ciardi*, and compare the criticisms listed under his name.

A LIBRARY OF LITERARY CRITICISM: MODERN AMERICAN LITERATURE

Dorothy Nyrene Curley. *A Library of Literary Criticism: Modern American Literature*, 1904-1960. New York: Ungar, 1960.

This contains criticisms for about 170 authors. Many of the same writers appear in this one volume that are in the three-volume set.

A LIBRARY OF LITERARY CRITICISM: MODERN BRITISH LITERATURE

Ruth Temple and Martin Tucker. *A Library of Literary Criticism: Modern British Literature*. New York: Ungar, 1966. 3 vol.

This is similar to the three-volume *Library of Literary Criticism: Modern American Literature* except that it focuses on criticisms of the writings of about 400 modern British authors.

Problem 61

SEARCH QUESTIONS

1. What did Virginia Woolf say about James Joyce?

2. Edmund Wilson has a notable critical style. Read some of his criticisms.

3. What kind of writing has Peter Ustinov done?

CLUES

1. Find Joyce in the alphabetical arrangement of authors. Scan for a criticism written by Virginia Woolf.

2. Use the index to critics to find Wilson.

3. Look for Ustinov in alphabetical order.

BOOK REVIEW DIGEST

Book Review Digest. New York: H.W. Wilson Co., published since 1905.

Criticisms and book reviews are often difficult to locate. The *Book Review Digest* not only locates

The digests of the reviews are arranged alphabetically according to the author of the book being reviewed.

The author and title.

A brief description of the book.

Digests of three reviews are given for this book.

Additional reviews are annotated even though no digest is included.

Digests are annotated. This one is from the *New York Times Book Review*, p. 22, February 25, 1973. The review contains 160 words.

When looking for reviews of books about a certain subject, look in the index for the appropriate year or years under that subject.

Three books are listed under the general topic of *Comic books*.

Additional books are listed under the subtopic of *History and criticism*.

If you want reviews of a particular book, look under its title in the index.

Excerpts from *Book Review Digest*. New York, The H.W. Wilson Co. © 1974, 1975 by The H.W. Wilson company. Reprinted by permission of the publisher.

JACOBS, FRANK. The mad world of William M. Gaines. 244p col il $7.95; pa $1.95 '73 Bantam

B or 92 Gaines, William M. Mad (periodical). Comic books, strips, etc.
ISBN 0-8184-0054-4

A biography of the comic book publisher. Index.

"Although many studies of comic book history have appeared, Jacobs is the first author to broach the important subject of comics publishers. Unfortunately, however, he has produced an inferior beginning study, as his book is filled with so many anecdotal trivia and banality that his prominent subject—William M. Gaines . . . is played for laughs. . . . Nevertheless, the book should interest veteran Mad readers, if only for its gossipy tales about the magazine's writers and artists ('Madmen'). For more serious readers the book will be disappointing."
Choice 10:448 My '73 190w

Reviewed by Guernsey Le Pelley
Christian Science Monitor p11 Mr 28 '73 260w

Reviewed by Barbara Zelenko
Library J 98:734 Mr 1 '73 150w

"Jacobs shows Gaines's talent for bringing out the best in his staff members and captures both the man and the atmosphere he creates. Since 'Gaines and Mad, like a boy and his frog, are inseparable . . . ,' this is a biography of the magazine as well as the man. The struggles of the early days, the lawsuits, the problems of finding staff members and contributors, the emergence of Alfred E. Neuman as the Mad mascot, and current activities are interspersed with accounts of Gaines's obsession for order, love of gourmet food and rare wines, the failure of his two marriages, and the frustration he feels in his role as father. The result is a believable and funny picture of a remarkable man which Mad readers of all ages will enjoy." Joni Bodart
Library J 98:1024 Mr 15 '73 220w [YA]

"Frank Jacobs, a Mad contributor since 1957, never explains the Mad phenomenon; instead he offers a lighthearted history of the magazine and its improbable publisher William M. Gaines. . . . The book is studded with examples of the Mad-cap doings of Gaines and his staffers. Some of the humor is on the intra-office side, but the book entertains, and Mad fans will eat it up."
N Y Times Bk R p22 F 25 '73 160w

Comets
Juvenile literature
Asimov, I. Comets and meteors. (Ag '74)
Comets and meteors. Asimov, I. (Ag '74)
Comets, meteoroids, and asteroids. Branley, F. M. (D '74)
Comic-book book. Thompson, D., ed. (O '74)
Comic books, strips, etc.
Jacobs, F. Mad world of William M. Gaines. (N '74)
Kunzle, D. History of the comic strip. v 1. (O '74)
Thompson, D., ed. Comic-book book. (O '74)
History and criticism
Berger, A. A. Comic-stripped American. (Ag '74)
Comic mind. Mast, G. (Je '74)

Juvenile literature
Ancona, G. Monsters on wheels. (Ja '75) (1974 Annual)
Macmillan, Harold
Macmillan, H. At the end of the day, 1961-1963. (Ap '74)
McNamara, Robert Strange
Murdock, C. A. Defense policy formation. (S '74)
Macramé book. Bress, H. (Mr '74)
Macramé, weaving, and tapestry. Dépas, S. (My '74)
Maculan's daughter. Gainham, S. (O '74)
Mad (periodical)
Jacobs, F. Mad world of William M. Gaines. (N '74)
Mad dog blues & other plays. Shepard, S. (Ap '74)
Mad ducks and bears. Plimpton, G. (Je '74)
Mad world of William M. Gaines. Jacobs, F. (N '74)
Madame Vestris and the London stage. Appleton, W. W. (O '74)

reviews for you; it also gives brief digests of the reviews.

Issues of the *Digest* come out monthly and are cumulated annually. Each volume is arranged alphabetically by the author of the book being reviewed. There is an index arranged by subject and by title. These subject and title indexes are cumulated every five years for that five-year period. So, to find the reviews of a book, you have to know about when it was written, look in the index for the title of the book, and then turn to the appropriate volume of the *Digest*.

The entry for each book includes the author and the title, followed by the number of pages in the book, its price, and its publisher. Then there is a brief sentence or paragraph telling what the book is about. Then a digest, or condensed version, of a book review is given. This is followed by the name of the magazine the review is from, its volume and date, and the number of words the review contains.

If a book has been reviewed by many magazines, usually digests for only a few of the reviews will be included, but all the other sources of reviews will be given so you can find them.

Problem 62

SEARCH QUESTIONS[1]

1. What are some current books on jazz?

2. Find a review of a recent book called *Tolkien's World*.

3. Find a review of *The Palace Guard* by Dan Rather.

CLUES

1. Look in the subject and title index at the back of the book under *J*. Under *jazz* you will find a list of books by author and title. If you want to read more about these, look in the main part of the book under the author.

2. In the index under the title, you find the author is Helms, so look under *H* in the main part of the book.

3. You know the author, so turn to *R* in the main part of the book.

[1]These questions and clues were taken from the 1974 *Digest*.

THE GREAT BOOKS OF THE WESTERN WORLD

Mortimer J. Adler, ed. *The Great Books of the Western World*. Chicago: Encyclopedia Britannica. 54 vol.

The Great Books of the Western World includes writings which portray the ideas of Western man from the ancient Greeks to the twentieth century. Here is a unique collection of Western thought. It is exciting to realize that concepts and ideas we consider modern have existed through the centuries. Ancient Greeks like Homer and Aristophanes wrote about love, marriage, and family with many of the same ideas and observations found in a different form in the lectures of Sigmund Freud centuries later.

The first volume is an introduction to the set. The 2nd and 3rd volumes are called the *Syntopicon* and serve as an index to the set. This Syntopicon is organized by topics and refers you to various authors who have something to say about a particular subject. The large topics are listed as the table of contents of the two Syntopicon (index) volumes.

These large topics are arranged alphabetically in the two Syntopicon volumes. Each of these topics includes a long introductory essay which is followed by an outline of the topic. After this outline, references to the writings in the *Great Books* are listed in the order of the outline.

For example, suppose you want to know something written about civil liberties, especially censorship. Scan the table of contents of the Syntopicon for a large topic which would include the specific one you want. In this example, the large topic would be liberty. Turn to the given page in the Syntopicon. Following the introductory essay, you will find the outline of the large topic of liberty. Scan this for the smaller topic you are interested in. In this case, it would be item 2a, "Freedom of thought and expression: the problem of censorship." Look through the references which follow — they are arranged in accordance with the outline — until you come to section 2a. You will find more than 50 references including Sophocles, Montaigne, Kant, Cervantes, Gibbon, and the Federalist papers.

Problem 63

SEARCH QUESTIONS

1. Compare what two writers have said about the love of life and the instinct for self-preservation.

2. What did Galileo write about mathematical method?

CLUES

1. a. Scan the table of contents in the Syntopicon for a likely large topic which would include love of life or self-preservation. In this case "Life and Death" would be the large topic.
    b. In the Syntopicon, turn to the page given and look at the outline of the topic which follows the introductory essay. Under 8a you will find what you are looking for, "Love of Life: instinct for self-preservation."
    c. Turn through the references (they are in the same order as the outline of the topic) until you come to 8a and you will find more than a column of appropriate references. You could select any two to compare.

2. a. Check the Syntopicon table of contents for a likely large topic, in this case "Mathematics."
    b. Look at the page given and scan the outline of the topic which follows the introductory essay. Item 3 "Method in Mathematics: the model of mathematical thought" will probably contain what you need.
    c. Turn through the references (given in the same order as the outline of the topic) until you come to (3) and scan down the column for Galileo; the reference given will send you to the right page of the appropriate writing.

SCIENCE AND MATHEMATICS

General encyclopedias often refer to outstanding men and basic ideas in the fields of science and mathematics, but sometimes you want more complete, specific, or detailed information that is given only in a reference that specializes in science and mathematics. For example:

What is a pingo?[1]
How do a pi and an electron compare in size?[2]
What was George Gamow like?[3]

Many specialized references have been written to help answer your questions in science and mathematics. There are books that specialize in biographies of scientists; there are encyclopedias that contain articles about all fields of science and those that focus on only one aspect of science such as mammals or chemistry. There are also dictionaries of both mathematics and science.

Be careful when using a specialized reference in science that it is up-to-date enough for what you need. If you are checking the ancient Greeks' views of astronomy, it might not make much difference whether your reference volume is dated 1964 or 1974. But, if you are investigating black holes (in astronomy), it would make a big difference which date the book was published. If you are studying really current areas of science, remember also to check the *Readers' Guide* for articles in the periodicals.

We have described the contents of many of the specialized references available in mathematics and science and have provided Search Questions and Clues for most of these. Knowing what specialized references are available in these fields will help tremendously with your study and pleasure reading.

Biographies of scientists. There are several good sources of information about the lives of scientists. Two of these biographical references give very complete information: the *Dictionary of Scientific Biography* includes all scientists, while the *Modern Men of Science* volumes are concerned with only modern scientists.

DICTIONARY OF SCIENTIFIC BIOGRAPHY

Charles Coulston Gillispie, ed. *Dictionary of Scientific Biography.* New York: Scribner's Sons. Vol. 1 was published in 1970 and the series should be completed soon.

[1] A pingo is a "mound of earth raised and split by frost action." *Harper Encyclopedia of Science,* "Tundra," Vol. 4, p. 1207.

[2] A pi is a particle 270 times heavier than the electron." *Concise Encyclopedia of the Atom,* p. 187.

[3] George Gamow had a "legendary sense of humor . . . a greatly enjoyed reading and memorizing poetry." *Dictionary of Scientific Biography,* p. 273.

York, 1953); and *Vierteljahrsschrift der Naturforschenden Gesellschaft in Zürich*, **41** (1896), Jubelband 1.

R. S. HARTENBERG

CUMMING, JAMES (*b.* London, England, 24 October 1777; *d.* North Runcton, Norfolk, 10 November 1861), *physics*.

Cumming entered Trinity College, Cambridge, in 1797, graduated tenth wrangler in 1801, became a fellow in 1803, and was elected professor of chemistry in 1815, a position he held until the year before his death. He was apparently excellent as a teacher. Cumming's scientific accomplishments, however, were limited—reportedly by ill health and lack of ambition—to a ten-year period early in his career: his published works span the years 1822–1833.

He became fascinated by the developments in electromagnetism following Oersted's experiments and independently invented the galvanometer, describing it in greater detail than either Schweigger or Poggendorff. P. G. Tait gave Cumming credit for the independent discovery of thermoelectricity, but there seems to be no good reason to accept this. A brief announcement of Thomas Johann Seebeck's discovery appeared in the *Annals of Philosophy* in 1822; Cumming's first description was in the same journal in the following year. On the other hand, Seebeck's detailed paper was not available until 1825. By then Cumming had compared the thermoelectric order of metals with the voltaic and conductivity series, noting the lack of any apparent connection. He also recorded the inversion effect which occurs with certain couples at high temperatures (Seebeck had remarked on this, as had A. C. Becquerel); this anomalous behavior was finally explained by William Thomson on the basis of thermodynamic arguments and the assumption of the "Thomson effect." (Thomson had his attention drawn to this phenomenon by Becquerel's paper but later recognized Cumming's priority; he apparently never realized that it had been described in Seebeck's original publication.)

Cumming was active in the founding of the Cambridge Philosophical Society and from 1824 to 1826 acted as its fourth president.

BIBLIOGRAPHY

I. ORIGINAL WORKS. The galvanometer is described in "On the Connexion of Galvanism and Magnetism," in *Cambridge Philosophical Society, Transactions*, **1** (1821–1822), 268–279, and in "On the Application of Magnetism as a Measure of Electricity," *ibid.*, 281–286. The more important thermoelectric articles are "On the Development

of Electromagnetism by Heat," in *Annals of Philosophy*, **21** (1823), 427–429, and "A List of Substances Arranged According to Their Thermoelectric Relations, with a Description of Instruments for Exhibiting Rotation by Thermoelectricity," *ibid.*, **22** (1823), 177–180. The inversion effect was reported in "On Some Anomalous Appearances Occurring in the Thermoelectric Series," *ibid.*, **22** (1823), 321–323.

II. SECONDARY LITERATURE. A biographical sketch appears in the *Dictionary of National Biography*. Reference is made there to some collected papers, but this author has been unable to discover any knowledge of their existence. The galvanometer is discussed in Robert A. Chipman, "The Earliest Electromagnetic Instruments," in *United States National Museum Bulletin*, **240** (1964), 121–136.

BERNARD S. FINN

CURIE, MARIE (MARIA SKLODOWSKA) (*b.* Warsaw, Poland, 7 November 1867; *d.* Sancellemoz, France, 4 July 1934), *physics*.

Maria's parents, descendants of Catholic landowners, were intellectuals held in poor esteem by the Russian authorities. Her father, Wladyslaw, a former student at the University of Saint Petersburg (now Leningrad), taught mathematics and physics in a government secondary school in Warsaw. Her mother, the former Bronislawa Boguska, managed a private boarding school for girls on Freta Street[1] when Maria, her fifth child, was born. The mother subsequently contracted tuberculosis and gave up all professional activity. Misfortune struck the family again in 1876, when Sophia, the eldest child, died of typhus; in 1878 the mother died.

Denied lucrative teaching posts for political reasons, Professor Sklodowski decided, after moving several times, to take in boarders at his home on Leschno Street. Maria, known familiarly as Manya, gave up her room and slept in the living room; she worked there late at night and put everything in order before the boarders had their breakfast. A gold medal for excellence crowned her brilliant high school studies—in Russian—but her health was weakened (1883). A year in the country with her uncle Sklodowski, a notary in Skalbmierz, near the Galician border, restored her. During this period she formed her profound attachment to nature and to country people.

Upon her return Maria gave lessons to earn money. She was a passionate adherent of clandestine movements supporting Polish political positivism and participated in the activities of an underground university—progressive and anticlerical—whose journal, *Pravda*, preached the cult of science. Maria read everything in the original: Dostoevsky and Karl Marx, the French, German, and Polish poets; sometimes she even tried her hand at poetry.

This is an exciting and useful new source of biographical information about men of science, past and present. This series, sponsored by the American Council of Learned Societies, was begun in 1970 and will have approximately sixteen volumes when it is finished. It contains information about men and women in mathematics, natural sciences, and physical sciences. Scientists of the past and the present are included. Each article contains concise information that tries to show the personality of the scientist as well as how he or she fits into the knowledge of his time and of ours. The final volume is to include science of ancient Babylon and Egypt.

The articles are arranged alphabetically by name of the scientist, but the last volume is to have a topical index which enables you to follow any aspect of science through the various people involved with it. This index allows you to study the history of a scientific idea or concept.

Problem 64

SEARCH QUESTIONS

1. How did John Audubon develop his interest in science?

2. What fields did George Gamow work in?

CLUES

You should have no trouble using this set. All people are listed in alphabetical order by their last names, and the letters included in each volume are shown outside.

McGRAW-HILL MODERN MEN OF SCIENCE

McGraw-Hill Modern Men of Science. New York: McGraw-Hill, 1966. 2 vols.

The biographies in these two volumes are of men and women scientists from various countries who have been working since 1940. Both volumes follow the same format. The biographies are listed alphabetically, and there is a two-part index at the end of each volume. Volume 1 discusses more than 400 scientists and Volume 2 adds another 400 who have become famous more recently.

The first part of the two-part index in each volume lists the persons and subjects discussed in the biographies. The second part of the index lists the major scientific fields these people are working in. This is helpful in selecting scientists in a particular field. It may be necessary to check the index in each volume to find what you need.

Problem 65

SEARCH QUESTIONS

1. List five contemporary scientists who have made significant contributions to molecular biology.

2. Describe the work of Albert Sabin.

3. Who worked on the radio-carbon dating technique?

4. In what field was Lise Meitner a pioneer?

CLUES

1. Check the index by field under *M* (molecular biology). The names will be listed.

2. You could turn directly to Sabin or you could check the index of people and topics to locate the page.

3. Look in the index to topics under *R* (radio-carbon dating). You will be referred to W.F. Libby and a page.

4. Turn directly to *Meitner* or check the index of people and topics to locate the page.

WORLD WHO'S WHO IN SCIENCE

Allen G. Debus, ed. *World Who's Who in Science: A Biographical Dictionary of Notable Scientists from Antiquity to the Present.* Chicago: Marquis, 1968.

This is a one-volume collection of very brief biographies, arranged alphabetically by last name. It is useful for quickly identifying a scientist.

Encyclopedias of science. There are some science encyclopedias that include information from all fields of science. They are particularly useful for

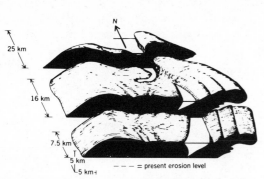

ANTIMATTER 101

--- = present erosion level

Fig. 3. Schematic block diagram of the Morin anorthosite, Quebec. Dotted line indicates present erosion level. (*From J. Martignole and K. Schrijver, Tectonic setting and evolution of the Morin anorthosite, Grenville Province, Quebec, Bull. Geol. Soc. Finland, 42:165–209, 1970*)

MOON in the McGraw-Hill Encyclopedia of Science and Technology. [B. F. WINDLEY]

Bibliography: J. W. Chamberlain and C. Watkins (eds.), *The Apollo 15 Lunar Samples*, 1972; J. C. Duchesne, *J. Petrol.*, vol. 13, 1972; B. F. Windley, *Nature*, vol. 226, 1970; B. F. Windley, *Grønlands Geol. Unders. Rapp.*, vol. 35, 1971.

Antimatter

Among recent studies of antimatter have been investigations of annihilation of antimatter with matter by way of nucleonium formation and investigations of x-rays from antiprotonic atoms.

Nucleonium formation. Antimatter is a substance made up of antiprotons, antineutrons, and positrons (antielectrons) in the form of antinuclei, antiatoms, and antimolecules in the same way that ordinary matter is made up of protons, neutrons, and electrons. The term antimatter can also be applied to collections of free antiparticles and to individual antiparticles. Such antiparticles along with other antiparticles that have short lifetimes have been observed in primary and secondary cosmic rays and are thought to have been present in the early stages of the formation of the universe. In addition, positrons are emitted in the radioactive decay of many nuclei. Along with the antideuteron, antiparticles have been produced in high-energy accelerator experiments. Antimatter in the form of antiatoms and antimolecules has not been produced, but there now appears to be some possibility that antimatter exists in large amounts in the universe. It has recently been shown that when atomic and molecular matter and antimatter come into contact under a large range of circumstances, annihilation occurs principally through the formation of nucleonium atoms. Previously, only direct particle-antiparticle annihilations were considered. *See* GRAVITY.

A nucleonium atom consists of a nucleus and an antinucleus in a bound state. A bound state is pos-

getting broad background information on scientific subjects. Two of these science encyclopedias have several volumes and contain rather long articles.

MCGRAW-HILL ENCYCLOPEDIA OF SCIENCE AND TECHNOLOGY

McGraw-Hill Encyclopedia of Science and Technology. 3rd ed. New York: McGraw-Hill, 1971. 15 vol.

This encyclopedia contains information on all the natural sciences and their practical applications. Clearly written and very readable, it is intended to be useful to both students and nonspecialists. No biography or history of science is included since this information is available in other sources. There are many diagrams and charts. A yearbook covers the important scientific advances of each year. Like any large encyclopedia, you can find a large general topic by turning directly to the alphabetical spot in the text. However, if you are looking for a specific bit of information or for complete information about a large topic, you need to go first to the index.

Problem 66

SEARCH QUESTIONS

1. How do hurricanes form?

2. What is the scientific name of the anteater?

3. What is the interior of the sun like?

4. What important scientific events took place in the year 1970?

CLUES

1. You could go directly to *hurricanes* in the text. If you check the index, however, you will find more than a dozen additional references.

2. Check *anteater* directly in the text.

3. Check the index either under *sun*, subtopic *interior*, or under *interior of sun*.

4. Use the 1971 yearbook. Remember yearbooks usually appear the year following the event they summarize.

THE HARPER ENCYCLOPEDIA OF SCIENCE

James R. Newman, ed. *The Harper Encyclopedia of Science.* New York: Harper, 1967. 4 vol.

This readable encyclopedia covers scientific topics from ancient times to modern times. It has a good index to help you find specific information. There are good cross-references to other articles which contain considerable information on a topic.

There is also a one-volume *Harper Encyclopedia of Science* which is useful. It too is arranged alphabetically by subject with an index.

Problem 67

SEARCH QUESTIONS

1. What is geochemistry?
2. What is an irrational number?
3. How many different references deal with maps?

CLUES

You could also locate (1) and (2) by going to the index first.

1. Check in the proper volume under *g*.
2. Look directly in the proper volume under *irrational*.
3. Check *maps* in the index. There is an article under *map*, but to find all the different references to maps, you must use the index.

THE SCIENCE LIBRARY

The Science Library. Chicago: Encyclopedia Britannica. 7 vol.

This set is intended to explain the "big ideas" of science to younger readers. Its high interest articles are arranged by large subject, and each volume deals with three subjects. For example, Volume IV contains sections on "Our Earth," "Rocks and Minerals," and "Weather." Volume VI deals with "The Moon," "Planets and Interplanetary Travel," and "Stars." You need to look at the outside of the volume to select the one which includes the subject you are interested in. It is difficult to find a specific bit of information, but this is a valuable source of general science material.

THE BOOK OF POPULAR SCIENCE

The Book of Popular Science. New York: Grolier. 10 vol.

This is a well-written general science encyclopedia for students. It is continuously updated, and its articles are well-illustrated. Material is classified into broad subjects like the earth, the universe, or plant life. An index helps you find specific items of information.

Problem 68

SEARCH QUESTIONS

1. What is the "lifting force" of a balloon?
2. What kinds of things can an elephant use his trunk to do?
3. Describe the saltiness of the Arctic Ocean.
4. How big is a particle of sand?

CLUES

Remember, articles in this encyclopedia are written about broad subjects. For this reason, you must always look in the index for a specific subject. Without the index you would probably never find any of these specific things.

1. Look in the index under *balloon, lifting force*. You will be referred to a page in an article on forces within liquids and gasses.
2. Look in the index under *elephant, trunk of*.
3. Look in the index under *Arctic Ocean, salinity of*. You would also find the information listed under *polar regions*.
4. Look in the index under *sand, particles of*. You will be referred to an article on "The Crust of Our Planet."

There are several good *one-volume science encyclopedias*. These usually define and briefly discuss terms and ideas. They are useful for getting information quickly.

142   COMPUTERS

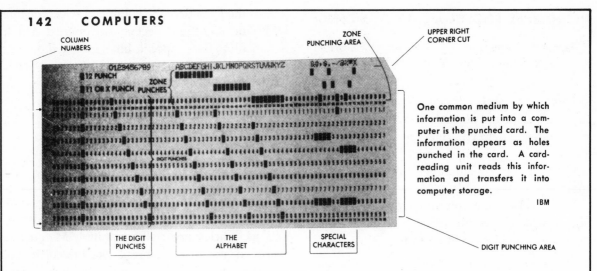

COLUMN NUMBERS

ZONE PUNCHING AREA

UPPER RIGHT CORNER CUT

12 PUNCH

11 OR X PUNCH

ZONE PUNCHES

One common medium by which information is put into a computer is the punched card. The information appears as holes punched in the card. A card-reading unit reads this information and transfers it into computer storage.

IBM

THE DIGIT PUNCHES

THE ALPHABET

SPECIAL CHARACTERS

DIGIT PUNCHING AREA

The central processing unit (CPU) provides the computer with arithmetic, logical and control capabilities. The arithmetic unit of the CPU provides for the simplest of arithmetic operations; namely, nothing more than addition, subtraction, multiplication and division. The logical operations are very little more than an ability to compare two numbers and determine whether they are equal, and, if unequal, which one is the larger.

The control unit of the central processor governs the operation of the computer electronically; it coordinates the various units that make up the computer and determines in what order these units are to become active and for how long. The processing unit accomplishes its tasks by executing instructions of a program. Each instruction causes the computer to take one very small step in carrying out some process. The set of instructions that makes up the complete directions to the computer is called a computer program. (See the article Computer Programming, in Volume 7 of THE BOOK OF POPULAR SCIENCE.)

Associated very closely with the central processing unit is a storage unit. This is the primary storage unit for the computer and is often called the "memory." This unit receives data, holds the data indefinitely without erasure or loss, and supplies the data upon command from the CPU for processing. Together, the primary storage and the CPU are the heart of the computer system.

The input and output units are the mechanisms by which data and other information are transferred between the computer storage and the outside world. One common input medium is the punched card. Data punched as holes in a paper card is read by a card-reading unit into the computer storage. One very important output device is some form of printer, perhaps as simple as a typewriter or as complicated as a high-speed printer that will print 2,000 lines per minute, with each line as wide as 132 characters.

Finally, human control over the computer is exercised through the console. Lights, switches and buttons not only enable the computer operator to control the computer, but also to monitor what the computer is doing at any moment. Very often the console is designed into the CPU so that physically the processor and console are in one box.

A simplified diagram of a computer is shown in Figure 1. The diagram represents a small computer with a punch card for input and a typewriter for output. The solid lines indicate the direction of flow for data values and instructions. For example, input values are transferred from the card reader to memory; output values from memory to the typewriter. Values are also transferred between memory and the arithmetic unit in both directions. Instructions are transferred from memory to the control unit. The dashed lines indicate the exercise of control. Thus, they connect the control

Sample page from the article on "Computers" by R. Clay Sprowls. This article appears in the mathematics section of *The Book of Popular Science*, N.Y., Grolier, Incorporated.

90

POPULAR SCIENCE ENCYCLOPEDIA OF THE SCIENCES

Popular Science Encyclopedia of the Sciences. Garden City: Doubleday, 1963.

This readable one-volume encyclopedia is arranged alphabetically by subject. There is an index to help locate specific ideas. Also, there is a useful six-page list of important events in science.

Problem 69

SEARCH QUESTIONS

1. What is the specific gravity of a diamond?
2. What is a galaxy?
3. What were the important events in science of the 1500s?
4. Who was Anders Retzius?

CLUES

1. Look in the *d*s for diamond.
2. Look under *galaxy*.
3. Look in the Important Events list. It is in chronological order, so the 1500s are easy to locate.
4. Retzius is not in the *r*s in the text, so you have to check the index and scan the page it refers to.

VAN NOSTRAND'S SCIENCE ENCYCLOPEDIA

Van Nostrand's Science Encyclopedia. Princeton: Van Nostrand, 1968.

This useful reference contains terms in science, engineering, mathematics, and medicine arranged alphabetically. Each topic begins with a simple definition and then gives more detail. The articles give cross-reference to other related terms. There is no index.

Problem 70

SEARCH QUESTIONS

1. What is a factor?
2. Describe the grasshopper.
3. What is a beta particle?

CLUES

Look for these in their alphabetical place:

1. *f*actor
2. *g*rasshopper
3. *b*eta

COWLES ENCYCLOPEDIA OF SCIENCE, INDUSTRY AND TECHNOLOGY

Cowles Encyclopedia of Science, Industry and Technology. New York: Cowles Book Company, 1969.

This is a useful one-volume reference. It deals with seven subject areas of science: history, chemistry, earth sciences, life science, mathematics, physics, and space sciences. It discusses industry and technology under five fields: communications and transportation, energy and power sources, food and agriculture, machines and processes, and materials and structures. There are a great many pictures, diagrams, and charts. Many of the sections include a glossary. There is an index which helps you locate specific information.

Problem 71

SEARCH QUESTIONS

1. Find information about liquid oxygen used in rockets.
2. How do telephones transmit sound?
3. What is the structure of a plant cell?

91

silver thaw. A silver thaw usually lasts only a few hours as the warm air soon warms all exposed objects above 32° F.

SILVERFIN. Pisces, Teleostei. A small fish **(Pisces)**, *Cyprinella (Notropis) whippli*, related to the shiners. Common in clear streams from New York to Alabama and west to Minnesota and Arkansas. It is silvery with a bluish tinge and the paired fins are pale white.

SILVERFISH. Insecta, Thysanura. *Lepisma.* One of the primitive wingless insects. It is about ½" long, broad in front and tapering behind, with two long slender antennae and three similar processes at the caudal end of the body. It is covered with lustrous grayish scales, whence the common name. The insect eats starchy materials and sometimes defaces book bindings, wall paper, and laundry, but as a rule it is not sufficiently abundant to be a pest. It is often found in damp buildings. Also called the fish moth.

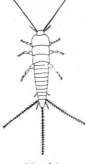
Silverfish.

SILVERSIDES. Pisces, Teleostei. Small slender fishes **(Pisces)**, of numerous species, found chiefly along the coasts of the warmer seas but in a few cases in ponds and streams. They make up the family Atherinidae.

SIMA. That portion of the crust of the earth, chiefly the sub-Pacific **lithosphere**, which is composed chiefly of rocks rich in the ferro-magnesian silicates. (See also **Geosyncline.**)

SIMILITUDE. The analysis of an engineering structure may be made by means of mathematics or by the use of models. A model is a small-scale reproduction of the prototype in all features which are pertinent to the particular problem under investigation. Model analysis is based on Newton's Law of Similarity. In general this law states that models must be geometrically and dynamically similar to the structures which they represent. No restriction is placed on the size of the model. Consequently the scale and the material of the model may be varied to produce the particular action which is required.

Methods of analysis have been developed which reduce the essential elements for similarity to certain fundamental characteristics. The methods of analysis require a proportionality or scale ratio of the respective forces acting on the model and on the prototype. These forces, depending upon their nature or origin, are expressed in terms of one or several physical characteristics such as **mass**, length and time. The engineer does not always use these characteristics as such but may use **density, velocity, gravity, viscosity,** etc. Often it is impossible to satisfy all of the requirements for similitude simultaneously. In this event skill is required in designing the model in order to reduce the error, which is the result of ignoring some of these requirements, to a negligible value.

Models are used to determine the action of **bridges,** building frames, **airplane** structures and **hydraulic structures.** The action of some structures is so complex that it is virtually impossible to make an exact mathematical solution which will have a practical application. Model analysis may then be used advantageously. Even fairly crude models are often quite useful in providing at least qualitative answers to complex problems.

SIMPLE BEAM. A simple **beam** is one which rests on two end supports in such a manner that the ends of the beam are free to rotate on the supports.

Simple Beam

The usual standard riveted beam connections are designed to transmit **shear** only and they offer relatively little end re-

straint. Therefore, beams and girders which are riveted to supports are generally assumed to be simply supported unless a special type of moment connection is used.

SIMPLEX OPERATION OF A RADIO SYSTEM. A method of operation in which communication between two stations takes place in one direction at a time. This includes ordinary transmit-receive operation, press-to-talk operation, voice-operated carrier, and other forms of manual or automatic switching from transmit to receive.

SIMPLEX TELEGRAPHY. Telegraphy.

SIMPLEXED CIRCUIT. A circuit used to transmit two signals simultaneously. (See **Phantom Circuit.**)

SIMPSON ONE-THIRD RULE. A numerical **quadrature** formula

$$\int_a^b f(x)dx = \frac{h}{3}[y_0 + 4(y_1 + y_3 + \cdots + y_{n-1}) + 2(y_2 + y_4 + \cdots + y_{n-2}) + y_n]$$

where h is the interval between equally spaced values of the independent variable x.

This rule can only be used where there are an even number of intervals.

SIMULTANEOUS EQUATIONS. An important type of **linear** equation occurs when a system of them is given, as

$$A_{11}x_1 + A_{12}x_2 + \cdots + A_{1n}x_n = y_1$$
$$A_{21}x_1 + A_{22}x_2 + \cdots + A_{2n}x_n = y_2$$
$$\cdots\cdots\cdots\cdots\cdots\cdots\cdots$$
$$A_{n1}x_1 + A_{n2}x_2 + \cdots + A_{nn}x_n = y_n$$

where A_{ij} and y_i are known and it is desired to find values of the n unknowns which satisfy the equations. The notation is considerably simplified in **matrix** form, $Ax = y$. If A is non-singular, the equations have a unique solution; if A is **singular,** they are either incompatible or not linearly independent. These cases can best be considered separately.

1. If $y \neq 0$, the equations are inhomogeneous; if the determinant of A does not vanish, $|A| \neq 0$, A is non-singular and its reciprocal A^{-1} exists. Then, $x = A^{-1}y = \hat{A}y/|A|$, where $\hat{A}$ is the adjoint matrix. This solution, when written in terms of cofactors, is known as **Cramer's rule.**

2. If $y = 0$, the equations are homogeneous and two cases occur: (a) $y = 0$; $|A| \neq 0$. The only solutions are the trivial ones $x_1 = x_2 = \cdots = x_n = 0$ and the equations are inconsistent. (b) $y = 0$; $|A| = 0$. Assume that the rank of A is $m < n$, then at least one cofactor $A^{ik} \neq 0$, unless all $A_{ij} = 0$. The solutions are then $x_i = cA^{ji}$, where c is any constant. This is the case where the unknowns x_i are not linearly independent. The given equations are then equivalent to a system of $(n + 1)$ linear equations in n variables and the condition that it be consistent is that the determinant of the augmented matrix vanish.

In a practical case, two or more simultaneous equations can be solved neatly by Cramer's rule. However, the evaluation of the determinants in that method becomes very laborious for four equations or more. A suitable procedure, especially adapted for a desk calculating machine, is as follows. Divide the first equation by some coefficient, say A_{11}, the second by A_{21} and so on to make the coefficients of x_1 become unity. Then subtract the second equation from the first, the third from the second, and continue until $(n - 1)$ equations remain but none of them contains x_1. Repeat until one equation is left with only one unknown. Proceeding backwards through the various equations one can determine all of the x_i. Several short-cuts and modifications of this general method are possible. They are discussed in detail by P. S. Dwyer, "Linear Computations," John Wiley and Sons, Inc., New York, 1951.

CLUES

1. Check the index under *liquid-oxygen*, subhead *rockets*; or under *rockets*, subhead *fuel systems*.

2. Check index under *telephones*, subhead *transmission*.

3. Check index under *cells*, subhead *plant structure*; or look under *plants*, subhead *cells*.

There are many *encyclopedias that specialize in an area of science or mathematics* rather than try to include something about the entire field. Their titles generally indicate clearly the subjects they contain.

ENCYCLOPEDIA OF EARTH SCIENCES

Rhodes Whitmore Fairbridge, ed. *Encyclopedia of Earth Sciences*. New York: Van Nostrand.
Vol. I *The Encyclopedia of Oceanography*, 1966.
    II *The Encyclopedia of Atmospheric Sciences and Astrogeology*, 1967.
    III *The Encyclopedia of Geomorphology*, 1968.
    IVa *The Encyclopedia of Geochemistry and Environmental Sciences*, 1972.

According to the preface, other volumes are planned on minerology, geophysics, hydrology, and paleontology. In other words, in this reference set, the earth sciences have been divided into specific areas dealing with the ocean, air, the planet as a whole, space, astrogeology, and the surface of the earth. The names may frighten the layman, but these encyclopedias are well-written and could be easily read by any high school student or adult interested in science. They are not meant for the professional to use in his own field. The main articles are arranged alphabetically within each volume. Each volume has an index that helps you find specific topics, and there are many cross-references to other related material.

Problem 72

SEARCH QUESTIONS

Vol. I, *The Encyclopedia of Oceanography*

1. Describe the Indian Ocean.

2. Explain the dynamics of ocean currents.

3. What is a hydrophone?

CLUES

1. Go directly to the article in its alphabetical place under *Indian*. You could also check the index.

2. Check the index under *currents* or *ocean*. If you check the index under *currents*, you will be referred to *ocean*. If you check under *ocean currents*, you will see a subtopic, *dynamics* of ocean currents.

3. Check *hydrophone* in the index. You will have to scan the page it refers you to.

THE ENCYCLOPEDIA OF THE BIOLOGICAL SCIENCES

Peter Gray, ed. *The Encyclopedia of the Biological Sciences*. New York: Reinhold, 1961.

This one-volume encyclopedia contains brief articles on biology for nonspecialists. It could be used by high school students and adults. These articles define and explain the terms used in biology. There are some biographies included. There is an index, although usually you can go directly to the entry.

Problem 73

SEARCH QUESTIONS

1. What is meiosis?

2. What is the nitrogen cycle?

3. What is biological warfare?

CLUES

1. Go directly to *meiosis* in the encyclopedia.

2. Look under *nitrogen*.

3. It would probably be faster to check the index for this. Look under *warfare, biological*.

Descartes' Vortex Theory

Descartes, whose principal work appeared in 1644, is often called the father of modern philosophy, and can also be called the father of modern cosmogony, although his work was published before the general law of gravitation had been established by Newton.

Descartes made the relevant remark that even if God had created the world without much regularity, the laws of nature would select from all possible configurations those that have the greatest stability.

Descartes showed that the vortex shape of the solar system is a stationary one. He assumes that space is not empty but filled with something later called "ether." In a universe filled with ether and matter, the only possible motion would thus be a vortex motion. The primordial matter tends toward the center of the vortex, forming the sun. Pieces of matter tend to fly out of the vortex forming the transparent heavens, while the coarser bodies are captured in the vortex; this third kind of matter forms the earth and the other planets. Around these planets, secondary vortices are formed, in which the satellites are captured. This picture is remarkably similar to the cosmogonical ideas of von Weizsäcker, to be discussed below.

There are many objections to the vortex theory in its original form. First, the analogy between the plane of the ecliptic and the surface of a whirling waterpool is completely fortuitous. The vortices

The First Tidal Theory

In 1745, Buffon suggested that a comet encountering the sun might have been responsible for tearing from the sun sufficient material to produce planets. A skew or grazing collision could have produced solar rotation, the planetary material, and planetary rotation and, in turn, the satellite systems and their respective rotation.

It must be remarked here that in Buffon's time fantastic ideas about comets were common. Buffon estimated the mass of the comet of 1680 as about one solar mass. Therefore, Buffon's theory shares the difficulties encountered by modern tidal theories.

One difficulty is that if a mass of dimension a and density ρ is under the influence of the solar gravitational field, the differential rotation will dissipate the system. The gravitational self-attraction F_1 is given by

$$F_1 \cong G\rho a^2 \qquad (3)$$

while the solar gravitational field will produce a shearing force of the order of

$$F_2 \cong \frac{GM'_0}{a} \qquad (4)$$

where M_0 is the solar mass. Comparing the two we see that

$$\frac{F_1}{F_2} \cong \frac{M}{M_0} \qquad (5)$$

where M is the mass of the material torn from the sun. We

CONTINENTAL TERRACE

In cases where there is a continental borderland (q.v.) or marginal plateau seaward of the continental shelf, the continental slope is liable to be divided into two sectors, one at the inner edge and the other at the outer edge of the borderland. The latter has been termed the *marginal escarpment* by Heezen *et al.* (1959).

The continental slope, from the sedimentary point of view may be either:

(a) A site of nondeposition, over which there is flow or slumping of sediments (Fairbridge, 1947) destined to come to rest on the continental rise or to be swept by turbidity currents out onto the abyssal plain. In this case, coring and dredging may reveal traces of continental rocks (e.g., massive rocks like granite, as off southern California, or horizontally bedded Mesozoic-Cenozoic rocks, as in parts of the Atlantic coast), or

(b) A site of slope deposition with foreset beds, where the finer terrigenous neritic materials carried across the shelf come to rest. Such sites are to be

Rich, J. L., 1951, "Three critical environments of deposition, and criteria for recognition of rocks deposited in each of them," *Bull. Geol. Soc. Am.,* **62**, No. 1, 1–19.

Wagner, H., 1900, "Lehrbuch der Geographie," Hanover, Hahn.

Cross-references: *Continental Rise; Continental Terrace; Submarine Plateaus.*

CONTINENTAL TERRACE*

Introduction

The *continental terrace* (Fig. 1) is defined as the sediment and rock mass underlying the coastal plain, the continental shelf, and the continental slope. The *continental shelf* is the shallow submerged platform bordering the continents. It slopes gently seaward to the *shelf break*, an increase in slope at an average depth of about 130 m. There is considerable variation in depth of the shelf to a few meters

Vol. I, *The Encyclopedia of Oceanography.* © 1966. Reprinted by permission of Van Nostrand Reinhold Company.

Vol. II, *The Encyclopedia of Atmospheric Sciences and Astrogeology.* © 1967. Reprinted by permission of Van Nostrand Reinhold Company.

94 Sample pages from Rhodes Whitmore Fairbridge, ed., *Encyclopedia of Earth Sciences,* Van Nostrand Reinhold Company, N.Y.

MAMMALS OF THE WORLD

Ernest P. Walker. *Mammals of the World*. Baltimore: The Johns Hopkins Press, 1968. 2 vol.

Mammals of the World is organized according to the scheme of classification by order, family, and genus. The table of contents equals an outline of the sequence used in the book. The common names for each family are also used so you can locate the mammal you want, even though you are not familiar with the scientific names. There are many photographs, almost one for every living genus of mammal.

The first page for each order includes general statements which describe that order. A page follows for each family in the order giving general statements applying to each family. Generic descriptions with their photographs follow.

Problem 74

SEARCH QUESTIONS

1. List the characteristics of chiroptera (bats).

2. Find a picture of a kangaroo.

CLUES

1. Scan the table of contents to look under the major order headings at the left. It might be faster to check the index under *c*.

2. Look in the index under *kangaroos*, or scan the table of contents for *marsupialia* or *pouched animals* and scan down for kangaroos.

COWLES ENCYCLOPEDIA OF ANIMALS AND PLANTS

Cowles Encyclopedia of Animals and Plants. New York: Cowles, 1968.

This encyclopedia contains very short, easy to read descriptions of many animals and plants. It is almost a dictionary, but the entries include more than a definition. For example, they tell where an animal lives, what it eats, how it is classified. There is an index.

THE ENCYCLOPEDIA OF CHEMISTRY

George L. Clark and Gessner G. Hawley, eds. *The Encyclopedia of Chemistry*. New York: Reinhold Publishing Corp. 2nd ed., 1966.

The preface to the first edition of this one-volume encyclopedia says it hopes to be useful to "anyone with a bowing acquaintance with chemistry." The first edition includes biographies of great chemists; these are omitted in the 2nd edition. The easily read definitions and descriptions are arranged in alphabetical order. There is an excellent index.

Problem 75

SEARCH QUESTIONS

1. What is colloid chemistry?

2. What are the properties of lipides?

3. Discuss napalm.

CLUES

1. and 2. can be easily found by going directly to the body of the encyclopedia under *colloid* and *lipides*.

3. There is no entry under *napalm*, so you need to check the index. There you find two references, one to *chemical warfare* and the other to *soaps*. Napalm appears as part of these articles.

INTERNATIONAL ENCYCLOPEDIA OF CHEMICAL SCIENCE

International Encyclopedia of Chemical Science. Princeton: Van Nostrand. 1964.

This one-volume encyclopedia is intended for chemists and chemistry students. It has brief definitions and descriptions arranged in alphabetical order. One interesting feature is the four-language appendix which translates all the English terms used in the book into French, German, Russian, and Spanish.

The International Dictionary of Physics and Electronics and the *International Dictionary of Applied*

Mathematics (both published by Van Nostrand) are one-volume encyclopedias that perform the same functions in physics and in mathematics. They are organized in the same way and written in a style similar to the *International Encyclopedia of Chemical Science*.

Problem 76

SEARCH QUESTIONS

1. Describe the carbon cycle.
2. Describe the properties of water.
3. Discuss the nomenclature of organic chemistry.

CLUES

1. Look under *carbon*.
2. This will be found under *water*.
3. If you look under organic chemistry nomenclature, you will be referred to *nomenclature, chemical*. There you will find several subtopics, among them organic chemistry.

THE CONCISE ENCYCLOPEDIA OF THE ATOM

Paul Musset and Antonio Lloret. *The Concise Encyclopedia of the Atom*. Chicago: Follett (Larousse), 1968. There are other titles in this series.

This one-volume encyclopedia is useful to the nonspecialist who needs information about atoms. It is arranged alphabetically, like a dictionary, and there is no index to its entries. The more general entries do have subtopics, so it is good to scan the headings before you read.

In the same series there are other titles:

Concise Encyclopedia of Astronautics
Concise Encyclopedia of Astronomy
Concise Encyclopedia of Electronics

Their format and style are similar to the *Concise Encyclopedia of the Atom*. They provide a useful, quick reference for the nonspecialist in these fields.

Problem 77

SEARCH QUESTIONS

1. Explain the concept of strangeness.
2. What is meant by the capture of an electron by an ion?
3. Who was Henrik Lorentz?

CLUES

1. Look in its alphabetical order for *strangeness*.
2. Check *capture*. Here there is a subtopic referring to *electrons,* so if you scanned the headings first, you saved time.
3. Look under *Lorentz*.

WORLD OF MATHEMATICS

James R. Newman. *World of Mathematics*. New York: Simon and Schuster, 1956. 4 vols.

The title page states well the purpose of these volumes: "A small library of the literature of mathematics from A'h-mosé the Scribe to Albert Einstein, presented with commentaries and notes." A valuable reference for the serious, older mathematics student.

There are articles on the history of mathematics, laws of change, statistics, infinity, logic, and mathematics related to other fields such as the physical world, literature, or music. The table of contents in Volume 1 outlines all four volumes. The tables of contents in Volumes 2, 3, and 4 repeat that portion of the outline which applies to them. An index at the end of Volume 4 helps find material on people and concepts in the series.

Dictionaries. There are dictionaries that specialize in defining words in science and mathematics. Some of them include words from all fields of science, others focus on a smaller area such as natural science or biology. You can almost always tell from the title what areas are covered in any science dictionary.

COMPTON'S ILLUSTRATED SCIENCE DICTIONARY

Charles A. Ford, ed. *Compton's Illustrated Science Dictionary*. Chicago: Compton, 1963.

This is useful for both younger and older students. It is arranged in three columns. One column gives the word and its pronunciation, another lists its definition or definitions according to the areas and fields of science it is used in, and the third uses each meaning of the word in a sentence. There are many pictures and illustrations.

The end of the book includes several helpful tables and diagrams such as the classification of plants and animals, the periodic table of elements, and systems of the body. These special tables are all listed in the table of contents.

Problem 78

SEARCH QUESTIONS

1. What is a ligament?

2. What is the photosphere?

3. What field of science uses the word *analygesic?*

4. Find a list of scientific symbols.

CLUES

1. and 2.   Check in alphabetical order for *ligament* and *photosphere*. They will be clearly defined in the middle column.

3. Check *analygesic* in alphabetical order. The definition tells you what field of science uses the word.

4. Look in the table of contents for the list of scientific symbols and abbreviations. It is one of the special helps at the back of the book.

SCIENCE DICTIONARIES OF THE ANIMAL AND PLANT WORLDS

Michael Chinery. *Science Dictionary of the Animal World*. New York: Watts, 1969.

Michael Chinery. *Science Dictionary of the Plant World*. New York: Watts, 1969.

These two specialized dictionaries are both helpful to high school students or adults interested in biology.

THE PENGUIN DICTIONARY OF SCIENCE

E.B. Uvarov and D.R. Chapman. *The Penguin Dictionary of Science*. New York: Schocken Books, 1972.

This is a useful and up-to-date dictionary that emphasizes scientific words. There are several diagrams, and the appendix includes useful tables.

NEUTRINO

S.G. 20·45, m.p. 640°C., produced as a *by-product* by *nuclear reactors* in the manufacture of plutonium.

NERNST EFFECT. If a *temperature* gradient is maintained across an electrical *conductor* (or *semiconductor*) which is placed in a transverse *magnetic field*, a *potential difference* will be produced across the conductor. Named after Walter Nernst (1864–1941).

NERNST HEAT THEOREM. The *entropy* change for *chemical reactions* involving crystalline *solids*, is zero at the *absolute zero* of temperature. See also *thermodynamics, laws of*.

NEROL. $C_{10}H_{17}OH$. A colourless *liquid unsaturated alcohol, isomeric* with *geraniol*, b.p. 224°C., used in perfumes and obtained from *neroli oil*.

NEROLI OIL. An *essential oil* obtained from the flowers of orange trees.

NERVE CELL. See *neurone*.

NERVE FIBRE. An *axon* or *dendrite*.

NERVE GAS. A war-gas which attacks the nervous system especially the nerves controlling respiration. Most nerve gases are *derivatives* of *phosphoric acid*.

NESSLER'S SOLUTION. A *solution* of potassium mercuric iodide, $KHgI_3$, in *potassium hydroxide* solution. Used as a test for *ammonia*, with which it forms a brown coloration or precipitate. Named after Julius Nessler (1827–1905).

NEURON (E). Nerve cell. A special type of biological *cell*, being the unit of which the nervous systems of animals are composed. Consists of a *nucleus* surrounded by a *cytoplasm* from which thread-like fibres project. In most neurones impulses are received by numerous short fibres called *dendrites* and carried away from the cell by a single long fibre called an *axon*. Transfer of impulses from neurone to neurone takes place at junctions between axons and dendrites which are called *synapses*.

NEUROTOXIN. A poison which attacks the nervous system.

NEUTRAL (chem.). Neither *acid* nor *alkaline*. Containing equal numbers of *hydroxyl* and *hydrogen ions* and having a pH of 7.

NEUTRAL (phys.). Having neither negative nor positive net *electric charge*.

NEUTRAL TEMPERATURE. The temperature of the hot junction of a *thermocouple* at which the *electromotive force* round the circuit is a maximum and the rate of change of E.M.F. with *temperature* is a minimum.

NEUTRALIZATION (chem.). The addition of *acid* to *alkali*, or vice versa, till neither is in excess and the *solution* is *neutral*.

NEUTRETTO. A *meson* with zero *electric charge*.

NEUTRINO. A stable *elementary particle* with no *electric charge* or *rest mass*, but with *spin* ½. Originally postulated to preserve the laws of *conservation of mass and energy* and *conservation of momentum*. The existence of the particle has since been established experimentally, and it is known to exist in two forms; the neutrino, which is emitted with *positrons*, and the anti-neutrino, which is emitted with negative *electrons* (e.g.

257

Sample page from E.B. Uvarov and D.R. Chapman, *The Penguin Dictionary of Science*, Baltimore: Penguin Books Inc., 4th ed., 1971. © E.B. Uvarov and D.R. Chapman, 1943. New material © Alan Isaacs, 1964, 1971. Reprinted with permission.

Problem 79

SEARCH QUESTIONS

1. What is an electron?

2. What is mercury?

3. What is a pulsar?

CLUES

You should have no problem with these. Look in the right alphabetical place for each term: electron, mercury, and pulsar.

Notice that words often have two different meanings — as is true here with *mercury*. So you need to be careful to get the one you need.

CHAMBERS' DICTIONARY OF SCIENCE AND TECHNOLOGY

T.C. Collocotr, ed. *Chambers' Dictionary of Science and Technology*. New York: Barnes and Noble, 1971.

This dictionary contains terms used in both modern science and technology. There are quite a few cross-references. Useful appendices include chemical elements, periodic tables, igneous and sedimentary rocks, and plant and animal kingdoms.

Problem 80

SEARCH QUESTIONS

1. What is the epidermis?

2. What is meant by hyperbola?

CLUES

1. Check epidermis in its alphabetical place.

2. Under *hyperbola* you find a cross-reference to conic (you will find the meaning of hyperbola under conic).

WORDS OF SCIENCE

Isaac Asimov. *Words of Science – And the History behind Them*. Boston: Houghton Mifflin, 1969.

This is not a traditional dictionary. It is more an explanation of basic words in science. Almost a page is devoted to each word, and the explanation contains a history of the concept. A wide range of concepts is included, such as absolute zero, pachyderm, glucose, and square root.

In addition to being a valuable reference for science students, *Words of Science* is interesting to browse through.

THE CRESCENT DICTIONARY OF MATHEMATICS

William Karush. *The Crescent Dictionary of Mathematics*. New York: Macmillan Co., 1962.

This is a useful reference for students in high school or for older students. It contains terms and concepts in algebra, geometry, trigonometry, calculus, and logic theory. It gives formulae and also diagrams where these will clarify. The appendix lists famous mathematicians and briefly describes their contributions.

Problem 81

SEARCH QUESTIONS

1. What is the cosine function?

2. What is the Königsberg Bridge problem?

3. What is a base?

4. What is Boolean algebra?

CLUES

Look in alphabetical order for each of these:

1. *Cosine*.

2. *Königsberg*.

3. *Base*.

4. *Boolean*. If you looked under *algebra, Boolean*, you found a cross-reference to the right place.

Other. There are two other specialized reference sources students in the sciences should be acquainted with: *The Handbook of Chemistry and Physics* and the *Field Guide* and *Field Book* series.

THE HANDBOOK OF CHEMISTRY AND PHYSICS

The Handbook of Chemistry and Physics. Cleveland: Chemical Rubber Co. Earlier editions were revised annually. Newer editions are dated for two years.

This handbook provides a mass of tables and formulae which are important to chemistry and physics students. It is well-indexed. By using this index you can easily find a specific gravity, a molecular weight, or a formula you need.

PETERSON FIELD GUIDE SERIES

Roger T. Peterson. *Field Guide Series.* Boston: Houghton Mifflin. Various titles are in the series.

PUTNAM'S NATURE FIELD BOOKS

Putnam's Nature Field Books. New York: Putnam's. Various titles are in the series.

The field guide or field book helps identify specimens and, therefore, usually includes many good pictures, along with other helpful, specific information. These two series are both very useful.

The *Peterson Field Guide Series* includes such titles as *Field Guide to Animal Tracks, Astronomy without a Telescope,* and *Field Guide to Landforms. Putnam's Nature Field Books* include titles like *Field Book of American Wild Flowers, Field Book of Ponds and Streams,* and *Field Book of the Skies.*

The individual titles usually are clear enough to help you select the field book you need.

GATHERING INFORMATION FOR REFERENCE PAPERS

Up to this point we have concentrated on how to use each library skill separately. You should now know the basic skills involved in getting information from the library. You should know how to use the card catalog, how books are arranged on the shelves, how to use indexes and general references, and how to select special references related to your questions. These are all valuable skills needed to get information you need from the library. However, we have been assuming that the answer to your question could be found in one particular source. Sometimes this is not possible because the breadth or depth of the question demands that we search for parts of the answer in many different places. This is usually the case in writing a reference paper.

I once visited a large family where there was always food around; everyone was snacking all the time, but there was never a real meal. In a sense we have been snacking in the library; we have seen how the whole library is organized to help you get the information you need to answer your specific questions. Now it is time for the full meal: the in-depth pursuit of a topic. The kind of study required by a reference paper demands all of the skills you have learned so far plus the elements of *selecting* and *coordinating* these skills.

The purpose of a reference paper (sometimes called a term paper, a research paper, or a report) is to bring together information from many sources which will clarify a problem or topic. In such a paper you summarize and pull together what others have said on the subject, evaluate what they have said, and draw conclusions about the subject based on your readings and your evaluations.

In one sense you are not being original in writing a reference paper because you are using what others have written; but in another sense you need real creativity in your selection of the problem, in your selection of the material to be used, in your organization of this material, in your evaluation of the material, and in your general conclusions. The overall logic holding the paper together is yours, and the writing style and language, except for the direct quotes, are yours.

Before dealing with how to write a reference paper, we will focus on all of those steps involved in using the library to collect the information needed to write the paper. This includes choosing a topic, locating sources of relevant material, recording the information, keeping a search record, and organizing the information into a sequence to fit an outline so that the actual writing can begin. The secret to preparing information for the reference paper is to have some *system* so that you can be methodical, thorough, and efficient. Without some tested system, you can waste endless hours and become hopelessly tangled in a disorganized mass.

If you have not already built up a successful reference paper-writing procedure for yourself, try the procedure we are going to suggest. You may want to vary some of the suggestions, but to be sure of consistently good results you must include all of these basic steps.

101

CHOOSING A GOOD TOPIC

The choice of the topic is a step you may be inclined to shrug off, but it is the heart of a successful reference paper, so it is worth investing considerable thought. Sometimes you have no choice of the general subject of the paper; but even when your teacher has given you an assigned subject, you need to think through what the subject could mean and limit the definition for the purposes of your paper. For example, suppose you had been assigned to write a paper on communication. You might want to limit or define the subject for yourself in one of several ways:

- The importance of communication to the stock market.
- Communication without words: a study of gestures.
- Heiroglyphics in ancient Egypt.
- The communication industry today in the United States.
- Public versus private ownership of the means of communication.
- Communication satellite systems.

Whether you are choosing your own topic or defining a subject assigned, be sure to choose some specific topic that interests you. After you have tentatively chosen a topic of interest, live with it a few days to see whether you can arrive at the necessary restricting or limiting questions or whether you want to discard it and substitute another.

Be sure that it is a topic that you can work with effectively within the limits of the assignment. For example, if you have been assigned to write 1,000 words (about four pages), you don't want to start on a vast topic like the discovery, development, and importance of atomic energy. Also be sure that you have a topic that you can work with effectively within the time limits of the assignment. A one-week product obviously has to be more limited than a five-week product.

After you have selected a topic and can give a brief statement of what your paper will be about, work out some tentative but specific questions about the topic you want to deal with.

At this phase it is often helpful to go to the library to consult some general references on your subject. Browse through them and see what areas are covered, what questions they deal with under your topic. Discover the scope of the information involved. As a result, you may decide to shift the focus of your questions, to narrow or to broaden them, or even to deal with another topic. Remember it is easy to ask questions that are impossible to answer.

These answerable questions eventually will develop into the outline for your paper. There should be only a few major ones, although each could have subquestions. Before you begin in-depth reading, you should clarify what you want to answer or what you want to focus on when you write. This makes it easy to select and organize material. You can avoid the common danger of grabbing two or three books and stringing summaries of them together like beads.

As you read, your questions may be refined or changed, but you need sound, specific questions before you begin your library work to serve you as a framework for thinking, a guide for selecting appropriate reading, and later as an outline for your writing. Once you have these questions, you are ready to make your working bibliography.

MAKING A WORKING BIBLIOGRAPHY

A working bibliography is a list of all the sources you plan to consult in researching your subject. You are setting out to find all the materials the library has that might help you. Ask yourself: should I check a general reference for a quick overview of my subject? Is there an appropriate specialized dictionary or handbook or encyclopedia that would be helpful? Is there an index I could use to find in-depth information? What books does the library have which deal with my subject? You are going to see what is available and then select from this what you need.

One trip to any source is enough — once through the card catalog, once through the indexes, and once through the references. Avoid the time-consuming trudging back and forth by making complete bibliography notes as you check each place.

The bibliography may be kept either in a notebook or on a set of cards (either 3 × 5 or 4 × 6 size). I recommend the cards for several reasons. First, they can be divided into high and low priority on the basis of how relevant they seem from the titles. Second, after each item is scanned to evaluate its actual relevance you can easily pull out those not used. Third, after you have read the item and taken notes about the relevant materials, you can rearrange the cards to fit the sequence in which they are to be used. Fourth, they can be rearranged again into alphabetical order by author when it is time to type a complete bibliography of materials used. In general it is clear that the card system provides the flexibility needed to select, record, and organize the materials. If one card, front and back, is not large enough to hold all the notes (summaries or quotes) you need from the one volume, simply add as many additional cards as needed and clip them to the title card.

Whatever system you adopt, you should be consistent — and you must be complete. Bibliographic information on each source must include three things:

		For Books Note The	For Magazines Note The
(1)	Identify the usable *item*	title author (or editor)	title of the article author (if given)
(2)	Identify the *source* of the item	publisher place date	magazine name date volume number page number
(3)	Identify the *location* of the item	call number	does library have? if so, where?

One student started to write a paper evaluating Franklin Delano Roosevelt. After a preliminary look at an encyclopedia and at the card catalog, he found he needed to narrow his topic. He decided to focus on the Presidential years of FDR as seen through the eyes of his contemporaries, and to reduce the scope of the paper further, he tentatively choose the title ''Franklin Delano Roosevelt: Democrat or Demagogue?'' Here are some of his working bibliography cards for this paper.

WORKING BIBLIOGRAPHY CARDS

First he checked for his general subject in an encyclopedia article.

> "Roosevelt, Franklin Delano"
> *Encyclopedia Americana*, 1973 ed.,
> Vol. 23. pp. 680-84.

Then he looked for any helpful special references.

> "Roosevelt, Franklin D(elano)"
> *Current Biography*, 1943,
> pp. 706-14.

He looked in the card catalog under his subject.

> Perkins, Frances.
> B
> R6767p *The Roosevelt I Knew*
>   N.Y.: Viking Press,
>   1946

> Smith, A. Merriman.
> 923.17 *Thank You, Mr. President*
>   N.Y., Harper, 1946

> Sherwood, Robert Emmet.
> 973.917 *Roosevelt and Hopkins:*
>   *An Intimate History*
>   N.Y., Harpers, 1948

> Lash, Joseph P.
> B
> R6765l *Eleanor and Franklin*
>   N.Y., Norton, 1971

> Schlesinger, Arthur
> 973.91 *Coming of the New Deal*
>   Houghton, 1958

He then checked the indexes. First the *Readers' Guide.*

> *Presidency il por Time,*
> *28:9-15, Jl 6, '36*

> *President needs a gadfly*
> *H. Brown, Nation 143:577*

> *Pussyfooting about the*
> *President Sat. Eve. Post*
> *208:22 Je 20 '36*

> *Roosevelt and the spoils*
> *system H.B. Elliston*
> *Forum 147:267-76 Mr. '37*

> *Case against Willkie*
> *B. Bliven il por Life*
> *9:104+ O14 '40*

> *Case against Roosevelt*
> *R. Moses il por Life*
> *9:105+ O14 '40*

Then the *New York Times Index.*

> *Col. R.R. McCormick calls theories*
> *monarchial*
> *N.Y. Times Ja 9 15:1 1936*

> *editorial on indications of*
> *popularity*
> *N.Y. Times Ja 12 IX 8:1 1936*

Since you are setting out to find all the materials the library has that might help you, like a detective you must keep a record of where you look. For a very simple or a very limited topic, you can skip this kind of record, but if you have a complex topic that requires several visits to the library to complete your preliminary working bibliography, it is helpful to keep a search record sheet in which you keep track of all your efforts. This is part of a search sheet the student kept for his Franklin Delano Roosevelt paper when he was doing his working bibliography.

```
                Bibliography Search Sheet
                    (sources checked)
General references

     Ency. Americana - Roosevelt, Franklin Delano


Special references

     Current Biog. - Roosevelt, Franklin D.



Card catalog subjects

     Roosevelt, Franklin Delano
     U.S. History  History, U.S. - 1932-45
     World War 1939-1945  Depressions - U.S
     New Deal , not used.
Indexes   subjects and dates

     Readers Guide: Roosevelt, Franklin Delano - about
        check 1932-45 vol '9 '10 '11 '12 '13 '14
     N.Y. Times Index: Roosevelt (Pres. F. D.) - administra-
        tion Vol 1932 '33 '34 '35 '36 '37 '38 '39 '40 '41 '42 '43 '44 '45

Pamphlet file subjects

     ✓ Roosevelt, F. D.
     ✓ Depression
     ✓ New Deal


Other: resource people, museums,
       TV programs
```

Sometimes I jot down my intended sources ahead of time on a search sheet and then check them off as I consult them. Sometimes I just keep a record of where I've looked. It depends on the topic. A search sheet insures that you have been thorough, and it avoids backtracking later when you wonder, "Did I check under such-and-such?" When you have finished your working bibliography cards, you know everything your library has that might help with your topic.

PRELIMINARY SELECTION

Now it is time to assemble the materials you have found and to select those which suit your purpose. Avoid grabbing the first book that looks promising and beginning to read on page one.

Get *all* the books that your working bibliography search has turned up. Check the tables of contents and the indexes to see what parts of each book may be relevant.[1] Very few whole books will apply to your own properly limited topic. Make brief notes to yourself on your bibliography cards about what parts of the material looked useful and put aside cards for books that are not useful to you.

If you are allowed to go to the shelves, check the call-number sections for your books. There may be other titles that did not show up in your card catalog search. Do a preliminary check of any new titles that turn up this way.

Next do a preliminary selection of your periodical articles and pamphlets. Skim what the writer has said; if his points are relevant to your topic, make a note on your bibliography card and put it aside to be gone over more thoroughly; pull out the bibliography cards that are not useful.

This quick preliminary overview can select which books look promising, and you can leave the others. This is a more efficient approach than sweeping the shelves clean and getting sore muscles carrying books back and forth, intending to look at them some day.

Here is what some of the preliminary bibliography cards for the paper on Roosevelt looked like after the student skimmed for relevant information.

NOTES FOR PRELIMINARY SELECTION

The books and articles found in the preliminary bibliography search are skimmed and notes added to the cards.

Sources that look useful will be more carefully read later.

Sources that are not useful are weeded out.

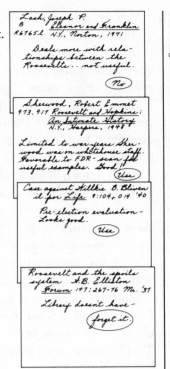

While doing the preliminary scanning, you may find an additional new source and add a card for it.

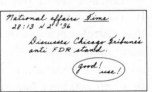

This preliminary sorting for even a complex paper can usually be done in a few hours. You have eliminated sources of no relevance to your topic and know for certain how much material you have to work with. You can now settle down to the next step of a careful reading and note taking.

READING AND TAKING NOTES

Your critical reading and thoughtful note taking are the core of your successful reference paper. Begin with the sources that looked best in your preliminary selection of materials. As you read carefully, you need to take notes on the author's main ideas, striking examples, and important conclusions. It is useful also to jot down specific details like names of people, dates, or figures that you may want to use in your writing.

You must remember that you are not reading and taking notes so you can summarize the book or magazine article. You are trying to get from your reading only the material that relates to your problem or questions. Again, you are not a book reviewer, you are investigating what different people have to say about two or three related questions that are the focus of your reference paper.

Some times it helps remind you of your focus if you take notes that deal with each of your subquestions on separate cards or pages. Thus if there is no suitable question under which to put the information, no question of yours that it deals with, you either skip it or consciously change the scope of your paper.

Students some times argue, "I can just prop a few books up in front of me and write my paper directly. It's much faster." And they are right. That is exactly what they can do, and it is faster; but this process short-circuits the essential part of writing a reference paper. It eliminates thinking. It avoids your sifting through material and thoughtfully evaluating and using it to develop your own point. Such a procedure will get by when you are trying to learn as little as possible or when you have begun your paper a few hours before it is due. But these are first-aid measures, and you don't get much out of it except a check mark in a grade book and more practice in typing.

Good notes should be made so that you do not have to look at your source again. This means that you must have some short but accurate and consistent way to identify your sources. One way is to number your bibliography cards and then use that number on all note cards that come from that source. Another is to briefly identify the source on each note card with a key word in the title or with the author's last name.

You should take notes in a notebook or on cards not on bits and pieces of paper or the backs of old envelopes. Take your notes as briefly as possible. You can use key words rather than sentences, and use abbreviations. Just be sure you will be able to understand what you have written later.

You may summarize in your own words, but use quotes if you use the author's words or phrases. Be sure to note the page numbers. They will be useful for footnotes later. Notes should also include your own evaluation or reaction to what the author has said.

Again, there is no single proper way to take notes, but your system must be complete, consistent, and accurate. The following notes were made for the paper on Roosevelt and illustrate one form of good note taking.

SAMPLE NOTE CARDS

The author's last name is enough to match with the bibliography card.

Notes can paraphrase.

Notes can contain your evaluation.

Notes can contain direct quotes.

Notes which paraphrase or quote need page numbers.

To review, let's follow one source through locating, skimming, and reading.

Looking in the card catalog our student found a likely-looking title and made a bibliography card.

After he had all his bibliography cards made, he skimmed the material to select what he wanted to use. When he did this, he jotted enough on his bibliography card to remind him what the book contained.

Sherwood, Robert Emmet.
973.917 Roosevelt and Hopkins:
An Intimate History
N.Y., Harpers, 1948

Limited to war years Sherwood was on whitehouse staff. Favorable to FDR-scan for useful examples. Good!!
(Use)

After he had narrowed down and selected the material he wanted to use, he read it more carefully and took notes on cards.

Sherwood
Argues there is too great a gap between the Presidency and Congress. In crisis the Pres. will use tremendous Constitutional powers for better or worse. FDR did not create this situation but made it apparent. pp 586-89
"... history must record the unalterable fact that Roosevelt in 1940 was indispensable." p. 589

After you finish note cards for each source, take time to reread the notes. You will catch omissions like forgotten page numbers and incomplete thoughts while you still have the book to check with. Also, it is a good idea to check your bibliography cards to be sure that the information is complete. Such checks take very little time and avoid the frustration of trying to get hold of the book again later to fill in missing information or decode a cryptic scribble.

Continue reading and taking notes until you have enough material for your purposes. You have started with the sources that looked the best in your preliminary selection. If you stop reading before you finish them all, you will be leaving out the sources that had appeared less useful. You need enough material to deal adequately with your topic, but not so much that it becomes repetitious and difficult to organize.

When you have enough material, if your notes have been properly taken, they can be sorted by subtopic or question and the organization of your paper is practically done. You are well on your way to a successful reference paper. You are finished with the library part of your reference paper and are ready to write.

WRITING THE REFERENCE PAPER

Begin with enough time and with the determination that you will write at least two drafts of your paper. The less experienced writer always tends to underestimate the amount of time needed to write a paper in comparison with the amount of time needed to do the library research. If you do not allow enough time for thinking about the relevance of the information you have gathered and about how to show its significance to your audience, much of the value to you and to your readers will be lost.

When shifting from the search phase to the writing phase of your project, your whole approach and attitude needs to shift from the search-and-accumulate mode to the display-demonstrate-and-convince mode. No matter how diligent you have been in digging, sifting, and sorting for nuggets of knowledge, no one will be influenced or impressed unless you succeed in displaying your valuable ideas in an orderly and attractive way.

Do not try to cram every crumb, every tidbit of trivia, into your paper at all costs. It is better to display fewer ideas more clearly so that your communication will have impact on the audience. The art of writing expository reports is like the art of displaying jewelry. It is better to display one diamond on a black velvet background than to put five in a coffee can of marbles.

In writing, the jewels are your main ideas and the black velvet background is the context in which your ideas appear. This context includes the way you pose your main question to show its importance, the way you organize your subques-tions and information to show their relationship and importance to the main question, and the order in which you unfold your material to give emphasis and dramatic impact to your most valued ideas.

You began work on this reference paper by choosing a good and manageable topic. Before you started reading, you worked out a brief statement of what your paper is about. You have some specific questions about this statement and you have selected and read material which helps answer these questions. You have taken notes on these sources according to which question they deal with.

Now sort these note cards according to the questions they deal with and put the piles in the order you think they should be written about.

AN ORDERLY PLAN

There is no necessary right order, but you should have some plan. For example, when the student was writing the paper referred to earlier on "Franklin Delano Roosevelt: Democrat or Demagogue?" he thought about two possibilities for arranging his material. Since he was focusing on the presidential years of FDR as seen through the eyes of his contemporaries, the student could arrange his material chronologically according to Roosevelt's first, second, third, or fourth term in office. Or, he could present materials supporting the idea that Roosevelt was a great democrat;

then he could discuss those contending that he was a dangerous demagogue; and then in the conclusion, the student could summarize and comment on or evaluate these. He chose the latter, although either way would have worked.

While there is no one right order in which to present your material, you must have some orderly plan or you will lose your reader.

If you are writing a paper which does not follow a chronological history, it will usually have a logical flow in which questions and subquestions are raised, information related to these questions is presented, arguments are given about the pros and cons of the questions in view of the information presented, and conclusions are drawn. Even though it may sound somewhat vague to you at this point, it is helpful to think of the organization of any paper as having some type of sequence. After all you must start some place, you have to end some place that gives the reader a feeling of completion, and, obviously enough, you have to do something between the start and the finish. Therefore, it helps to think of the paper as having an introduction, a body, and a conclusion. Each of these three phrases of the presentation has a special function.

In the introduction you should tell the reader what you are going to do in the body of the paper. What are the major problems, questions, or ideas you are going to deal with? Why are you dealing with these? Why are they important? How do you propose to go about answering the questions? Whether or not you tell the reader in advance the answers you have found or the conclusions you draw will depend upon whether you feel it would whet the reader's curiosity about the types of information and arguments you will present, or would detract from the dramatic impact of your conclusions.

Once you make your promises to the reader in the introduction, you try to deliver what you promised in the body of the paper. Later we will show some of the principles of organizing this part of the paper.

The longer and more complicated your paper, the more necessary it is to include a final section which presents a summary of your paper and the conclusions you have drawn. In this section it is often useful to remind your reader of the purposes you stated in the introduction, to summarize the key parts of your information, the general slant of the evidence presented in the body, and then to draw your conclusions about the answers to your questions. You should also evaluate how reliable you feel your conclusions are in view of the kinds and the sources of information you used.

WRITING THE FIRST DRAFT

After you have your orderly plan in mind, get your pencil or typewriter and write. This is the moment when many students freeze because they are too eager to do a "good" job. For this first draft do not worry about the literary quality or the precision of your thoughts; that is the function of the revision. The purpose of this first draft is to get your material on paper in some organized form. If you worry about the perfect opening, you may never get anything down on paper.

You have already, before you started reading, worked out a general brief statement of what your paper is about. Begin your paper with that, and then continue by discussing the material you have been reading in the order you have arranged your note cards. Pretend you are telling your friend about what you have read. Do not worry about precision, focus on getting all your information in some organized fashion.

After you have presented and discussed all your material, conclude it by briefly summarizing what you have written; then give your own interpretation or evaluation of this material.

REVISING THE FIRST DRAFT

The rough draft is done. The next step is to revise, but wait until the next day if possible. You will have a better perspective on your work.

Your rough draft should be read to check for four large areas: contents, organization, style, and mechanics. Some people like to read through the rough draft considering all four of these areas at once. I find it easier for me to read a rough draft four times, each time concentrating on one of these areas.

First check the contents. Is it clear? You know what you meant to write, but would your reader understand?

Is it complete? Remember that your reader knows nothing about your subject. Are there gaps in your writing which would make it difficult for him to understand what you mean?

Does it avoid irrelevant information? Remember your brief statement of what your paper is about and the questions related to this statement. Is your information concerned with these? Every student occasionally has to add to what has been written in order to meet the requirements of the assignment. However, be sure that everything you include is related to the topic of the paper.

Assume, for example, that you are writing a paper evaluating Washington's role as a revolutionary leader and you find that you are a page short of the minimum you need. It would probably be better to add an anecdote from a particular revolutionary meeting Washington attended, such as the First Continental Congress, than to add some personal facts about his height or his set of carved false teeth.

Is the information you give accurate? Check to be sure that you have correctly copied the material you quoted. Is your information documented where necessary?

To document is to tell the source of information: what book did you find the information in? who wrote it? who published it? where and when was it published? These things are noted at the bottom of the page in a *footnote.*

You need to footnote the source of a quotation or statistics you use and all original ideas or opinions of an author. Since your reference paper is based completely on what you have read, you have to use judgment in selecting what ideas are unique enough to need to be footnoted. Your bibliography will take care of sources of general information.

You have all the information you need to footnote your material on your bibliography cards, and a good form to use for giving these sources will be discussed later. Now, when you are revising for contents, it is enough to be sure that you mark each spot in the rough draft which you need to document, as was done in the following example.

". . . history must record the unalterable fact that Roosevelt in 1940 *was* indispensable.[1] It seems useless to debate whether Roosevelt should have continued to seek the Presidency. The United States could not have done without him.

[1]Sherwood, p. 589.

The writer has marked the information that needs to be footnoted and has identified the card which has the information he needs to make the footnote. After a little practice most of this documentation can be done as you write the rough draft.

Your rough draft has been revised for contents. You have checked it for clarity and completeness; it contains no irrelevant information; it is accurate and documented where necessary.

Read your rough draft for its organization. Organization is the orderly plan you had in mind when you were writing. Does your draft present your ideas in the sequence you intended? Do you need to change the order of your material? Are the right ideas emphasized? The structural emphasis is affected by such things as the amount of space or words devoted to a particular point and whether it has a prominent position in the format of the paper.

If in reading the rough draft you find that the amount of detail and the number of words devoted to a particular idea are out of proportion to its importance in the argument, if it interrupts the chain of ideas and threatens to derail the reader, there are several things you can do. If the offending part can be reduced without losing meaning, simply make it shorter. If it is a point which must be included and must be described in detail to be clear, you can put the description in an explanatory footnote. This avoids a long interruption in the trend of your main ideas in the paper. If the detailed section is one or more whole pages, it might be well to put it at the end of your paper as an *appendix* and give a short explanation in a footnote referring to that appendix.

No matter how the ideas of the paper logically follow one another, or what their relative importance is to the argument you are trying to develop, a particular idea is given greater emphasis in the reader's mind if it is spotlighted by using a separate subheading that labels the idea.

The larger the print used for the heading, or the higher up the ladder it is in your outline of topics and subtopics, the greater the emphasis communicated to the reader. For this reason the importance of the idea should correspond to its position in the hierarchy of the outline. Sometimes it is necessary to add, eliminate, or combine headings to get the emphasis you want.

Now read your rough draft for style.[1] Is your vocabulary appropriate? Have you avoided extremes of stiffness and folksy chit-chat? Is your choice of words interesting and varied? Go to your thesaurus for help here.

Is your material presented actively rather than passively?

- *passive:* It was noted by Whitman during the Civil War that . . .
- *active:* During the Civil War Whitman noted that . . .

While passive wording is good for some effects and for occasional variety, it becomes heavy and dragging when used too much.

Have you given specific details or examples rather than general statements?

- *general:* Workers labored in worrisome factory conditions.
- *specific:* Riveters had to be constantly alert for the unguarded overhead crane while continually worrying about missing one of the whitehot rivets being thrown to them.

Too many general statements make your writing less forceful. Your reader generally knows what you mean, but never exactly envisions it.

Is your material precise rather than vague?

- *vague:* Paganini had regular attention from his father.
- *specific:* Paganini had daily lessons from his father.
- *vague:* The townspeople were influenced by the curfew.
- *specific:* The townspeople complained the curfew was too early.

Precision helps communicate to your reader exactly what you intend. Vagueness allows him to stray from your point.

Check the mechanics. Your rough draft has been read for contents, organization, and style. Now is the time to look at the mechanics. Reach for your dictionary as you check your spelling. Is your grammar all right? Sometimes reading your paper aloud is helpful when you are checking grammar. Is your punctuation correct?

Once you have attended to these details, put the material in your footnotes in order.

Footnotes are usually put at the bottom or "foot" of the page on which you have written the material referred to. Sometimes they may be listed together on a separate page at the end of your paper. The notes are usually numbered consecutively in the paper, and the same number is used beside the material which needs documentation and the note which gives its source.

Footnotes need to include the author, the title, the publishing information, and the specific page referred to in some generally understood and consistent manner. There are many ways to do this. Check to see whether your instructor has a recommended form for footnotes. If not, I would suggest using a very simple form:[1] separate each part of the footnote with a comma and end with a period. Look at the following example of the footnote for the material quoted from Sherwood:

[3]Robert E. Sherwood, *Roosevelt and Hopkins: An Intimate History*, New York, Harpers, 1948, p. 589.

This footnote gives all the necessary parts and uses the suggested simplified punctuation, as follows: author, *title*, place published, publisher, date, page referred to.

Write your complete footnotes either in the margins of your rough draft or on a separate page. Your bibliography cards contain all the information you need to do this.

After you have completed your footnotes, take the bibliography cards for all the sources you used in writing your paper. Arrange these in alphabetical order by the *last* name of the author (or by the first important word in the title if there is no author). These titles make up your bibliography, or the list of sources from which you got your ideas for the paper. It is the list of things you read or consulted.

---

[1]If you are not already familiar with a good manual of style, you might want to look at one of the following:

W. Strunk, Jr., and E.B. White, *The Elements of Style*, 2nd ed. (Riverside, N.J.: Macmillan Co., 1972).

Porter G. Perrin and Wilma R. Ebbitt, *Writer's Guide and Index to English*, 5th ed. (Glenview, Ill.: Scott, Foresman & Co., 1972).

---

[1]One manual which deals thoroughly with more complex documentation is Kate L. Turabian, *A Manual for Writers of Term Papers, Theses, and Dissertations*, Chicago: University of Chicago Press, 1955.

These sources are listed on a separate page or pages at the end of your paper. You can use the same simplified form you did for your footnotes except you need to put the author's last name first. See the example of the student's bibliography for the paper on Roosevelt.

Notice that whether the source is a book or an article, it is listed alphabetically by author or by the title if you do not know the author. If you made certain that your bibliography cards are in proper alphabetical order, it usually is not necessary to make a rough draft of a bibliography. The final draft can be made from your cards.

WRITING THE FINAL DRAFT

Once you have your rough draft revised, you are ready to make the final copy. This final copy is the packaging for your ideas, and it is important to keep the paper easy to read. Different schools may have slightly different requirements for written work; but, in general, standards of good form are similar.

Keep your final draft neat. Use ink or type on one side of standard size paper. If you type, make a carbon, which you need not correct. Double space your writing. Keep margins of about one inch all around. If you have major divisions in your paper, capitalize and center these. Subdivisions stand at the left margin. Number your pages consecutively at the top. Look at the sample page showing the headings.

The final draft should include a title page which gives your name, the title of your paper, the course, and the date. See the example of a title page.

If your paper is long, there should be a table of contents which gives the main divisions of the paper and the number of the page on which each division begins, as is done in the sample table of contents.

We have already discussed the form of the bibliography. It should follow the paper.

Proofread your finished copy and make your corrections neatly in ink. Even if your paper is typed, minor ink corrections are usually acceptable.

If you have written your paper in ink, keep the rough draft; if you have typed it, keep the uncorrected carbon. It does sometimes happen that a student is certain he has turned in a paper which the instructor does not remember seeing and cannot find. You should keep a copy of every paper you write as a kind of insurance until the original is returned by the instructor. If you have no carbon, a lost paper can be tragic.

Your final draft is finished and proofread, and your paper is ready.

SAMPLE BIBLIOGRAPHY PAGE

The kind of source:

(1) article in magazine by named author

(2) article in a reference

(3) encyclopedia article

(4) article in magazine by author not named

(5) book

(6) book

BIBLIOGRAPHY

Bliven, B., "The Case Against Wilkie," Life, Vol. 9, October 14, 1940, p. 104.

"Franklin D. Roosevelt," Current Biography, 1943, pp. 706-14.

"Franklin Delano Roosevelt," Encyclopedia Americana, 1973 ed., Vol. 23, pp. 680-84.

"National Affairs," Time, Vol. 28, November 2, 1936, p. 13.

Perkins, Francis, The Roosevelt I Knew, New York, Viking Press, 1946.

Sherwood, Robert Emmet, Roosevelt and Hopkins: An Intimate History, New York, Harpers, 1948.

SAMPLE TEXT PAGE

This sample shows correct format for headings and footnotes:

(1) pages numbered consecutively at the top

(2) main division headings centered and capitalized

(3) subheadings at the margin and underlined

(4) footnotes at the bottom of the page

14

x x x x x x x x x x x x x x x x x x x x x
x x x x x x x x x x x x x x x x x x x x x
x x x x x x x x x x x x x x x x x x x x x
x x x x x x x x x x x x x x x x x x x x x

THE THIRD TERM (1941–1944)

x x x x x x x x x x x x x x x x x x
x x x x x x x x x x x [4]

Lend Lease

x x x x x x x x x x x x x x x x x x x
x x x x x x x x x x x x x x x x x x x x
x x x x x x x x x x x x x x x x x x x x
x x x x x x x x x x x x x x x x x x x x
x x x x x x x x x x x x x x x x x x x x
x x x x x x x x x x x x x x x x x x x x
x x x x x x x x x x x x x x x x x x x x
x x x x x x x x x x x x x x x x x x x x
x x x x x x x x x x x x x x x x x x x x
x x x x x x x x x x x x x x x x x x x x
x x x x x x x x x x x x x x x x x x x x

---

[4]author, *title*, place published, publisher, date, page referred to.

SAMPLE TITLE PAGE

This sample title page includes:

(1) title of the paper

(2) student's name

(3) the course name

(4) the date

**FRANKLIN
DELANO
ROOSEVELT:**

DEMOCRAT OR DEMAGOGUE?

Karen Gregory
History 101
May 15, 1976

SAMPLE TABLE OF CONTENTS PAGE

This sample contents page shows:

(1)   major headings and the page each begins on

(2)   indented subheadings

(3)   the bibliography is also included

APPENDIX A

ANSWERS TO SELF-CHECKING EXERCISES

PROBLEM 1 — CARD CATALOG

1. card catalog

2. author, title, and subject (in any order)

3.
   a. 5
   b. 1
   c. 3
   d. 4
   e. D

4.
   a. 2
   b. 3
   c. X
   d. 1
   e. M

5.
   a. 2
   b. 1
   c. X
   d. 3
   e. F

6.
   a. 3
   b. 4
   c. 2
   d. 1
   e. U

7.
   a. A
   b. M
   c. W
   d. O
   e. A
   f. D
   g. F

8.
   a. 5
   b. 6
   c. 3
   d. 4
   e. 2
   f. 1

9.
   a. 7
   b. 6
   c. 4
   d. 1
   e. 2
   f. 5
   g. 3
   h. 8
   i. 9

10.
   a. yes
   b. no
   c. can't tell

PROBLEM 2 — LOCATING MATERIAL

1.
   a. 2
   b. 3
   c. 1
   d. 4

   e. 2
   f. 5
   g. 1
   h. 4
   i. 5

2.
   a. M
   b. D
   c. A
   d. R
   e. N
   f. P
   g. L

3.
   a. K
   b. J
   c. C
   d. C in 920s — This book is a collection of biographies and has to be kept within the 920s (collective biography) under the author's last name.
   e. P
   f. B
   g. M
   h. D in 920s
   i. B

4. Nonfiction books are shelved together by subjects represented by numbers in the Dewey Decimal System. These books would be found in the following order, left to right on the shelf:

616.24	616.3	616.8	616.9	616.94
B81	K82	J15	Z69	B91
616.99	620	620	620	921.5
S36	B51	B81	M18	W93

PROBLEM 3 — READERS' GUIDE

1. 1
2. 4
3. 3
4. 6
5. 2 and 5
6. 8 and 13
7. 10
8. 12
9. X

7, 9, and 11 were not used to answer the questions.

APPENDIX B

PARTS OF A BOOK AND PRELIMINARY SCANNING

When you look at books, you can see that they are organized in a fairly similar way. They usually contain some preliminary material, the text or main part of the book, and some supplementary material. The preliminary material usually includes the following parts in the order they are given.

The frontispiece. This is an appropriate illustration which faces the title page.

The title page. The title page contains the title (the name of the book) and sometimes a subtitle which clarifies or explains the title. The author's name is given, and there is occasionally information about his or her background or the titles of other works by the writer. The names of other people contributing to the work are also given: the editor, the illustrator, or the translator. The title page also includes publishing information: the name of the publisher and the place and date of the printing.

The copyright page. This is the back (or *verso*) of the title page. It shows the date of the copyright and the name of the copyright owner.

The preface or foreword. In the preface the author tells why the book was written and what readers the book was meant for. The author also explains any special things the reader should know about using the book, and often acknowledges the assistance received from other people.

The table of contents. The table of contents lists the important things the book contains. It lists the sections or chapters of the book in order and shows the pages where they begin. Some tables of contents are so detailed that they almost equal an outline of the book; others are like skeletons.

This preliminary material is followed by the text or body of the book. This is the main part of the book. While the preliminary pages are usually numbered in small Roman numbers, the text usually begins with page 1 and continues with Arabic numbers.

Supplementary material comes after the main text, often in the following order.

The appendix. Nonfiction books often have a section of supplementary materials which are helpful to the reader but which do not fit well into the text. These materials are referred to but not explained in the text, and they follow the text in a separate section called the appendix. An appendix may include a table or a list or statistical information. Sometimes an appendix includes an explanation which would interest only some of the readers. The appendices are listed in the table of contents.

The glossary. The glossary explains vocabulary used in the text. It is especially useful in a book that includes many specialized terms which would be unfamiliar to the average reader. Such terms are often used in discussing a specific field such as sculpture or computers.

The bibliography. A bibliography can be a list of references the author has used in writing the book, or it can be a list of additional reading related to the subject that the author recommends to the reader. Sometimes a book will contain both a bibliography and a suggested reading list. At times these lists of references and of additional reading are included at the end of each chapter. Often however they are included in a separate section at the end of the book.

The footnotes. If footnotes are not placed at the bottom of each page or at the end of each chapter, they may be put together in a separate section at the end of the book.

The index. The index is the last section of the book. It lists in alphabetical order all the important topics, terms, and names appearing in the text, and it gives a page number where each can be found.

After you have located the books whose titles seem to be appropriate for your topic, do a preliminary scanning to choose which to look at in more detail. Knowing what can be found in different parts of a book will help with your preliminary selection of material.

The preliminary material and the supplementary material are especially important in this first sifting for useful reading.

Look at the title page. Does the author appear qualified to write in this field? Is the date of the publication appropriate for what you need? A book on atomic theory dated 1945 might be perfect for a paper on the history of atomic discovery, but it would not serve so well for a paper describing current work with the atom.

Check the preface. Is the author's stated purpose one that includes material you need? Is the author intending to write at a level useful to you? A book on the atom written for preschoolers would probably not be of much benefit but neither would one written for specialists in the field.

Scan the table of contents. Would the book be useful for general background for your project? Are there sections or chapters that deal specifically with the area you are interested in? Scanning the table of contents should tell you whether the material you need is included in the book, and it should also give you an idea of approximately how much material is included which might be useful. You can see whether one section, several chapters, or the whole book looks helpful.

Look in the index under the important ideas contained in your questions. Do the areas included in your questions appear in the index? Does there seem to be much material about them?

As you do this scanning for preliminary selection of material, you will find chapters listed in the table of contents or concepts listed in the index which look useful. Note these sections which you want to check later on your bibliography card. This saves repeating the process when you are ready to sit down to read.

INDEX

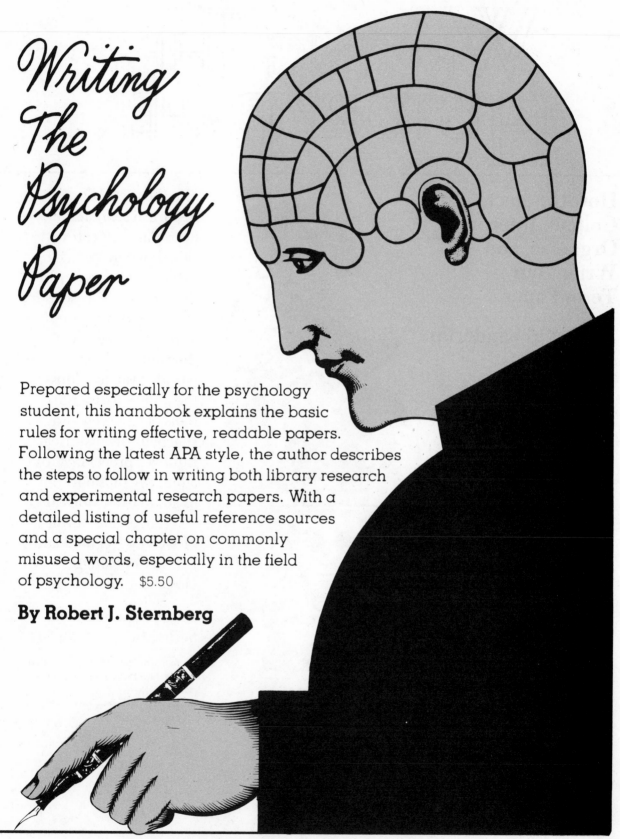

Writing The Psychology Paper

Prepared especially for the psychology student, this handbook explains the basic rules for writing effective, readable papers. Following the latest APA style, the author describes the steps to follow in writing both library research and experimental research papers. With a detailed listing of useful reference sources and a special chapter on commonly misused words, especially in the field of psychology. $5.50

By Robert J. Sternberg

Barron's Educational Series, Inc.

Writing The History Paper

How to Select, Collect, Interpret, Organize, and Write Your Term Paper

By David Sanderlin

Use the methods of historical scholarship to produce a professional paper. With extensive discussion of the reasons for research and suggestions for applying the topic to the contemporary world. Also develops the ability to use the tools of research and sharpens the historical thinking process. With a lengthy bibliography of standard historical references and outlines of Dewey Decimal and Library of Congress classification systems.

Barron's Educational Series, Inc. $5.50

At your local bookseller or order direct adding 10% postage plus applicable sales tax.